SALESMANSHIP

SALESMANSHIP

Earl E. Baer

Highline College

McGraw-Hill Book Company
New York St. Louis San Francisco Düsseldorf Johannesburg
Kuala Lumpur London Mexico Montreal New Delhi
Panama Rio de Janeiro Singapore Sydney Toronto

SALESMANSHIP

Library of Congress Catalog Card Number 77-175180

07-003012-X

1234567890 MAMM 798765432

This book was set in Theme Medium by Allen-Wayne Technical Corp. and printed and bound by The Maple Press Company. The designer was Paula Tuerk; the drawings were done by Vantage Art, Inc. The cover was designed by Jo Jones. The editors were Jack R. Crutchfield and Helen Greenberg. Sally Ellyson supervised production.

Dedicated to Helen and the children

CONTENTS

PART FOUR   SALES MANAGEMENT

PREFACE

A textbook on salesmanship can be judged in terms of how successfully it develops the student's skills. However, it is important for the reader to understand one basic point: To become useful, skills must be applied. It is only through application that the student truly experiences the joy of a successful sales effort. And it is only through application that he becomes aware of how the principles of salesmanship are used to attain this success. The experience is not of the same type as that gained in other areas of business study. In accounting, for example, the student applies his knowledge in a manner quite similar to classroom theory. In sales, on the other hand, the relationship between customer and salesman is unique. If the student accepts this fact at the beginning, then this book will have special significance. Too often one of two extreme attitudes will result from a formal course in salesmanship: Either the student is lulled into believing that the course qualifies him as a salesman, or he takes the attitude that a formal course has no value unless it is directly applied to selling.

This book is designed to provide the framework for a successful sales career in any field of salesmanship. The material is presented systematically and can therefore be remembered easily. When the student gains first-hand experience, he will find it even more valuable.

Of particular relevance to salesmanship is the development of those personal characteristics that are important for *any* sales activity. Although everyone has the desire for individuality, certain characteristics are by nature common to all men. For instance, man's personality is a combination of materialism and idealism. Materialistically, man yearns for tangible rewards. Idealistically, he desires to develop fully his abilities and capabilities, ultimately reaching a state of self-actualization.

Keeping in mind this dual nature of personality, the salesman can further develop two important characteristics, not only to gain greater success in sales, but also to lead a fuller life. These characteristics, attitude and enthusiasm, can be acquired through product knowledge and the development of customer benefits, two areas which will be fully discussed throughout this book.

Many people have contributed significantly to this book. I would like to thank F. L. Lucke, my district manager with the Mobil Oil Corporation, for his time and patience in helping me develop a degree of selling competence, and David C. Hughes of the J. C. Penney Company and Elmer Prather, district sales manager, Parke Davis Pharmaceutical Company, for their time and professional advice. Special thanks are due to Patty Von Behren, our faculty secretary, who gave much of her time and interest in preparing this text.

The hallmark of salesmanship, like that of law and medicine, is service to society. And like the lawyer or doctor, the salesman must undergo a period of apprenticeship. It begins with this course and continues into the actual sales efforts taking place in the business community.

Earl E. Baer

SALESMANSHIP

PART ONE
THE SELLING SYSTEM

You are starting on what will be an interesting and rewarding study. During the coming weeks you will learn new skills and techniques. You will gain a new understanding of yourself and of selling. This course of study will help you develop yourself more fully in order to achieve greater satisfaction and security in your chosen field. Many of the things you learn will apply to your daily personal, family, and social life, for you will gain a deeper understanding of human motivations and behavior. You will also gain a thorough understanding of salesmanship — its principles, analyses, and techniques. You will learn how to recognize what goes on in the buyer's mind at all times and how to convince him of the merits of your proposition without pressure, tricks, or gimmicks. You will learn the modern methods of selling, with each technique firmly based on enduring principles of human nature. You will learn what to do at each step of the sale, how to do it, and the reasons for it.

The *selling system* will become the means by which you will start on the road toward becoming a professional salesman. The systems approach is utilized because it offers the student a device by which he can understand the *relatedness* of the material, for the systems concept is based upon an ability not only to understand the material, but truly to comprehend its significance and act accordingly. When you understand the strength of the selling system, you will be able to use your complete range of abilities in selling with full honesty, integrity, and power — that power which comes from taking pride in yourself and your work and which consequently allows you to earn more money more easily. Others have found that this is true. It will be true for you.

Chapter One
Why Be a Salesman?

The typical college student rarely sees himself as a salesman. This is understandable for various reasons. One, the student associates salesmanship with particular activities within a rather limited field. Two, the student does not feel qualified to perform as a salesman. Three, he does not realize the broad spectrum of sales work available. And fourth, he does not realize the many training opportunities offered by marketing organizations. Here are a few reasons why every student in business administration should give serious consideration to a sales career.

There is no reason to believe that the opportunities will diminish. Increasing reliance upon sophisticated technology results in a wider variety of goods being made available to more market segments, ultimately requiring sales personnel capable of bringing these goods to the consumer. Perhaps it would be helpful to develop a clearer understanding of the various types of sales positions available. It might be well for the student to appreciate that, as he progresses within the field of salesmanship, he becomes involved with marketing principles as well. The important point here is that in order to progress within the sales organization an understanding of these marketing functions becomes important. In fact, many firms use such terms as "manufacture representative" in referring to a sales function in order to relate the function of selling more closely to the total marketing organization.

SELLING DIRECTLY TO THE CONSUMER

Primarily this would be retail salesmanship. Students entering this field usually are involved in a formal training program which leads to the position of assistant buyer or buyer. The opportunities in this field will continue to grow, particularly with chain store organizations such as Marshall Field, Sears, Roebuck, Montgomery Ward, and J. C. Penney, to name a few.

SELLING TO THE RETAIL OUTLETS

This function of salesmanship offers a wide variety of opportunities, some of which are listed below.

Pharmaceutical Salesmen

These are company representatives calling on retail drug outlets. Once the representative has established himself in the territory, one of his primary objectives is to gain a clear understanding of the particular needs of his accounts. For example, the market for a new formula children's cough medicine may be greater in suburban locations than in older, established neighborhoods. This sales function would probably include calling upon both drugstores and members of the medical profession within a specified geographical area.

Petroleum Representatives

These sales representatives usually begin their careers in metropolitan locations (where training assistance is nearby) and are responsible for a given number of service stations, probably numbering between fifteen and twenty-five. It is not unusual for a representative also to be assigned other accounts within his particular geographical area — parking lots, small local industry, etc. This is the classic example of how marketing principles are directly related to the sales activity.

Basically there are two types of leasing agreements between the petroleum firm and the retail outlet. One is when the dealer owns the service station property and facilities or independently leases such property from a third party. In this instance only a *gasoline contract* is signed with the petroleum firm. The second class of agreement is most common. This is a situation in which the petroleum firm owns or leases the property and also owns or leases the physical plant. In this case a gasoline contract and a *rental agreement* are signed. Obviously the dealer who has personal ownership of the service station has a higher degree of flexibility as to products sold in the service station. This could have an impact upon his attitude and personal relationship with the firm.

From a sales viewpoint, the petroleum representative is concerned with selling ideas as well as products. In selling ideas, the emphasis is upon selling the dealer or operator on particular management principles, standards of operation, or perhaps hours of operation. Since the lessor is an independent businessman, he has the right and privilege to buy products (other than gasoline) from whomever he chooses. It becomes the responsibility of the sales representative to provide the environment which will encourage the dealer to buy from the petroleum firm. Quite often special promotions of tires, batteries, oil, and the like will require special emphasis.

Food and Beverage Salesmen

Firms such as Procter & Gamble, General Mills, and Rainier Companies (brewing) have sales representatives who devote their efforts to retail food markets. Here is another area where the functions of salesmanship become interwoven with broader marketing functions, particularly in the food line.

For the food salesman, the primary concern is moving the product onto the grocer's shelf. In order to do this, the salesman must understand how the product will satisfy particular needs for the outlet and make the manager aware of the relationship between his product and the need. Once the product is in the store, the representative must be ever vigilant to maintain the shelf space necessary to sell his product, especially if there are several sizes or varieties. Probably at certain times of the year he will assist store managers in setting up promotional material.

The initial task for the beverage salesman is, again, to develop a need for the product in retail outlets. Once this need is established, maintaining adequate cooler space, reserves, and proper assortment becomes important. To accomplish this, adequate control measures must be established by the representative.

Automotive Representatives

General Motors, Ford, and Chrysler spend considerable sums developing representatives to call upon automobile agencies. Since this is also a franchise arrangement, the selling function is one of selling ideas, possibly a new promotion program, specialized training programs for the dealer's salesmen, etc. Here again is a job function where marketing and sales play a dual role. Marketing offers a framework for a particular course of action, while salesmanship plays a significant role in developing and bringing the plan into action — and results.

These represent only a cross section of the opportunities available in sales. These brief job descriptions may also dispel the myth which the young aspirant to the business profession often believes in: the picture of the salesman as someone with a flashy smile, a fast sales technique, questionable morals, and a more questionable future. Nothing can be farther from the truth. The professional salesman has as his hallmark an ethical background, from which emerges high principles of conduct and positive benefits to the customer. These become the basis for evaluating the success of the salesman and his future growth within the firm. This can be accomplished only through positive action, which in turn originates from strong moral values.

GROWTH POTENTIAL

The reason that sales offers an opportunity for promotion is because the function of salesmanship involves many of the activities of a manager. It is a decision-making function requiring the courage to continually commit oneself to a particular course of action or objective. Both the firm and the salesman learn under fire whether or not the salesman possesses the temperament to make these kinds of decisions daily. Salesmanship also involves a high degree of planning: planning of personal selling time and of how to accomplish sales objectives.

CONCLUSION

Students who have limited knowledge of sales as a profession tend to stereotype salesmen. One is depicted by Arthur Miller in *Death of a Salesman*. Willy Lowman is shown wearing a slouched hat and a seedy suit, carrying a beat briefcase, and badly in need of a haircut. Another stereotype is the sharp-looking individual with an oversharp suit, a constant smile, and a keen desire to make money — any way. Neither portrays a professional salesman. A true representation of the professional salesman is not unlike that of any other professional. He has at least two years of college and a balanced education in the business field, and he is strongly motivated to do well in his chosen field. If you see him at church on Sunday, at a ball game, or at a club, he is but another symbol of the group.

It is difficult here to do much more than point out that each field of salesmanship has a specific set of requirements for success. Some firms require a four-year degree in business administration, some a two-year degree, and others have no requirements regarding education. If the sales activity involves a technical area, such as drugs, machinery, or computers, it may be necessary to have a knowledgeable background in these areas before entering the selling profession. If a particular area of salesmanship appears attractive to you, it would be advisable to contact firms in that business and find out specifically what the technical requirements are.

PROBLEMS

1. Present a one-page position paper stating why you would like to be a salesman.

2. What background should a student acquire to sell computer systems for IBM?

3. What background should a student acquire to sell business forms?

4. Why are attitude and enthusiasm two important factors for a successful sales career?

5. Write a one-page report listing courses you have taken that can be valuable in preparation for a selling career.

6. Discuss three reasons why college students rarely see themselves as salesmen.

7. If your business department has a placement board for potential interviews, list all the interviewing companies that are looking for salesmen. What percentage of the total position interviews is this?

8. Discuss in detail one selling function found in the food industry.

9. Under the concept of professionalism, how are the doctor, lawyer, educator, and salesman alike?

10. Why is it often said that the successful salesman has a secure future?

See pages 247-248 for a case study.

Chapter Two
Professional Salesmanship:
A Conceptual Scheme

The *selling system* is the nerve center of the selling approach presented in this book. Although the terms used here may be new to the student, the basic concepts are not new. For example, the human body is a "system." Within the boundaries of this system we have two processes, or two flows of activity: the mental process and the physical process. By itself, the mental process can reach a *degree* of effectiveness; a blind person can mentally visualize a sunset and to this extent fulfills the functions of his human system. By contrast, a person gifted with sight responds to the sunset by first using his physical process (sight) and then directing this vision to the mental process. With the full utilization of both processes, the human system is better able to reach a valid conclusion: "This is a beautiful sunset." This example also demonstrates the various results that may occur within two separate systems that are of a common nature (the human system) when there are varied inputs within the particular systems. For instance, due to his lack of sight, the blind person may develop an extraordinary sense of hearing and mental capacity relative to the individual possessing sight.

Each selling organization possesses certain characteristics of a general nature. Essentially they are concerned with determining the needs of consumers and satisfying these needs. Each salesman within the sales organization will have certain abilities and certain characteristics which will distinguish him from other salesmen.

THE SELLING SYSTEM DEFINED

The systems approach is based upon a group of activities, functions, or components that can be bounded within a particular framework.[1] What do we find within the boundaries of the selling system? We find all relevant interdependencies, interactions, and relationships essential to perform selling functions. By definition a "system" is *a particular linking of processes which has a facilitating effect on carrying out the overall goals and objectives of the selling organization.* "Particular" suggests that although two systems may be contributing to carrying out similar processes, System 1 may be different in some respects from System 2. For example, selling petroleum products and selling life insurance would not be accomplished in exactly the same manner, although in both cases the selling system would be applied. In addition, a given component of one system may be similar to a component in another system, or it may have unique

---

[1] Martin Kenneth Starr, *Production Management*, Prentice-Hall, Inc., Englewood Cliffs, N.J., 1964, p. 4.

characteristics. "Facilitating effect" suggests that systems are ordinarily designed as a means of *accomplishing something positive in nature*.

Process

A "process" may be defined as a *flow of interrelated events moving toward some goals, purpose or end*. "Flow" implies movement through time and in the direction of a consequence; it may be mental or physical. "Interrelated" implies interaction in that the events are highly relevant to one another. "Events" are changes or happenings that occur at one point or period of time and may be of an infinite number of phenomena.[2]

The function of selling has several characteristics that relate directly to the merit of a systems approach. One, the salesman may influence but he cannot control the satisfaction of consumer needs. Only the consumer himself can say if a product fulfills his needs. Two, the selling organization cannot regulate its competitors, but rather may be influenced by them. Three, the salesman has no control over the remarkable technological advances which create new products to fulfill newly discovered needs. Because of these conditions the selling function is referred to as an "open" system as compared to a "closed" system. An electrical system is a closed system — that is, one in which activities can accurately be predicted if the system is functioning properly. It is also one in which the causes of disturbances, or happenings which run counter to productive results, can be readily diagnosed and corrective action can be taken. The selling system is an open system in the sense that the variances of the inputs and outputs cannot be predicted with absolute certainty: the salesman cannot predict with complete accuracy the results of his inputs into the selling system. Consequently the professional salesman must continually adjust his selling technique to meet the changing conditions or variables within the boundaries of the system.

Within this environment we find the importance of analysis and synthesis playing an integral role in the systems-process approach. Through analysis we proceed to take the selling system apart. We study the pieces individually and attempt to improve them. It is through synthesis that action is taken. Synthesis is required to put the factors back together in a relationship which leads to a specific end — the sale. For example, in selling investments the salesman must, through analysis, relate each of the six customer buying decisions in such a way that what he says and does will have a positive impact upon the customer. Thus the action taken by the salesman — synthesis — should involve a supportive interrelatedness between the needs of the customer and the product characteristics.

In this chapter we will list the inputs of the selling system: the component parts found within the boundaries of the system. These inputs will be discussed

[2] Wendell French, *The Personnel Management Process: Human Resources Administration*, 2d ed., Houghton Mifflin Company, Boston, 1970, pp. 33–43.

in greater detail in later chapters. It is the relatedness of the various inputs and processes, diagramed in Figure 2-1, that will be our primary concern.

INPUTS OF THE SELLING SYSTEM

Why People Buy

There are five buying decisions which enter into a final decision to buy a product: (1) the need to be fulfilled, (2) the product or service to fulfill the need, (3) the source for the product, (4) the price to pay (value), and (5) the time to buy. From a systems approach every decision to buy is actually the sum of five decisions; it is the interacting of the three processes with all the inputs. Each of these decisions fits into a particular place in the steps of selling — another group of inputs — and is a key to overcoming resistance and objections, ultimately leading to a successful sale.

How People Buy

There are six steps of selling: (1) preapproach, (2) attention, (3) interest, (4) conviction, (5) desire, and (6) close. In ordinary sales, the following three steps are emphasized:

2. *Attention*: Approaching the customer, getting attention, making a good impression, selling yourself and your personality

4. *Conviction*: Telling your sales story with product knowledge, making your sales presentation

6. *Close*: Conquering the buyer, making him see your point of view, getting the order

The systems approach completely develops all the steps of selling. From an overall view of the selling profession, it appears that the three steps of selling that are usually neglected are actually the most important:

1. *Preapproach*: The sale is completely planned and made in the salesman's mind. The salesman actually buys on behalf of the prospect — and then must tell the prospect what he bought and why.

3. *Interest*: The customer actually tells the salesman exactly why and how he will buy and how he wants to be sold. He tells the salesman how to make the sale.

5. *Desire*: This step is important because it is the one in which the buyer sees the product in terms of its meaning in his life. He feels its human values. He assumes ownership of the product in his mind. This step, often ignored or neglected, makes the close easy and automatic.

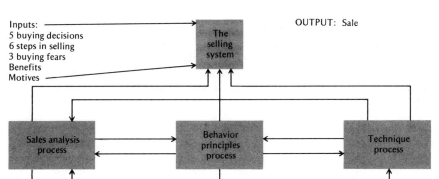

Fig. 2-1   A conceptual scheme of the marketing system.

Three Fears of Buying

Another group of inputs of the selling system are the three fears of buying that underlie much sales resistance and result in many lost sales. These are (1) the fear that the product will not do what the salesman says it will do, (2) the fear that the product is not worth the money (or that it might be obtained at a lower price than is asked), and (3) the fear that other people may not approve of the product or of the purchase.

What People Really Buy: Benefits

People do not buy products or services; they buy benefits. Benefits are facts translated into human values. They are the features and abilities of the product or service translated into what they can *mean* in the individual prospect's life. In systems selling, benefits are what the product will *do* for the buyer and what it will *mean* to the buyer.

Traditional sales training sometimes puts great emphasis on buying motives. Psychologists have made lengthy lists with dozens of possible buying motives carefully classified. They talk about the desire for gain, profit, or economy, for comfort, convenience, or ease, for satisfaction of pride or ego; they talk of the desire to avoid pain or loss. Actually, all buying motives come under three basic motives, and their corresponding negatives or opposites. The first is existence (life or self-preservation); its negative is death. The second is self-gratification (pleasure, adventure, prestige); its negative is self-denial. The third is gain (profit, growth, accomplishment); its negative is loss.

The important thing to remember about buying motives is that they are not the *reasons* people buy — they are the *reasons behind the reasons*. They are the deep human drives behind every purchase or action, the deeply felt drives people wish to satisfy. For this reason, we can seldom appeal to buying motives success-fully by name. They are labels used so frequently and widely that they have be-come empty and meaningless in selling. For instance, there is little selling power in the statement, "This product will make your family happy." The statement is meaningless because it is vague, even though we know that the customer wants to make his family happy, which is a basic desire. We must illuminate and illustrate our statement. We must show the customer *how* and *why* the product will make his family happy. We must speak of specific benefits rather than generalized buying motives:

> Mr. Swanson, I can see you and your family just a few weeks from now. You're sitting in your easy chair, reading the paper, and listening to your daughter play this electric organ. You look at her; you watch her for a few minutes. In her face you can see her interest, her complete concentration, her sense of accomplishment and pride in creating something truly beautiful. Nothing else has ever held her attention like this — this organ and the music it helps to create has become the most important thing in your daughter's life. Suddenly, she looks up at you and smiles, and in her eyes you can see her happiness and gratitude, her feeling that she has the most wonderful, understanding Dad in all the world.

When a salesman *talks about* buying motives, he is analyzing the underlying drives that lead people to buy. This may be worthwhile when talking to other salesman, but it is useless in talking to customers. But when a salesman *appeals* to buying motives, he is selling. And the way to appeal to buying motives is to talk in terms of benefits. Each benefit is an arrow that automatically will hit one of the targets called buying motives. To become a skilled archer, you study not the target but how to shoot the arrow. To become a professional salesman you study not the buying motives but benefits. They are the most important things you can study to build your sales ability and effectiveness. The emphasis here is upon the benefits, but this does not mean that motives have no significant role to play within the selling system. Before the salesman is in a position to discuss benefits, he must understand the source of consumer needs. In Chapter Four there will be a comprehensive discussion of this source within the consumer's personality.

Possibly real estate salesmen lose sales simply because they fail to realize the significance of benefits within the selling system. As a salesman turns the key allowing Mrs. Housewife to enter what may become her new home, a classic selling point is: *"This* is the living room!" It is probably quite obvious to Mrs. Housewife that the space vacant represents the living room, but there must be something about that living room that would have particular value to the prospective buyer. For example, there may be a grove of trees outside the window. The salesman could point out how in the spring of the year the picture window affords a bird's-eye view of nature. He could mention how much enjoyment will be theirs in enjoying the quiet hush of evening while watching the setting sun filter through the leaves as the last birds of evening give their chirps. Rather than stating, *"This* is the patio!" he could explain how the small children will enjoy riding their tricycles for hours on this fine cement patio, while Mrs. Housewife will never worry for the safety of her children.

THE THREE PROCESSES

Under the title of "Inputs," the system is now structured with all the component parts that will lead to a satisfactory completion of its outputs — sales. The processes, or particular flows of activity, are now presented.

Analysis: This process studies each step of the sale. It develops an understanding of what happens during a sale, but does not necessarily tell how to sell. It discusses theory rather than practice.

Principles of behavior: The emphasis here is upon the underlying principles of human nature and human behavior as they show themselves in buying and selling. This process studies what goes on in the buyer's mind and why it happens, teaching understanding rather than either the mechanics or the techniques of selling.

Techniques: This process is the practical side of the selling system, with emphasis on "how to do it." It concentrates on the mechanics of selling.

Again, the systems approach develops an overall understanding of salesmanship. It develops all three processes relative to the inputs: *analysis* to know what happens during the sale, *principles of behavior* to understand why it happens, and *techniques* to teach the salesmen how to make it happen, on a foundation of knowledge and understanding. Throughout the text we will discuss all the inputs in the framework of these processes.

Approach the selling system with an open mind. Try to forget everything you may already know or have read about selling (there is certainly plenty of material available). The selling system is a new way of looking at salesmanship — a complete, organized, logical, effective way to sell. If you try to edit or twist it to fit the ordinary concept of selling, it will lose its unity and lose its power. You will gain only a fraction of the help this training offers, emerging with a mongrelized salesmanship and trying to go in two directions at once. But if you can open your mind, if you will work to see the selling system as it is, the system will give you a solid framework, a method of automatically organizing all your knowledge and experience of sales. Each bit of information in your mind will automatically fall into its proper place, ready for effective use whenever it is needed. Your knowledge and experience will add their full strength and power to your selling.

CONCLUSION

Professionalism in any field denotes an aptitude by the professional to interpret events within a chosen activity and effectively react to these events. The concept of a selling system is developed as a device properly to relate those factors involved in the selling situation. The selling system allows the student of selling fully to develop an awareness and understanding of those factors which influence the selling situation. Once the inputs are mastered, the salesman through experience is able to grow continually in his professional skill.

The inputs of the selling system involve two basic areas. First are those factors the customer brings into the selling activity. These include the five buying decisions (need, product, source, price, and time); the three buying fears (fear the product will not do what the salesman says it will do, fear the product is not worth the price, and fear of what others may think about your purchase of the product); and benefits and motives.

The second basic area of inputs includes the factors which involve the direct activity of the salesman: the six steps of selling. These inputs are studied in terms of processes, or flows of activity. The processes are sales analysis, principles of behavior, and techniques. The salesman will deal principally with the three processes, but in doing so he realizes that inputs of the customer and the salesman are what create the environment for the three processes to exist. Of particular significance to the selling system is a recognition that the customer will not make a decision to buy unless he is aware that the salesman's product will produce benefits — significant personal values that the product can bring to the customer.

The selling system is an open system as compared to a closed system such as an electrical system. In a closed system, activities can accurately be predicted if the system is functioning properly. The selling system is an open system in the sense that the salesman cannot predict with complete accuracy the results of his inputs into the selling system. Thus, when a salesman deals with the thinking process of a customer, he cannot be entirely certain that the results will be as intended. This is why it becomes so important to use the selling system in developing, through effective communication, a firm bond of need awareness. This becomes the significant role of the selling system.

PROBLEMS

1. Define the term "system."

2. What is the significant distinction between an electrical system and the selling system? What does the term "open system" mean?

3. Discuss how awareness of the fear that others may not approve of what the customer buys would be relevant to a salesman of men's suits.

4. Discuss the importance of motives to the selling system.

5. Why are benefits of singular importance to the selling system?

6. Why is the systems approach of significant value in the function of selling?

7. What selling steps are most commonly used in selling? Which are frequently eliminated?

See page 249 for a case study.

Chapter Three
Consumer Need: The Basis for All
Professional Sales Approaches

In developing a systems approach to salesmanship, it is important to understand how and why a conceptual scheme is developed. The elements which result in successful salesmanship are not new — actually these factors go back to man's creation. Possibly Eve was the first known saleswoman, for it was she who sold Adam on the advantages of eating the forbidden fruit. Man's nature is today the same as it was at that time; however, there has been a constant shifting of his environment, values, beliefs, and needs throughout history. Therefore, the challenge in learning salesmanship is understanding not only the factors which lead to successful sales but also the *relatedness* of these factors.

The conceptual scheme, or systems approach, is a means by which the salesman may develop a framework. It includes all possible inputs and meaningfully *relates* those inputs. As a result the systems approach presents a mental process of developing the proper sales presentation for each customer. Through an understanding of the selling system, the student emerges with a professional approach toward any selling situation.

NEED AWARENESS

There is a classic sales story which you probably have heard before, but which merits attention here. The scene depicts an enthusiastic sales manager discussing with his sales force why their brand of dog food is not selling. "Haven't we the best advertising program in the industry?" the sales manager belts out. "You bet!" echoes the chorus of sales personnel. "Haven't we the most attractive package in the industry?" again exclaims the sales manager. Once again there is a responsive answer from the salesmen. "Haven't we the most effective sales organization in

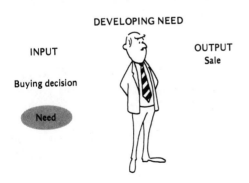

Fig. 3-1   The selling system.

the business? " he continues to ask. To this there is a thundering answer: "You bet we do!" booms the sales force. "Then why can't we sell more dog food? " The critical question is accompanied by silence, until a salesman in the back of the room, still entranced with the extreme honesty of the moment, shouts, "Because the dogs don't like it!" All the sales activity in the world will be of no benefit until there is a clear need established for the product.

In Chapter 2 the five buying decisions necessary for a completed sale were introduced:

1. The need to be fulfilled

2. The product to fulfill the need

3. The source for the product

4. The price to pay (value)

5. The time to buy

Everything is dependent upon the first decision, the need. It is the power behind the sale. Need is defined as a condition demanding supply or relief — a lack of something necessary, useful, or desired. It is also a feeling of inadequacy; it is the restlessness which results from dissatisfaction with the present state of affairs. It is desiring what you do not have. It is a feeling of not enjoying maximum personal satisfaction or of not receiving desired benefits. It is the desire to have more or be more.

For successful selling, the prospect must be aware of his need which the product will fulfill. He must feel this need, and he must acknowledge it. If this is not done, the prospect is almost certain to object during the sales interview. He will resist, or refuse to buy, or seem unable to make up his mind. The objection may *seem* to be on price, product, time to buy, or source, but it will actually be the prospect's way of saying, "I do not feel a strong enough need for your product to buy it right now."

DEVELOPING THE NEED

As we meet various prospects we run into a number of possible situations. Some prospects are strongly aware of their needs and ready to buy. Some are generally aware of their needs, but have not defined them; they may be "thinking about" buying. Some are not yet aware that they have a need for your product; they may not know that the need exists, or that it can be satisfied. The salesman cannot create needs, but he can create an *awareness* that a need already exists. The salesman's job is to do the following:

1. Determine and develop awareness of need in the buyer's mind.

2. Confirm the need so that the prospect knows his needs, the salesman knows what they are, and the prospect knows that the salesman knows. The

salesman and the prospect must have a common basis for communication, and starting with the prospect's need establishes this basis and ensures that the communication will be interesting and important to the prospect.

3. Match or link the buyer's needs with benefits offered by the product to show how the needs will be satisfied by the product.

THE FIRST COIN OF SELLING: NEEDS/BENEFITS

For every need that exists, there is a possible benefit that will fulfill it. Every benefit exists only because it satisfies a need. They are two sides of the same coin. This concept is called the "need/benefit coin"; it is the first coin of selling. Whichever side you see, the coin has the same value and can be turned over to show the other side. Throughout your study of the selling system you will encounter other important coins of selling. Each is the embodiment of one of the basic concepts of professional selling, and each is a way to keep that concept fresh in your mind when selling.

THE STEP CLOSE

People do things gradually. They buy in five decisions, not just in one. The first decision, the need, is made in a number of gradual steps. The buyer's need for the product is usually the sum of a number of needs, some of major importance, some of less importance. The sum total of the selling system consists of matching or linking needs with benefits, using the three processes of analysis, principles of behavior, and techniques to accomplish this. Benefits are linked in the salesman's presentation and in the buyer's mind. The process continues until the benefits, or value, are greater than the cost, and the sale is made.

Figure 3-2 is a diagram of the step close. It shows how the buyer is led over the hurdle of cost. Professional selling is gentle, convincing, and effective. The step close is built by starting with the needs. They must be determined in order to chart the steps: the salesman must find out what needs the buyer has and which are most important in his mind. Once he knows the buyer's needs, he can begin to present the benefits that will satisfy them, without wasting time or effort on anything that is not important to *this* prospect. Determining the buyer's needs

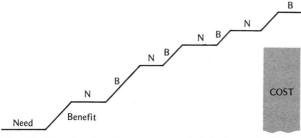

Fig. 3-2 The step close to overcome cost obstacles.

and developing his awareness of them take a little time but lead to a successful sale by the quickest possible route.

The first three steps of selling (see Figure 3-3) are concerned primarily with determining and developing needs for each individual prospect. You will study and learn how this is done, in detail, as the steps of selling are discussed in detail in later chapters.

DEVELOPING BENEFITS

The final three steps of selling are concerned with the other side of the needs/benefits coin — the other side of the step-close stairway shown in Figure 3-2. These three steps — conviction, desire, and close — are concerned primarily with presenting the benefits we can offer to fulfill the buyer's needs. The features of the product sold must be presented in terms of the benefits they offer. We must continually translate what our product offers into what it will mean in the buyer's life. Thus we use the phrase "is-do-means" in referring to this selling approach: we describe what the product *is*, what it will *do* for the buyer, and what it will *mean* to the buyer.

Selling Points

Analysis of the product is one of the beginnings of the scientific approach to selling. The doctor examines the patient to find out his specific symptoms. The lawyer questions the client to find out the specific circumstances. The housewife studies the recipe to learn the specific ingredients of the cake. These people realize that knowledge leads toward success in treating the patient, pleading the case, or baking the cake. The same is true of the professional salesman. He wants specific facts about his product. These specific facts are known as *selling points* or selling features. Selling points are significant facts about the product. They are the beginning framework of the conviction step. They are as important to the salesman as diagnostic symptoms are to the doctor and circumstances are to the lawyer. The success of the doctor, the lawyer, and the salesman in their respective fields will hinge on the accuracy and value of the facts they gather.

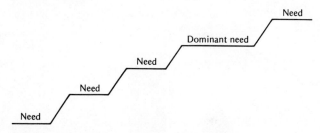

Fig. 3-3 Step close related to dominant need.

TABLE 3-1 STEPS OF SALESMANSHIP

Buying decision	Buying decision	Buying decision	Buying decision	Buying decision	Buying decision
Need	Need	Need	Need Product Source	Price	Time
Determining and developing need			Developing benefits		
Preapproach	Attention	Interest	Conviction	Desire	Close

Product Analysis

The salesman must know his product and its selling points in order to translate the selling points into benefits. The process is known as product analysis. Knowledge of the product is one of the keys to natural enthusiasm; knowledge of the benefits it offers is the other key. Complete knowledge of his product and its human values is of first importance to the professional salesman. It creates true self-confidence and abounding natural enthusiasm. It marks the expert, professional salesman.

This is one of the main reasons why many firms spend so much time and money training and developing their sales force. It is not uncommon for a trainee to spend up to one year in various phases of a training program. Firms specializing in technical products, such as International Business Machines Corporation, may require an even greater amount of training. The firm wants to assure itself that it has developed a high degree of product knowledge, so that trainees will have the opportunity to grow in confidence and enthusiasm.

Differences Make Sales

For a buyer to make a choice, he must see a difference between the choices open to him, a difference that means one choice will better satisfy his needs. It is one of the paradoxes of human nature that although man does not wish to be completely unique among men, he does reserve for himself a degree of difference, something which distinguishes him from others. He carries this concept of difference over to making a purchase.

The difference that makes the sale is frequently a difference in the product itself, a special or exclusive feature. Or it may be any of these differences:

1. A difference in the salesman's ability to determine the prospect's needs and make him aware of them

2. A difference in presenting the features and abilities of the product, even when they are the same for competitive products

3. A difference in the source

4. An actual difference in the price at which the buyer can satisfy his needs

5. A difference in the time the purchase *can* or *should* be made

PRODUCT ANALYSIS FOR EFFECTIVE SELLING: SP IS-DO-MEANS

Analyzing a product and translating it into human values involve the following steps:

1. *Determine the selling point.* Any significant feature of the product, whether it is exclusive or not, may constitute a selling point.

2. *Explain what the selling point is,* in specific terms. Define or explain the selling point, in a few direct sentences. When you talk about what a selling point is, you are selling *product quality.* You are working to remove one of the basic buying fears, the fear that the product is not worth the money. Talking about what a product *is* is a start in removing this fear.

3. *Discuss what the selling point does* — and how and why it does it. This particular step is most important to the buyer. Every buyer is most interested in what a certain product will do for him. Sales sentences giving this information should be phrased so they contain within them a benefit which will appeal to more than one buying motive. The *how* and *why* of what the product does is explanation that helps the buyer be sure the product will do what you say it will do.

4. *Explain what the selling point means to the buyer.* Up to this point the discussion has been about the product — from the buyer's point of view. Now the focus is upon the buyer and how his needs will be fulfilled. To illustrate, in selling the idea of drinking his orange juice to a child, you might say: "If you drink your orange juice (product) it will help cure your cold (what the product will do) and you'll be able to go outside to play with your friends" (what the product means to the buyer). A *do* benefit comes from the product and its abilities. A *means* benefit comes from the buyer and his needs. The same needs can be satisfied in many ways by many different features or many different products.

5. *Appeal to the buying motive or motives.* This is a valuable point to add in product analysis, particularly for the salesman's understanding of the selling system. A product analysis using the is-do-means approach described above is given in Table 3-2.

TABLE 3-2   PRODUCT: THE ZOOMO MOWER

1. Selling point	2. What it is	3. What it will do for the buyer; why or how it will do it	4. What it means to the buyer	5. Buying motives
Soft tires	Semi-pneumatic rubber 1½" wide	These tires won't dig into the soft turf of your lawn. Wheels will not break. Will not chip sidewalk. Are quiet on sidewalk.	This will keep your lawn trim; you won't be digging up the grass when you turn sharp corners, or mar the beauty of your sidewalks by chipping them. You will never have to replace the wheels as you may have had to replace the cast iron type.	Beauty Money
Saber cutting edge	Has five precision-ground steel blades	It will cut a 16" swath of grass cleanly and smoothly to selected height.	You will save time in cutting your lawn, and have a more attractive lawn. It can be done with the same ease as cutting a standard narrow swath.	Ease Beauty
Flexible underknife	A spring steel bar	Automatically adjusts itself to the blades. Acts as a self-sharpener. Absorbs shocks that would break a rigid underknife.	Saves you the time and effort of adjusting your mower; assures a perfect cut every time. Reduces sharpening costs. Prevents breakage and repairs.	Ease Beauty Money

CASE STUDIES IN NEED DEFINITION AND PRODUCT ANALYSIS

THE ABC FERTILIZER CO.

The sales manager is telling his men: "Over half the job of selling is done with the hands and feet. Anyone can increase sales by increasing his physical effort. He can contact more people, carry his sample case into the presence of more prospects, and increase his sales without increasing his knowledge one bit.

"You've heard many times that it is important that you present a product in terms of the prospect's wants and desires. His chief and only interest is most often the answer to one question: 'What's in it for me?'' You've been told that you have to think on the customer's side of the fence. Many of us have wondered how it could be done. Today we're going to lay those principles right on the line.

"In the average call, the salesman opens his case, goes through the presentation of the feed facts, the merchandising of the period special, and then the display and suggestion selling. Usually the products are picked up one by one, shown, described, and analyzed for the prospect. He is then questioned to find if the product fits his needs or desires.

"Suppose you were to take a small boy to the zoo. In one section you find an elephant. You know about elephants, so you explain it to your small friend. You tell how strong it is, how it has been brought from India, how much feed it eats, how tough its hide is, the wonders of its trunk — yes, you tell all about it. There is no doubt that your small friend will be amazed at this two-tailed beast. He will probably be open-mouthed at your explanation. He might even tell all his friends about it. *But, believe me, he probably wouldn't want to own one.* He couldn't imagine it doing anything constructive for him, or giving him any pleasure. He would know that it is strictly a zoo animal, something to amaze and intrigue people, but of little practical value to him.

"Now move down a few steps to the pen where they keep the Shetland pony. You're an authority on ponies, too. You tell him that many boys have ponies, how they can ride them to school, how ponies are friendly, how much fun it is to feed them apples, how they can be hitched to carts. And, as you go on, your friend's excitement grows. Certainly he can see himself riding that pony. He can see himself feeding it lumps of sugar. He begins to lick his lips and he gets downright emotional about it. He would work all summer — he would take every cent he has — he would coax money out of his Dad and Mom and his friends to buy that pony! Why? *Because of what it will do for him!*

"Many prospects look at our products like a visitor looks at an elephant in a zoo. They are amazed, they didn't realize our products are what they are, but they have no feelings about owning them. Our products are the answers to the wants and desires of the farmers, ranchers, and stockmen in your territory. If it isn't one product it may be another. You're not selling feed, you're selling benefits, you're satisfying wants. When you get a prospect interested and thinking about the *benefits he wants*, you're in a position to show him how you can help him realize those benefits. That's the time to bring out your product as the solution to his wants and desires."

A CASE STUDY OF THE ABC MACHINERY CO.

The sales manager poses this situation to his sales staff:

"Suppose we were selling machinery, and we told a buyer: 'Our machine has this new double reduction framistat that is brand new and completely exclusive with us. It is the result of millions of dollars in research, and is covered by ninety-six American and international patents.'

"Any prospect would be justified in saying: 'So what? What does it mean to me?' He might say this to us, or he might say it only to himself. Only the rarest buyer, assuming he understood us, would be able or willing to translate the information in his own mind. *How much simpler and more effective to do it for him — and for every buyer.* For example:

"As you know, one of the big problems on machines of this type is that the vibration can shake them out of adjustment, and they start turning out parts that don't meet specifications. It's been a tough problem, and it took a long time to solve. But it has been solved, with this automatic unit we call the double reductive framistat. Here's how it works. When you first set the machine, you lock this dial. As the machine runs, it automatically inspects each part it produces, and adjusts itself back to the original setting. Every piece the machine produces will automatically meet specifications.

"Naturally, this feature is patented — with ninety-six patents, in fact. There's no other make of machine that is self-inspecting and self-adjusting. But the important thing is what this framistat means: Every part produced will meet specifications. You'll eliminate one source of wasted materials, labor, and production time. You'll be able to turn out more perfect parts in less time at a lower cost per unit. You'll be able to set exact production schedules, and be sure of meeting the deadline. You'll be rid of those production stoppages and bottlenecks that usually come at the worst time. And you'll cut your labor costs, for this machine has its own inspector and adjustor built in. You won't have to pay anyone $4.50 per hour to stand and watch it run. Your inspectors and machine setup men will be freed to work on other machines where they are needed."

If you were the prospect, which explanation would do more toward leading you to buy? Which framistat would have more meaning and value to you?

CONCLUSION

Conceptually, the systems approach is as old as man's nature, and its logical approach is very much in harmony with man's approach to action. The Romans expressed it in this manner: *bonum ex integra causa* ("good results from the integrity of its component parts"). From the systems approach the challenge in learning salesmanship is understanding the factors which lead to successful sales *and* the relatedness of these factors. It is in meeting this challenge that the salesman develops integrity between the component parts of the selling system. Above all, the system itself must be related to the *needs* of the customer: developing this need awareness becomes an initial activity within the selling system. Needs must be understood in their broadest terms as a lack of something necessary, useful, or desired. It is not the salesman's responsibility to question the value judgment of the customer. The salesman's job is to determine what the customer's needs are and through *product analysis* (is-do-means) present the benefits of the product which will fulfill these established needs. The salesman is not in a position to create needs — only the customer can do this. But the salesman can make the customer aware of needs not previously recognized. This we call "creative selling." The professional salesman who can develop this particular skill cannot help but reach a high degree of personal satisfaction and achievement.

PROBLEMS

1. Why is the term "related" of importance to any system? To the selling system?

2. Why is need so fundamental to successful selling?

3. Define the term "need." Relate this definition to the need a recent purchase satisfied.

4. Discuss the importance of developing need awareness.

5. How does the customer become aware of his needs?

6. Discuss the needs which an automobile would fulfill for the following persons: housewife, salesman, vice-president of an insurance company.

7. How is the systems approach used in developing need awareness?

8. Why do we say that needs/benefits are two sides of the same coin?

9. Discuss the concept of the step close.

10. Define the term "is-do-means."

11. Take an advertisement from a local newspaper. Using the is-do-means approach, develop a sales analysis with three selling points. See Table 3-2.

12. In rereading the ABC Fertilizer case, discuss how you would use the ideas presented by the sales manager in a systems approach. Use the material found in the chapter.

See pages 250–251 for an additional case study.

ASSIGNMENT 1

List three products and give three selling points and three benefits for each.

PRODUCT OR SERVICE THAT I SELL:

Selling point:

Benefit:

Selling point:

Benefit:

Selling point:

Benefit:

PRODUCT OR SERVICE THAT I BOUGHT:

Selling point:

Benefit:

Selling point:

Benefit:

Selling point:

Benefit:

Check one: _____ These are the three most important benefits I wish to receive from this course.

_____ These are my three most important selling needs.

First:

Second:

Third:

ASSIGNMENT 2

Prepare a sheet similar to the one for the "Zoomo Mower" (see Table 3-2 on page 19). List selling points, what they are, what they will do for the buyer, why or how they will do it, the benefits, and buying motives.

The product you are to analyze this way is a regular lead pencil. List at least *five* selling points and carry them across the analysis sheet through each item. To help you analyze the pencil, here is some information:

It has six basic parts: the lead, the wood, the paint, the printed identification, the brass ferrule, and the rubber eraser.

It has shape, size, and weight.

It is used for certain purposes.

Each part, each physical characteristic, each function of a pencil is your clue to a *number* of possible selling points. Look at it closely. Ask yourself how it is made and why it is made that way.

ASSIGNMENT 3

Develop three selling points for any one product or service.

PRODUCT OR SERVICE: _____

Selling point:

The selling point — what it *is* in specific terms:

  Examples of what each selling point is:

What each selling point will *do*; how or why it will do it:

  Examples of what it will do; how or why it will do this; what it has done for others:

What each selling point *means* to the buyer (specific benefits):

  Examples of what it means to the buyer or what it has meant to other buyers:

Buying motive or motives appealed to:

Chapter Four
Consumer Needs and Their Satisfaction

In Chapter Three we mentioned the five buying decisions and the initial importance of understanding and developing consumer needs/benefits. In order to relate these buying decisions ultimately to a purchase decision, two broad areas are of particular significance to the professional salesman. The first is the product analysis, discussed in Chapter Three, whereby the salesman becomes knowledgeable of his product (and consequently capable of relating needs to benefits), and the second is an understanding of the source of consumer needs. This chapter deals with the source of consumer needs and their satisfaction.

On the night of March 8, 1971, Joe Frazier fought Cassius Clay for the heavyweight championship of the world. Because of legal restrictions the fight could not be carried "live" by network radio. However, one of the major networks presented a clever fight program structured around a fifty-word summation (by decree of the courts) of each round eminating from UPI. Obviously, there was much discussion time between these fifty-word summations. For the sake of developing some "fight talk," one of the commentators made the observation that Joe Frazier has a *six*-car garage and may even buy another car if he wins the fight. The typical family man would wonder why Joe would even consider buying another car; it is not difficult to conclude that there is *no* way that one man can effectively utilize all those cars. And yet, as salesmen we would have to conclude that if Joe were to buy another automobile he would do so because of some need. Is it possible to have a need for the seventh? If we broaden our understanding of needs to include a lack of something related to attitudes, motives, or knowledge, there is valid, logical reasoning used in determining that a need would be fulfilled.

In order to show this logic, let us compare Joe Frazier's need to that of Frank Carroll, who has just been graduated from college, has recently married, and is looking forward to a new selling career with the ABC Aluminum Corporation. To function as a sales representative, it is necessary that Frank have an automobile. He is already in debt to the local department store, so he approaches the credit union for ABC asking for a $1,500 loan to buy a late-model used car.

What is the difference between the needs of Joe Frazier and Frank Carroll? Frank needs a car in order to earn an income and thereby provide basic needs for his new family, while Joe is possibly satisfying the need for social prestige. As car salesmen, do we have the right *or* the obligation to determine which of these needs are of greater value? Must they not be evaluated in terms of the *particular* needs of each customer? In order to determine which specific needs the product will satisfy for a customer, it is helpful for the salesman to understand needs in terms of the customer's personality. This chapter offers three avenues of introspection by which the salesman can develop basic needs in a manner significant to the customer.

To use another example, a man's suit could be purchased for a variety of needs. It might be a necessity to function at the job; it may be a device to become a part of a particular reference group; it could be a symbol of success; it could be simply to keep him warm.

After studying the areas of *motives, attitudes,* and *knowledge*, the professional salesman will have a much wider spectrum in his determination *and* understanding of the needs of his customers. It is entirely possible that a salesman is literally allowing sales to pass him by because he is not aware of customer needs.

"Wouldn't you *really* rather have a Buick?" is an advertising phrase used by the General Motors Corporation. From an *analysis process* viewpoint, the question as to *why* a consumer would rather have a Buick becomes critical. Is it because the consumer has "arrived," and the Buick becomes a symbol of the newly found success? Is it because of the special riding features of this car? Our objective in this chapter is to find some answers as to how the salesman can understand the source of consumer needs and thereby be more qualified in satisfying them.

It is not the intent of this customer analysis to present a buying motive list: as far back as 1923 Arthur Kornhouser argued against the buying motive list approach,[1] while Douglas McGregor felt that the normally listed motives were observations rather than explanations of behavior.[2] Rather, the concern here is to study the broad determinants that affect a buying decision. Once these determinants are understood, the salesman will be in a position to appraise intelligently the relationship of customer satisfaction and the product he sells.

PSYCHOLOGICAL DETERMINANTS IN FULFILLING CONSUMER SATISFACTION NEEDS

Salesmen are basically practical men who deal in tangible problems — problems of what product will attract a particular customer, what prices will be acceptable to consumers, how best to attract the customer with advertising. The sales manager is concerned daily with how he may direct his sales organization in bringing the product message to the customer. The salesman is concerned daily with how he can prepare a sales presentation that will sell the product. These daily challenges require an understanding of the processes through which the consumer progresses in deciding to buy a particular product. In order to gain a keener insight into the reasons for a buying decision, the salesman can look toward the fields of psychology and sociology. It is within these purely academic areas that certain fundamental concepts will be found that provide an understanding of what influences consumer satisfaction through the purchase of goods and services.

Individuals clearly differ in the factors that dominate their purchase decisions. Some are far more deliberative than others, some are better informed, some are

[1] Arthur W. Kornhouser, "The Motives in Industry Problems," *Annals of the American Academy of Political and Social Science,* 1923.

[2] Douglas McGregor, "Motives as a Tool of Market Research," *Harvard Business Review,* vol. 19, no. 1, Autumn, 1940, p. 44.

concerned with the best value, some seek attraction by purchases while others prefer to remain inconspicuous. However, customer behavior seems to vary widely according to types of products. Factors that dominate choice of soap, floor wax, cigarette, or canned soup, for instance, appear to be very different from those that dominate choices among houses, cosmetics, furniture, deodorants, jewelry, and automobiles. To expect a single theory to apply equally well to such diverse product choices places an undue and unnecessary burden on any theory. Not only are there vast differences in an individual's usual purchase behavior and the factors that dominate product choice, but there is great inconsistency in the way an individual buys different products. For example, a man may buy national brands of shirts but not shoes, or a national brand of television but not washing machine. A man may insist on the "best" when he buys food but be very economical when buying house furnishings.

ANALYTICAL VIEW OF CONSUMER BUYING SATISFACTION

From a time prospective, consumer needs are viewed in the future. The number and types of sales made today, yesterday, or last year are certainly useful in judging future trends and sales potential, but the prime impetus resolves itself in satisfying *future* needs — tomorrow, next week, or next year. In analyzing how the salesman can most effectively satisfy these needs, it is necessary to relate the future to the consumer. Based upon this important premise, the flow of activity generated within the marketing system begins with the personality of the consumer. Personality is the *present* disposition of the consumer and forms the basis upon which the selling system will develop its potential in satisfying future needs. Personality includes the consumer's *present* goals, fears, expectations, aspirations, frames of reference, and values. The consumer's personality is the product of knowledge, attitudes, and motives gained through experience in the *past*. This

TABLE 4-1   PROCESS OF NEED DEFINITION AND SATISFACTION

Past	Present	Future
Knowledge	Personality	Consumer need satisfaction.
Attitudes	Goals	Project one's personality into the future.
Motives	Fears	This involves a mental process by which the mind projects into the
	Expectations	future.
	Aspirations	How the purchase will satisfy needs.
	Opinions	
	Frames of reference	

personality is directed by the selling system into the *future* when consumer need satisfaction is achieved. Once a sale is made (the end result of the system), the need has been satisfied, and in the form of experience the need now becomes a element of the past. The cycle has been completed.

Through analysis of consumer satisfaction, the selling system must answer this critical question: How can the attitudes, motives, and knowledge developed in the past be related to the consumer's personality (present) so as to provide need satisfaction in the future? Since attitudes, motives, and knowledge are the factors which result in personality, these three factors require further study. Even though the consumer tends to act consistently and thereby to stabilize his personality, there is an opportunity within his framework for flexibility and variety of behavior. The next concern, therefore, is to develop an understanding of these psychological factors affecting consumer satisfaction.

PSYCHOLOGICAL VIEW

ATTITUDE

Attitude is a readiness to respond with a defined course of action in relation to an object in a given stimulus situation.[3] Attitudes basically serve as organizing forces by which the consumer perceives the need value of a product or service. They are an outgrowth of heredity, group experiences, and culture. Because attitudes are based upon values, they tend to remain constant. For this reason, an understanding of attitudes here is not for the purpose of *changing* attitudes, but rather to use these existing attitudes as a basis for need satisfaction. Attitudes apply in three areas: preference, product image, and symbolism.

Preference

Through attitudes consumers develop specific preferences for products. Through research it is possible to determine what these preferences are and thus develop a product focused upon this specific consumer need.

Product Image

Product image represents the pattern of consumer attitudes toward a product. Two problems arise: (*a*) determining what the image should be and (*b*) determining how distinct the image should be. In deciding what the image should be, the selling organization must determine the general attitude of the consumer toward the product. For example, State Farm Mutual Automobile Insurance Company found that the ideal automobile insurance company must be reputable, well

---

[3]Raymond B. Cattell and Andrew R. Baggaley, "The Objective Measurement of Attitude Motivation: Development and Evaluation of Principles and Devices," *Journal of Personality*, vol. 24, no. 4, p. 421, 1955.

known, prompt in payment, initially selective with respect to policy holders, and "on the side of the customer." State Farm decided to bring its image closer to the ideal by emphasizing in its advertising that it was on the side of the customer.

In determining how distinct the image should be, it can be stated as a general rule that the more specific the image, the narrower the segment of the population to which the product appeals. For example, PepsiCo, Inc. developed an advertising program relating its product, Pepsi Cola, to the younger generation. Although it might be debated who is represented by the younger generation, PepsiCo committed itself to a specific market segment in projecting its product image.

Symbolism

Symbolism refers to the thinking about the *meaning* of a product purchase rather than the *function* of a purchase.[4] The purchase of a Lincoln Continental automobile might be based more upon what it means to the customer (business success, stature in the community) than upon the engineering and other functional qualities of a Lincoln Continental. Sales tactics are often directed toward the achievement of an image with a symbolic meaning. Hallmark Cards, Inc., has developed the image that Hallmark greeting cards symbolize "those who care enough to send the very best."

The establishment by the Procter & Gamble Company of Blue Cheer is another example of appealing to attitudes through symbols. In 1950, four years after introducing Tide, Procter & Gamble decided to introduce a new laundry detergent. Even though Tide was by far the leader in the field, the company recognized a marketing potential in the form of housewives who did not like Tide. Although Cheer was not a bad product — in cool water it was considered by Procter & Gamble to perform better in some ways than Tide — the company could not at first get women interested in buying it. Then it was decided to appeal to the consumer's attitude in relating a white wash to cleanliness, personal satisfaction, and the symbol of a successful housewife. On this basis, the company tried a scheme to give Cheer a new and distinctive personality. Like other detergents on the market, Cheer contained an optical bleach — a dye that makes clothes *look* very white in sunlight by causing them to reflect some of the sun's ultraviolet rays in the form of blue light. The scheme was to add blue coloring matter to Cheer, which had been sold up to then as a white product, and to make a great point of the "blue whiteness" it imparted to shirts and sheets. This worked so well that by 1953 the new Cheer ("It's New! It's Blue! Only Cheer has the Blue-Magic Whitener!") was outselling every other brand of laundry soap or detergent except Tide.

[4]Walter A. Woods, "Psychological Dimensions of Consumer Decisions," reprinted from *Journal of Marketing*, vol. 24, no. 3, pp. 15-19, January 1960.

MOTIVES OF CONSUMERS

Motives are the impelling force behind need-satisfying behavior. Basically our search is a causal one: what cause can we discover within the consumer which will effect a purchase? As will be discovered, many of the causes will be subtle, but this does not mean that the salesman cannot intelligently arrive at *some* reasons why a particular purchase is made. Remember, there will always be factors which will be unpredictable. However, with greater insight into the consumer behavior patterns, the salesman increases his probability for success.

Basic Needs

To develop a framework for interpreting the basic needs, the studies of A. H. Maslow[5] deserve serious consideration. Maslow presents a need hierarchy, theorizing that *generally* the individual follows this pattern in need satisfaction. Once a need is fulfilled, it no longer is a motivator for fulfillment and the individual progresses up the need hierarchy.

Physiological needs These needs are basic to human existence: the need for shelter, food, drink. Undoubtedly these physiological needs are the most important of all needs. A person who is lacking in food, safety, love, and esteem would most probably hunger for food more strongly than for anything else. If all the needs are unsatisfied and the organism is then dominated by the physiological needs, all other needs may become simply nonexistent or be pushed into the background.

Safety needs With fulfillment of basic needs, higher needs emerge, for a want that is satisfied is no longer a want. The organism is dominated and its behavior organized only by unsatisfied needs, which, in the need hierarchy, now become safety needs. These too may wholly dominate the organism. They may serve as the almost exclusive organizers of behavior, recruiting all the capacities of the organism in their service. Unfulfilled safety needs in the extreme would characterize a man living almost for safety alone. An example would be the "compulsive-obsessive" neurotic who tries to order and stabilize the world so that no unmanageable, unexpected, or unfamiliar danger will ever appear. He hedges himself about with all sorts of ceremonies, rules, and formulas so that every possible contingency may be provided for.

[5] For a more complete discussion of these need patterns refer to Abraham H. Maslow, in *Psychological Review*, vol. 50, pp. 370–396, 1943, and Maslow, *Motivation and Personality*, Harper & Brothers, New York, 1954. Maslow is recognized as a noted psychologist. The reader is urged also to review his discussion of creative thinking in *Toward a Psychology of Being*, D. Van Nostrand Company, New York, 1962, p. 175.

For normal individuals, safety needs are related to job assurance, savings accounts, various insurance programs, and a religious philosophy which accepts an unknown future.

Love needs With the fulfillment of physiological and safety needs there emerges the love and affection and belongingness needs. Here the hunger is for affectionate relations with people, for a place in the group. Love needs here are not synonymous with sex; sex may be considered as a physiological need.

Esteem needs Within this category are considered the needs for self-respect and for the esteem of others. Satisfaction of the self-esteem need leads to feelings of self-confidence, worth, strength, capability, and adequacy, the feeling of being useful and necessary in the world.

Need for self-actualization Even if all these needs are satisfied, we may still often, if not always, expect that a new discontent and restlessness will soon develop, unless the individual is doing what he is suited for. A musician must make music, an artist must paint, a poet must write, if they are ultimately to be happy. What a man *can* be, he *must* be. This need we may call self-actualization. The clear emergence of this need rests upon prior satisfaction of the physiological, safety, love, and esteem needs.

Characteristics of the Basic Needs

This hierarchy has been presented as if it were a true hierarchy, but actually it is not nearly as rigid as may be implied. There are a number of exceptions. (1) There are, for example, some people for whom self-esteem seems to be more important than love. (2) In certain people the level of aspiration may be permanently deadened or lowered. That is, the less prepotent goals may simply be lost and may disappear forever, so that someone who has experienced life at a low level, for example, because of chronic unemployment, may continue to be satisfied for the rest of his life if only he can get enough food. (3) Perhaps the most important exceptions are the ones that involve ideals, high social standards, or high moral values. With such values people become martyrs: they will give up everything for the sake of a particular ideal or value. People who have been satisfied in their basic needs throughout their lives, particularly in their earlier years, seem to develop exceptional power to withstand present or future thwarting of these needs simply because they have a strong, healthy character structure as a result of basic satisfaction.

Again, this theoretical discussion of Maslow's hierarchy may have given the impression that these sets of needs are somehow in a stepwise, all-or-nothing relationship to each other. We have spoken in such terms as the following: if one need is satisfied, then another emerges. In actual fact, most normal members of our society are partially satisfied in all their basic needs and partially unsatisfied at the same time. A more realistic description of the hierarchy developed by

Maslow is in terms of decreasing percentages of satisfaction as we go up the hierarchy of prepotency. For instance, the average person may be satisfied 85 percent in his physiological needs, 70 percent in his safety needs, 50 percent in his love needs, 40 percent in his self-esteem needs, and 10 percent in his self-actualization needs.

Maslow's theory does not give the practical marketer a great deal to use specifically in analyzing people as customers. Nevertheless, it does offer an important key in specifically analyzing consumer needs. It is not unusual for motives to conflict with each other in the mind of the customer. The strong motivation to save for future security may conflict with the motivation to join his friends on a trip to Europe; or the cost to join a particularly fine social club might require funds previously allotted to college education.

KNOWLEDGE

Knowledge is a primary fact of human life and experience. Everyone understands what it means "to know," "to have knowledge." But when we attempt to explain and analyze this idea, we immediately encounter difficulties. In order to gain some insight into what knowledge is, it is important to understand the three elements which enter into knowledge: the subject, the object, and the mental act of knowing. The *object* becomes known to the *subject* by the mental act of *knowing*, called the "unitive act" — that is, somehow uniting the object and the subject. The object must become *intramental*, intrasubjective, before it can be known. This takes place by means of sense perception and thought, having cognitive presence. It is upon this basis that a judgment, a *conscious effort to buy*, is made.

TECHNIQUES UTILIZING CUSTOMER KNOWLEDGE, ATTITUDES, AND MOTIVES

KNOWLEDGE

The initial purchase of any item requires the use of mental processes which ultimately result in the willing acceptance of a value judgment. After initial acceptance of this value judgment, the buying decision may become a habit requiring less conscious effort. Eventually it may become a conditioned response. The consumer learns constantly throughout life. His reasoning process continually accepts or rejects facts his senses bring to his cognitive attention. Knowledge received through the senses is reacted to in a conscious manner. From the salesman's viewpoint this knowledge becomes significant when it results in a judgment or decision to buy. The customer reaches this conclusion in three stages of the thought process:

1. *Determination of needs.* Through the sensory perception of a sales presentation or a store display, the customer may reach a conclusion that a particular

need exists. This conclusion begins with the acceptance of sensory perception (sight, feel, smell, hearing, taste) and is concluded in the form of logical or intellectual reasoning.

2. *Desire to fulfill needs.* This involves the emotional belief and wanting, based upon the knowledge acquired.

3. *Decision to buy.*[6] The customer, on the basis of knowledge, says first, "It's reasonable; it makes sense; I should." Next he says, "It appeals to me; I want to." Third, the prospect says, "I will." He makes a decision on the basis of knowledge and puts it into action.

Through knowledge presented to him, a customer's inner conditions, represented by attitudes and motives, may be altered. For example, a housewife may

Sensory perception of sight makes knowledge possible

Knowledge of the object takes place in the brain through the *cognitive process* (the mental act of knowing)

Fig. 4-1 Subject related to object through sensory perception.

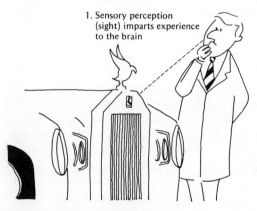

1. Sensory perception (sight) imparts experience to the brain

2. The brain accepts that which it chooses to accept—*selective perception*

3. *Cognition* occurs— interpretive analysis by which an awareness is made

4. *Decision making*: On the basis of this interpretive analysis an awareness is made

Fig. 4-2 The decision-making process.

[6] These three stages of the thought process are directly related to the five buying decisions made by the customer. Actually the buying decisions evolve from the thought process.

shop at a particular supermarket for years, and this consequently becomes a habit. She knows exactly where all the items are stocked (conditioned response). In fact she may no longer require a shopping list. She simply travels the store in a pattern, picking items from the shelves as she passes. She may have developed a favorable attitude (values) toward the store. She is pleased when the employees of the store greet her by name. Perhaps other women from the neighborhood also shop at this supermarket, thereby strengthening a group relationship within the store.

Before discussing how knowledge may alter the buying behavior of this housewife, it is imperative to recognize her personality (present) relative to developed patterns based on attitudes and motives (past). Certainly we can conclude that this store has become engrained in her disposition. Shopping for groceries is a buying action performed almost daily; it is very much a part of her life. If she feels comfortable in the store and can readily acquire the food items which will satisfy her family's needs, why should she change? Possibly a special price bargain might attract her attention to another store, but certainly she would weigh the prospect of traveling a new route to a store with which she is not familiar against the price advantage.[7]

Knowledge of new benefits sufficient in magnitude to alter present attitudes and motives could affect buying behavior. For example, an advertising campaign emphasizing the special quality of meat or vegetables could present sufficient information to allow the housewife a new learning experience of additional benefits she could offer her family. At this point, a new *motivating* factor is introduced, the welfare of her family. Attitudes would not be affected. To change her attitude toward the present store, a learning process involving experience is required. The factors may be the friendliness of clerks, the attractiveness of displays, cleanliness of the store, lighting, and other people who also shop at the supermarket. All these factors which will influence her attitude can be gained only through experience. If through the newly found knowledge of excellent meat she does shop at the new store, if she enjoys a pleasant buying experience, an alteration of motives and attitude may take place. Eventually a habit may be formed to shop at the new supermarket, involving less and less conscious effort, becoming more of a conditioned response.

The Use of Knowledge in Selling

The sales of Sears, Roebuck & Company have shown impressive gains; part of this sales increase is a direct result of the increased usage of the Sears catalog. In this area of consumer satisfaction, knowledge becomes an important factor.

[7]Basically this is the situation a salesman finds himself in when calling upon a new account. The prospective customer has developed a conditioned response — a habit of buying from a particular source based upon some positive features. He feels comfortable buying from the source. In the acquisition of a new medical group, insurance firms are often eager to have the new group present claims so as to develop quickly this comfortable feeling within the group.

The customer uses his senses in selecting and evaluating items in the catalog. He *sees* the item in attractive color (selective perception) and on the basis of the specific information defining the characteristics of the item (cognition) he makes a decision as to whether or not to buy. It should not be concluded that this is the only component of this process utilized, for certainly motives and attitudes will play a role, particularly in the desire to make a potential purchase. The example serves to emphasize the dominant position that knowledge plays in consumer satisfaction and show how it may be supported by an effective marketing strategy.

In 1970 $2.2 billion was ordered from Sears catalogs. This amounts to 22 percent of gross sales for Sears, Roebuck and Co., the world's largest retailer. At the same time, Americans bought approximately $1.1 billion worth of goods from the catalogs of Montgomery Ward and Co., J.C. Penney Co., and a handful of other general retailers.

Sears is now concentrating on the urban dweller, even the urban sophisticate. Today only about 15 percent of Sears' catalog business is truly mail order. The rest of the orders are placed by phone or in person at catalog offices in urban and suburban neighborhoods, where city dwellers can simply call in orders and, a few days later, pick them up without fuss. Sears now has 2,310 retail catalog and telephone sales offices in addition to catalog desks in all of its 827 retail stores across the country. In most cases, catalog buyers are lured by the convenience and the prices.

ATTITUDES AND MOTIVES

A manufacturer of men's suits presents a commercial depicting a young, well-dressed housewife awaiting the arrival of her husband. For the television cameras she states that, although her husband is quite successful, he is a "nice man" *and* wears XYZ suits. She further explains that even though the suits sell for $85, they bear the qualities of much more expensive suits. From a systems-process approach, let us analyze how this firm has used this commercial to fulfill the buying-decisions process involving the past, present, and future.

Future   Consumer satisfaction, through the purchase of XYZ suits.

Present   Personality. How might we analyze the consumer who would buy these suits? He is probably in the age group of twenty-five to thirty-five, holding a position in middle management with an income of $8,500 to $12,000 per year. He is interested in good grooming not only to please his wife but to reflect the position of success he now holds and the higher levels to which he is striving.

Past   Attitudes. This commercial is an excellent example of a firm analyzing the attitudes which are an integral part of the consumer's personality and appealing directly to these attitudes through image and symbolism. The predominant message of the commercial suggests that the successful young man need not spend $150 to $200 for a suit which will represent his success; he may reflect his success by purchasing XYZ brand for only $85. There is no effort to sell the quality or appearance of this suit; the emphasis is only on what it represents to the consumer's personality.

Noise Related to Attitudes

Researchers have discovered that for some products there is a direct relationship between the consumer's attitude toward the product and the sound it makes. In 1964 engineers for the Hoover Co. applied plastic material to muffle a whining motor in the company's Handivac portable vacuum cleaner. But along with the whine, they also eliminated most of the swishing air noise. Tests indicated that without the "whoosh" housewives would not buy the machine. So the engineers hastily removed some of the plastic, and in went the "whoosh."

The Remington typewriter division of Sperry Rand Corporation says it may soon be able to eliminate the clacking sound from its electric typewriters. Recently Remington asked a panel of secretaries to evaluate an especially quiet experimental typewriter. Except for the sound, it was identical with other models. However, girls who typed with it complained it was "much slower" than the noisier machines.

Acoustics engineers say the automobile industry, attempting to overcome the Tin Lizzie image of early mass-produced cars, was the first to deliberately manufacture noise. A prime target was, and still is, the car door. The same companies that today spend fortunes to reduce road noise and vibration also expend considerable effort to make car doors sound solid. The reason is that many prospective car buyers test showroom models by slamming the doors, listening for what they take to be the sound of quality construction. Ford Motor Company has a five-man engineering team that subjectively evaluates car-door slams, as well as the sounds of slamming hoods, trunk lids, and even glove compartment doors. Remedial action is often taken. For example, the 1969 Ford featured an inner door panel specially reinforced to create a more satisfying "thunk."

CONCLUSION

Attitudes and motives are based upon values and therefore tend to remain constant. In utilizing their significance to the selling system, the objective is to make the product attractive to the customer in *terms* of motives and attitudes, rather than to attempt to alter motives and attitudes. Consumer knowledge, however, is more flexible and therefore more subject to change. Here salesmen can develop an approach to attract consumers and as a result influence attitudes and motives.

Through the remainder of this book the emphasis will be more upon *benefits*, or facts translated into human values, than upon motives, attitudes, and knowledge. However, in determining what these human values, or benefits are, we must first have an understanding of their sources — motives, attitudes, and knowledge. From a practical selling standpoint, an understanding of these psychological variables plays a role in developing new appeals. Perhaps the following best relates these variables to the real world:[8]

> . . . As many astute businessmen have discovered, one added appeal for your product or service, properly employed, can mean the difference between success and failure, profit and loss.
>
> The real selling secret we have facing us is not concentrating on one appeal in your product or service as applicable to everyone. It's discovering how many different, directly personal appeals, based on major consumer thinking changes, you can send out, like a series of radar beams, seeking potential customers. Some must be used head-on, others obliquely. For while all basic human motivation boils down to a desire to stay alive as happily as possible, there are infinite ways to appeal to this desire — and to make your sale.

PROBLEMS

1. What is Maslow's theory of motivation?

2. In relating the importance of the consumer-satisfaction process to the marketing system, why is the ultimate sale viewed in the future tense?

3. Discuss the three areas that influence the consumer in making a buying decision.

4. Distinguish between a habit and a conscious act.

5. Explain the relationship between the five senses and the mind in the gaining of knowledge.

6. Why does the marketer first understand and then appeal to motives rather than try to change them?

7. Choose a friend or member of your family who recently purchased an automobile. List all the needs which the purchaser ought to fulfill and the benefits of the product which matched the needs.

8. How could a real estate salesman make use of an awareness of attitudes and motives in developing an insight into the sources of needs related to buying a home?

9. How could a sales catalog be instrumental in developing a customer's needs?

10. Pick any advertisement from a magazine or newspaper which portrays a product you would like to have. Develop one selling point in terms of this

[8] Ernest A. Dichter, "What Are the Real Reasons People Buy Today?" *Sales Management*, p. 37ff., Feb. 1, 1955. Dr. Dichter is founder and president of the Institute for Research in Mass Motivation, Inc., and is a pioneer in the use of psychological research for selling.

product (is-do-means) and then relate as many need sources as you can. Use attitudes, motives, and knowledge as the basis of your need sources.

11.   Use attitudes, motives, and knowledge to develop the cause of your need to attend college.

12.   If you were selling Chrysler automobiles and a prospect stated that he purchased General Motors cars all his life, would you utilize your knowledge of attitudes, motives, *or* knowledge as a means to develop needs? Discuss your answer.

13.   Describe in detail the motives which could be attached to buying frozen orange juice.

14.   Could the purchase of skis be related to the need for self-actualization? How? Could the purchase of a camera?

See pages 252–253 for an additional case study.

Chapter Five
Getting the Customer to Listen

This chapter is concerned with initiating the salesman-customer relationship in order to make a specific sale. The initial encounter may vary depending upon the particular sales situation. It may involve a salesman calling for the first time upon a customer he has not yet met. Or it may be a situation where the salesman calls on the account regularly and is not preparing to make another sales presentation. The setting may be a retail store, real estate office, or service station, where the customer approaches the salesman regarding possible need satisfaction.

ANALYSIS PROCESS

The attention step, also called the approach or introduction, is the second step of selling, but the first in which you are in contact with the prospect. The first selling step, the preapproach or planning step, will be discussed in Chapters Eleven and Twelve. The other five steps will be described first, because an understanding of the sequential buying decisions of the customer and the particular action taken in the selling steps is necessary before we can adequately *plan* the related areas of the selling system.

The attention step has two purposes. One is to get and hold the prospect's full, favorable attention. Unless this is done, your sales message will fall upon barren ground. Getting the right kind and degree of attention may be done in one second or less — or it might take days, months, or years of effort. The second purpose of the attention step is to sell the sales interview. The salesman must first convince the prospect of the value of giving his time and attention — the value of listening to what the salesman has to say.

The salesman's opening or approach statements should be considered the same as the headline of an advertisement, news story, or magazine article. They should be planned just as carefully, for they have the same purpose: to catch the buyer's attention and to encourage him to get the rest of the story.

In the attention step, the salesman is working on the first and most vital buying decision, the *need* decision. Therefore, so far as possible, the salesman talks about needs and benefits only. Figure 5-1 diagrams the attention step, using the step close as the foundation.

One last point regarding the analysis process: In selling, the salesman may return to the techniques of the attention step repeatedly. People have a brief span of attention, and it is cut shorter by interruptions. The salesman must continually work to hold the prospect's attention if he is to deliver the sales message successfully.

Perhaps the analysis process can be illustrated best by an example in which we relate the facts of what is happening in a particular situation. A pharmaceutical salesman is patiently waiting in the outer office to see the doctor. As he scans the

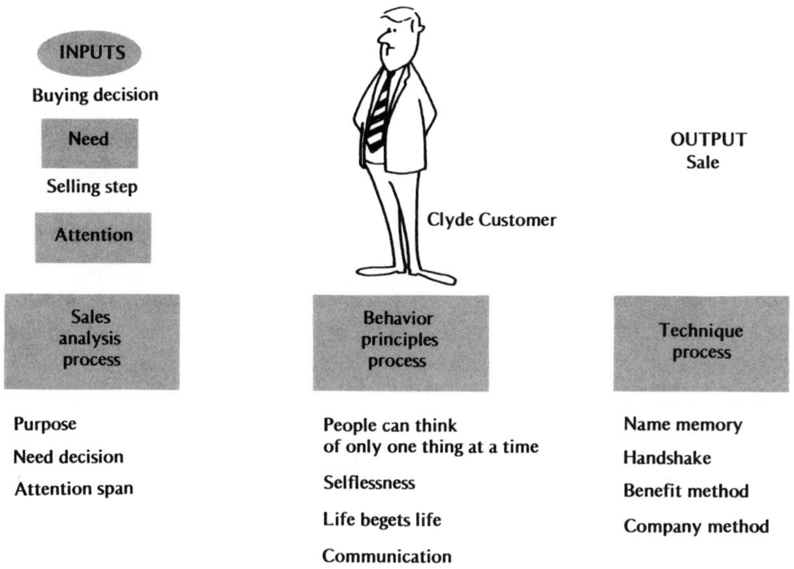

Fig. 5-1 Factors of the systems-process approach relating to the attention step.

office he realizes that the doctor will be busy with patients all afternoon and will have to *take time* to learn what the salesman has to offer. As the salesman is told by the receptionist that he may now see the doctor, he should be thinking clearly as to the needs which his firm may satisfy for the doctor and his patients. The doctor accepts taking time out from his busy schedule to see salesmen, because his professional background has developed within him a keen desire to seek all sources in learning better methods of aiding his patients. If, however, in the first few moments of the sales discussion it becomes obvious that the salesman is not capable of developing needs, or at the very least of presenting benefits, the doctor will mentally tune out from the discussion and end the presentation as soon as possible. Here, as in every other sales situation, the attention step becomes critical in getting *and* holding the prospect's full attention, as well as selling the sales interview.

TECHNIQUES OF THE ATTENTION STEP

Handshake

Probably one of the first actions to occur between a salesman and his client is the shaking of hands. In itself the handshake will not make a sale, but like other firm impressions it helps set a positive scene. The proper way to shake hands is with the right hand comfortably extended, a firm grip, and a simple one two — up and down twice and then release the hand. The other methods of shaking hands — the over-the-back grip, the limp grip, the continual pumping action, the hand over the arm — are not proper. Again, the handshake creates an impression which can have a positive influence upon the customer's attitude.

Name Memory

To remember a person's name is a compliment to that person. It indicates that you have enough interest in him to make that effort — and for most people it is an effort, particularly the first time they meet someone. But this is not the only case where name remembering may present a problem. Professional sales managers attending any kind of a meeting, whether with members of their own firm or with other groups, will make a list of the people likely to attend and review mentally the names of the people with their faces. Nearly everyone has had the experience of being with a group of people and seeing a recognizable acquaintance whose name he cannot remember. Even though the forgetful person may apologize and emphasize that recognizing the face is more important, there is something lost when the person's name is not remembered.

Here is a method of remembering names that may prove helpful. When first introduced, be sure to hear the name correctly. Under the pressure of making a new sales call, this may require mental training on the part of the salesman. As the salesman enters the office, his mind is naturally focused upon what his opening statement is going to be. Therefore, though he hears the name of the customer, it may not register in his mind. If you do not hear a name when it is given, do not hesitate to ask the prospect to repeat his name. After you hear it correctly, repeat it to yourself five times, trying to spell it once. You may not spell it correctly, but at least the phonetic expression will become fixed in your memory. Usually it is possible to associate an account's name in some fashion — business, rhyme, appearance, mental picture, meaning of the name, or a similar name or word. Using myself as an example, I always associate my name with "grizzly bear," and few customers forget the name.

Introduction

The salesman has two basic methods of introducing himself to the customer. The first is the *benefit method*, in which the salesman mentions first the benefit or service offered, next his name, and finally the name of the firm. If your firm is well known, the second method, or *company method*, may prove effective. First identify your company, then mention the office, branch, or department you represent. Your own name is actually of little importance to the prospect until he knows what you offer. If he is interested, he will ask your name later in the conversation.

Approach Methods

Basically there are two approach methods, or places the conversation can start. Using the first, the salesman talks about the prospect or his interest. Here the salesman develops the needs which the prospect may have. He may employ complimentary conversation related directly to the prospect or his family, his job, his product, or his company; or he may employ complimentary conversation not directly related, such as general conversation, jokes, stories, or possibly the prospect's general interest. He may use a direct statement of fact, such as, "Mr. Jones, the XZY had a problem of its rolling machine which apparently is common to all rolling machines. Perhaps our product can do the same for your firm as it did for the XYZ Company." Finally, he may encourage the prospect to participate, saying, for example, "Pull this switch, would you, Mr. Swanson?"

The second approach method is for the salesman to talk about himself, his product, or his company. The discussion here relates to the benefits which the salesman can offer: the selling points of the product (remember always to make use of product analysis) and how they apply to *this* prospect.

The salesman must continually relate the analysis process to the technique process, particularly in evaluating what is actually happening at that point in time. The customer is taking his time, or his company's time, to discuss the salesman's product. At this point he is not at all certain that this will be the best utilization of his time. Consequently, in the critical first few minutes of the presentation, he will be evaluating whether or not he should be spending this time with the salesman. To assure him that his time is well spent, pare your talk to essentials; make every word too important to miss. Speak with confidence and enthusiasm, putting your belief in your voice and manner. Perhaps change the pace: a change, something new, means a new reason for attention. Sometimes complete silence for 15 seconds can have great impact. Encourage the prospect to participate: get him into the act. Above all, concentrate on needs and benefits, the things most important to the prospect. You will find yourself saving time and selling with more power.

PRINCIPLES OF THE ATTENTION STEP

People Can Think about Only One Thing at a Time

This is a fact of life, a fact of how the human mind works. Some people believe they can think about a number of things at a time, but it has never been shown that this is possible. What they are doing is juggling several thoughts, touching on one and then another. If the salesman attempts to present his sales talk to a prospect who is dividing his attention, it is difficult to determine how accurately the sales talk is registering.

Recognition of this principle of behavior can lead to an easy mastery of the situation. The following are brief random samples to show how easy it is to make this principle a positive asset.

1. *Customer who is too busy*. If the customer clearly is occupied and concerned with other matters, perhaps the timing is not right to develop awareness of needs through the attention step. If this is the case, excuse yourself from the

scene *after* making sure you have another appointment date. The customer will appreciate this consideration and thus be more attentive the next time you call. The salesman should not need to be told to leave because the prospect is too busy; he should have the understanding properly to analyze the situation.

2. *Customer who likes to discuss problems with salesmen.* If a salesman remains in the profession, he will develop a group of accounts upon whom he calls quite consistently. In many cases these business relationships develop into lasting personal friendships. Sometimes a customer looks forward to the salesman's call because he knows that he has a captive audience and that what he tells the salesman about his firm is "privileged information." Such a customer believes he has someone to whom he can freely tell the troubles of the firm, a sympathetic ear. In this situation the salesman need only realize this principle of behavior and listen carefully, sincerely, and with understanding to what the customer is saying. The customer, after fully discussing his problems, may not only feel better but be in a more positive frame of mind to hear what the salesman has to offer. On the other hand, if the salesman attempts to force his product upon the customer while the customer is talking about himself, there will be a negative response, since people can think about only one thing at a time.

3. *Wholesale accounts as customers.* A wholesaler quite often is continually involved with some facet of his business, and while he is at his place of business it is difficult to keep his thinking process centered upon the salesman's product. There are several ways of overcoming this problem. One is to take the wholesaler out for lunch or coffee, preferably some distance from the warehouse. Another method is to ride with the wholesaler in his truck while he is making deliveries.

The Professional Salesman Has Selflessness

Throughout his selling the salesman thinks, talks, and acts in the prospect's interest, not thinking of himself. Selflessness is more than just being of service to somebody, for the service must be performed with a personal feeling of projecting yourself into your actions, which in turn satisfy a need for a customer. A teacher may be of service to his community, school, and class by teaching effectively, but only by being genuinely interested in the success of each of his students will he gain selflessness. A lawyer may wish to provide a service to society by defending the accused, but he does not achieve selflessness until he also feels a genuine interest in the personal needs of that accused.

The same principle of selflessness, the opposite of selfishness, is the basis of successful human relations. It is the basis of honest salesmanship: the only reason for a salesman to see a prospect is a sincere belief that he can offer something of value to the prospect. This sincere belief breaks down barriers. It automatically puts the salesman on the buyer's side of the fence. It makes the salesman welcome. It helps give the salesman confidence and power; it helps eliminate fear and nervousness. It enables him to be a "duck" — to let things roll off like water off a duck's back. Whatever the prospect says or does, the salesman feels it *professionally*, but never personally.

Each Thing in Life Begets Itself

Interest begets interest; confidence begets confidence; enthusiasm begets action. Whatever the salesman wishes to receive from the buyer he must first have within himself and transmit to the buyer.

Salesmanship Is Persuasion in Communication

Salesmanship depends upon the ability to communicate, to speak confidently and effectively. The best sales knowledge in the world is worthless without the courage and ability to put it to use. To sell effectively, a salesman must first be able to speak effectively. Communication must have *energy* behind it. To be received, it must be amplified and transmitted with power. To reach full effectiveness, communication must be keyed to human interest. Points and facts must be presented in terms of human meaning, human values, and human experience.

CONCLUSION

The attention step is the first step of selling in which the salesman has contact with the prospect. Within the selling system, it serves two functions: it gets the prospect's attention and sells the sales interview. In the attention step the salesman is concentrating upon the *need* decision, recognizing that he may find it necessary to return to this step again and again because interruptions may divert the customer's attention. The attention step involves these principles of behavior: people can think about only one thing at a time; selflessness is an important ingredient to a professional salesman; each thing in life begets itself; salesmanship is persuasion in communication. The techniques of the attention step include the handshake, name memory, and introduction methods.

PROBLEMS

1. You are a sales representative for the United Petroleum Corporation and have an important sales program to discuss with your largest and busiest dealer. How would you approach the attention step? What factors of the attention step would be helpful in developing your approach?

2. You are an account executive representative for the Apex Advertising Agency calling for the first time on the owner of a national department store chain. Your intention is to sell him on using your advertising agency for his national advertising. Develop an attention step approach, beginning with your

approaching the receptionist. Please detail your actions (techniques) and relate them to factors of the analysis process and the process of principles of behavior.

3. Can a salesman gain favorable attention without selflessness?

4. Write a one-page evaluation of a salesman you feel has selflessness.

5. Present the method of introduction you find best suits your personality. Why did you pick this particular one?

6. Give three examples illustrating the principle that people can think of only one thing at a time.

7. Why is the handshake an important ingredient in the attention step?

8. Why do we say that salesmanship is persuasion in communication?

See pages 254–255 for a case study.

Chapter Six
Developing Customer Enthusiasm and Need Awareness

The third step of selling, the interest step, is also called the need or exploration step. It is possibly the most important step of selling; often 85 percent of the sale is made by the time you complete this step. It is the step in which the need decision is made. Without the interest step, even the best-planned sales presentation is like a ready-made suit of clothes available in only one size. It may fit some people perfectly, but the chances are that it will usually be a misfit — almost fitting some people, completely wrong for others. The interest step is to the professional salesman what careful measuring is to the expert tailor: it enables him to know where and how to cut and sew the cloth for an absolutely perfect, individual fit. The interest step makes possible a custom-tailored sales presentation.

ANALYSIS PROCESS

The purpose of the interest step is to *determine* the buyer's needs (interests) and to *develop* his awareness of them. Then the salesman can *confirm* the needs as

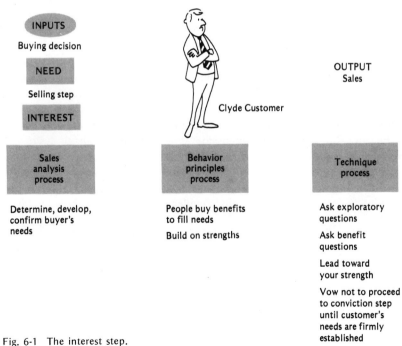

Fig. 6-1 The interest step.

the common ground upon which the salesman and the prospect will talk. You determine and develop the needs that relate to your product primarily by *asking questions*. You help the prospect explore his needs, but you do not cross-examine. You seldom talk about your product; you talk about the *buyer*, his *needs*, and the *benefits* he wants to receive. This is the key to understanding the true function of the interest step.

When the step is properly handled, the prospect organizes the salesman's complete sales presentation for him. He tells the salesman what he wants the salesman to tell him. The prospect also tells exactly what he wants the product to do — the benefits that are important to him. He further tells the salesman what he wants to buy and how he wishes to be sold; he tells what to emphasize and what to leave out.

In Figure 6-2 the interest step is charted on the step-close diagram for a particular prospect by showing the needs and the importance of each need. The salesman knows the sale from the buyer's point of view and can proceed in the conviction step to show each need matched by benefits.

The interest step used properly by a salesman can develop the natural enthusiasm and desire that will lead not only to a more enjoyable selling environment for buyer and seller, but to greater success and more effective efforts. There is nothing that can motivate a sincere salesman more than tangible success in his sales efforts. The reason that the interest has such impact in the selling system is that you as a salesman are creating the scene whereby the customer is given the opportunity to discuss *himself*, and in particular, the needs which *he* has. To give an example of how infrequently this is used in the sales field, think of the last time a salesman in the course of selling you anything somehow expressed a sincere interest in the product which would most effectively fulfill *your* needs. Probably it has been the exception rather than the rule. But that salesman who did sell in that manner probably still holds a favorable spot in your mind.

There are several pitfalls the unsuccessful salesman may encounter — not because he lacks ability but rather because he lacks adequate training or desire. It is appropriate at this point to mention two of these pitfalls: (1) improper product analysis and (2) improper use or nonuse of the interest step. Through product analysis the salesman will be in a powerful position to present the benefits of the product in the conviction step, thereby complementing the needs shown in Figure

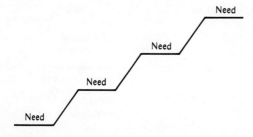

Fig. 6-2   Related needs.

6-1. Essentially it is difficult for the salesman to ask the proper interest questions unless he is completely aware of what the product analysis has to offer.

PRINCIPLES OF THE INTEREST STEP

People Buy Benefits to Fulfill Needs

As has been discussed earlier, people do not buy a product: they buy only the benefits the product will bring, the things the product will do or mean for them. Each benefit is the fulfillment of a need felt by the buyer.

In addition, each person is an individual; each person is different. The needs of one person, his reasons for buying, may be totally different from the needs of another. For this reason, the salesman must work to find out the individual prospect's needs that relate to his product. He must find out what he wants the product to do or mean to the customer. Also, the salesman must make the customer aware of his needs to help him make the decision that he has a sufficient need for the product.

For example, three people may buy a 1969 Chrysler Crown Imperial for three different reasons. For one the need to be satisfied may be prestige, for another it may be the comfort and enjoyment of traveling in such luxury, while for the third person it may be a fast and dependable method of transportation to a well-dispersed sales territory. Another situation, previously discussed, is the purchase of a man's suit. One man may need a suit that will withstand wrinkling, particularly if travel is involved. Another may need a suit that will portray the well-groomed executive based upon the material and color accepted by his firm; in this case good tailoring would be an important factor. Needs must be viewed through the customer's eyes, not through the salesman's. The interest step allows us to view these needs as the customer does.

Build upon Strengths throughout Life

This is perhaps one of the most important principles of success in selling and in life. It is worth studying very deeply. Everything has two sides: it has its strengths, its abilities, talents, and potentials, and it has its weaknesses, its limitations, liabilities, and shortcomings. Much advice for success looks at only one side, the debit side. We are told to correct our faults, work on our weaknesses, try to keep from becoming a failure. There is only one thing wrong with this advice: it does not work anymore than a business can succeed only by trying to eliminate its expenses. If you put your effort on your faults, the best you can be is mediocre. There may be nothing wrong with you, but neither will there be anything outstanding about you.

Building on strengths is creative and rewarding. It is the positive approach to self-improvement. It focuses your attention on your goal and your accomplishments. Working on weaknesses is only corrective, focusing your eyes on your shortcomings; it gives you the goal of mediocrity instead of the goal of greatness.

In selling, too, we build on strengths. We build on the strengths of our products, the benefits they offer, and particularly the exclusive benefits. We make the strengths outweigh the weaknesses in the buyer's mind, and especially the weakness of every product, the fact that it costs money.

TECHNIQUES OF THE INTEREST STEP

Ask Exploratory Questions

There are many types of questions, and many ways of asking questions. In the interest step, one of the most valuable types of questions you can ask is the exploratory question. An exploratory question is one planned to draw information from the prospect related to his needs and desires. It is a question that encourages the prospect to talk, explain, and volunteer information — a question that wants to know "who, what, when, where, why, or how" about the prospect's possible use of the product. It can seldom be answered with "yes" or "no."

You may have heard the advice, "Ask questions that will get the buyer to say 'yes'; get him in the habit." This may be valuable advice, but many buyers will say 'yes' out of curiosity only, or they will agree that something is important without telling you what they consider more important. At the crucial time, however, at the time for the decision to buy, they have no trouble saying "no." It is much more valuable in the interest step to ask questions that will help you explore the buyer's needs, questions that will get him to state and confirm his needs. Also, having the buyer state his needs is much stronger than your stating what you think they might be. They are accurate, and they are his ideas.

The way in which you ask questions is just as important as the questions themselves. Your manner and voice make the difference in how the prospect takes your questions. If they are asked properly, simple questions like "What are you doing?" or "Why did you do that?" can indicate friendly interest and express your desire to help the buyer define and fulfill his needs. Here are some suggestions to help you develop the proper manner of asking exploratory questions. Try for a soft tone of voice, a gentle manner. Remember that you are talking with a friend, not examining a witness. Pad the sharp edges with courtesy and with phrases like "Would you mind . . ." and "I wonder if . . .." Give a reason. Let the prospect know why you are asking and how the answer will help you help him. For example: "To help you find the perfect home, with the little things that will mean the most to your family, would you mind telling me some of the things you particularly like about your present home?"

Often it pays to be indirect, to ask questions that will bring out more information than they seem to ask. For example, to find out how much equity a person might have in a house, you might ask, "Could you tell me how long you've been living here?"

Ask Benefit Questions

A benefit question is simply a benefit expressed in question form. You are asking the prospect, in effect, "Would you like this benefit? Have you the need it fulfills?" To illustrate, the following example gives a sales feature of a product, develops it through the is-do-means approach in briefed form, and then expresses the benefit as a benefit question:

Sales feature: Snap-open top on a Thermos vacuum bottle.

Do benefit: Seals securely, yet opens easily with the touch of a finger. Even a small child can open it without spilling.

Means benefit: Since it does not have to be forced, the chance of splashing or soiling table or clothes is reduced. No lost tempers or broken fingernails when opening it.

Benefit question: "You know, children often have trouble opening ordinary Thermos bottles when they carry lunch to school. Sometimes they have to tug and force the cap — and the milk or soup can spill. It can splash on their clothes or schoolwork. It can spoil the day for them — and for you when they get home. Has anything like that ever happened with your children? Have you ever wished there was a Thermos can that even a small child could open easily, without a chance of spills?"

Lead toward Your Strengths

Every product has particular strengths, the ability to supply particular benefits. With your benefit questions, lead toward your strongest benefits and your special benefits. For example, in selling one model of refrigerator, the salesman might lead toward the benefits offered by its large capacity and its automatic ice cube dispenser. For another model, the salesman might stress the benefits offered by its swing-out shelves, ease of cleaning, and automatic defrosting. It is doubtful, in either case, that he would lead toward the benefits offered by the fact that this model (like all refrigerators) will keep food cool.

Remember and Use the Professional Salesman's Vow

The professional salesman makes this vow: he will not leave the interest step until he and the buyer are both clearly aware of the buyer's needs. He makes this vow to save selling time and effort and to have a successful sale. Unless he knows what the buyer wants, he does not know what benefits to offer. Unless the buyer is aware of his needs, he cannot make the need decisions. The salesman will be giving his presentation for practice, and if a sale is made, it will be made only by accident.

CONCLUSION

The means for developing customer enthusiasm and need awareness involves relating the interest step of the selling system to the need buying decision. In analyzing the interest step, we find its purpose to be a determination of the buyer's needs and a common awareness by the salesman and the customer of exactly what these needs are. Primarily this is done by asking questions about the buyer, his needs, and the benefits he wants to receive. The key to using the interest step correctly is that the salesman seldom talks or asks questions about his product; instead he concentrates on the buyer, his needs, and the benefits he wishes to receive. When the step is properly handled, the prospect organizes the salesman's complete sales presentation for him. He tells the salesman what he wants the salesman to sell him. The prospect also tells exactly what he wants the product to do — the benefits that are important to him. When used properly, the interest step can develop the natural enthusiasm and desire which will lead not only to a more enjoyable selling environment for buyer and seller, but to greater success and more effective efforts.

The concept stating that through building on strengths the sales activity becomes particularly effective has two principal ramifications. One, when the salesman is aware of his *personal* strong characteristics in selling activities, he focuses his attention upon positive goal achievement and consequently uses all facilities as backup to support these strong personal characteristics. Perhaps one of the truths which we all find hard to accept is the truth about our true abilities; these we should recognize and rely heavily upon. Two, in regards to the product, the professional salesman through product analysis can determine in a broad sense which of the product's strong characteristics merit being emphasized in terms of interest questions. An example might be a real estate salesman selling a home that has a large wooded lot which provides complete privacy. To determine whether or not this product strength would have relativity to the customer, the salesman might ask the question: "Would you and your family enjoy playing together without being constantly watched by your neighbors?"

The interest step is related to our discussion of attitudes, motives, and knowledge, particularly in developing need awareness. For example, if a real estate salesman learns that the customer prefers (attitude) a one-story house to a two-story house, he can then concentrate his interest questions in a manner which emphasizes the needs which relate to one-story homes. If the salesman is aware of Maslow's hierarchy of needs, he realizes that people are motivated in a purposeful manner to satisfy needs. He can then ask questions which determine if these needs are dominant in the area of physiological needs, safety needs, social needs, or possibly self-esteem needs. Sometimes the customer gives the salesman a clue as to which kinds of questions to ask. For example, if the customer indicates that he is interested in finding a home in an exclusive residential area, social needs and/or self-esteem needs will play a role in need determination and awareness.

CASE STUDIES OF THE INTEREST STEP

This section is presented to offer additional opportunity to develop a feel for the interest step and how customers might react.

THE CASE OF THE OIL BURNER

SALESMAN: I realize, Mr. P., that you are not the least bit interested in oil burners. Why should you be? You have a fine new furnace and a house that is easily and quickly heated. It is not much of an effort for you to care for your furnace properly. By the way, what did you spend for coal last winter? I am just curious to know what it costs to heat a well-built house like yours.

PROSPECT: I burned about 9 tons of good-grade coal. Not bad, is it?

SALESMAN: It certainly is not, Mr. P. Now would you mind answering two or three other simple questions before I go? In the first place, if you could, you would like to avoid the overheating and then cooling off of your furnace which results from draft firing, wouldn't you? That is almost unavoidable to some extent with your type of furnace.

PROSPECT: Yes, I guess so. We do leave the draft on too long at times.

SALESMAN: You and Mrs. P. would like to get away from the job of caring for the furnace three or four times a day if that were possible, wouldn't you?

PROSPECT: Yes, I would.

SALESMAN: And you will agree that in really cold weather you do have to get up a little earlier than usual to get the house warmed up for the family, don't you?

PROSPECT: Oh, yes, the house does cool off on cold nights.

SALESMAN: And in spite of everything you can do, you do know that many times your house is too hot, while sometimes it is too cool, owing to sudden changes in the weather that you cannot anticipate. Is that right?

PROSPECT: Yes, you are right about that.

SALESMAN: And there are days in the spring and fall when you wish you had a little heat mornings and evenings, but don't care to go to the trouble of building up a fire, so you just shiver. I know how it is.

PROSPECT: Yes, that has happened, but we learn to live with it.

SALESMAN: And I know that Mrs. P. would be happy to eliminate the dust from handling the coal and ashes. She could keep your home clean with much less effort, besides having more room in the basement. Now, Mr. P., just this final question. If you could avoid the over-heating and cooling; if you could get away completely from the drudgery of handling coal and ashes; if you could have 72-degree heat day and night just by touching a switch, and if, in addition, you would save $25 a year in fuel costs, would you be interested in hearing about it?

THE CASE OF THE MISSING REPORT FORMS

SALESMAN: Mr. Hansen, my name is Carter, Alan Carter, representing the Republic Systems Corporation, New York, designers of solutions to paper-work problems involved in accounting, inventory, sales, and personnel control.

PROSPECT: We're not interested in buying any more form printing now. We're well served by a printer who has supplied us for more than ten years, and we're not interested in making a change.

SALESMAN: Yes, I assumed you were not interested in buying more printed forms, but every well-managed business is finding it vitally impor-tant to have more and more timely information upon which to base intelligent management decisions. Do your executives ever ask you for facts or figures on accounting, credit, inventory, or sales problems which you cannot quickly or conveniently provide them?

PROSPECT: As a matter of fact, our sales manager called me yesterday for some information about our customers. He feels that some cus-tomers are not getting sufficient information from our salesmen. He wants to know about the situation of each buyer.

SALESMAN: Just what information was your sales manager looking for?

PROSPECT: He wanted to know which customers are buying regularly, the products each one is stocking, the customers who are promoting our line, the average inventory on each item, what percent of our customers we are selling, and other facts.

SALESMAN: Were you able to give him the information he wanted?

PROSPECT: I can get together some of the information he wants, but it will take me weeks to round it up. We have our accounting records, our salesmen's call reports, all separate records, but no compre-hensive picture of the customer's situation. Our customer records are not consolidated — some records duplicate others, a number are not needed, and the whole lot is practically useless for sales planning and supervision.

SALESMAN: Sales control records are worthless unless they are organized in a practical, workable system which provides facts quickly, clearly, and completely.

PROSPECT: That's what we need, but we're so snowed under with work right now that I don't see how we can do anything about it.

SALESMAN: Over the years, our company has gathered a great amount of know-how in solving record-keeping problems in a wide variety of businesses. Not long ago we worked on a problem similar to yours for the Benson Drug Company, and came up with a solution which they were good enough to say saves them more than $5,000 a year in record-keeping alone. It also gave them more facts for better sales supervision. I believe we can help you work out a similar system to reduce your costs and give your sales manager the information he needs about your customers for better sales management.

PROSPECT: Well, we'll be glad to get any suggestions you can make, with the understanding, of course, that we are under no obligation to buy. Our sales manager is the person who will have to be convinced of the value of your recommendations. If you can sell him, I'll be glad to go along.

SALESMAN: May I have your permission to see him?

THE CASE OF THE SHARP FOCUS

The prospect has entered a camera shop and stops at a display of Leica cameras. The salesman approaches.

SALESMAN: I noticed that you were looking at the new 3f Leica. Would you like to see it?

PROSPECT: Yes, please. (*Salesman removes camera from display case.*)

SALESMAN: You know, I'm always glad to show a man this camera; it's one of the finest we carry. Have you ever used one of these Leicas?

PROSPECT: No, I haven't. I've got a secondhand Rolliflex, and I've been thinking about getting another camera, so I thought I'd like to see this.

SALESMAN: Fine, I'm glad you stopped in. I think I can show you some features of this new Leica that you'll be interested in seeing. Now the main reason that you'd want a good camera is to get good pictures, isn't it?

PROSPECT: Well, yes, I guess so.

SALESMAN: Let me show you how the features of this camera are going to guarantee good pictures for you. What would you say causes most poor pictures?

PROSPECT: Well, there are lots of things. Aside from improper lighting, I guess being able to get the correct focus is as important as anything else.

SALESMAN: That's the thing that always bothered me the most. Now this Leica can completely eliminate that trouble. See this little focusing knob?

PROSPECT: Yes . . .

SALESMAN: Now look through this little window at the left. What do you see?

PROSPECT: Can't see much of anything. Looks like a double image. Blurred.

SALESMAN: Right. Now start turning the knob until the image becomes sharp and clear . . . got it? Now the camera is perfectly in focus.

PROSPECT: Say, that's pretty good.

SALESMAN: Without a doubt, I think it's one of the finest improvements ever put on a camera. And here's another feature of this camera. Have you ever tried to take a shot of something a long way off, and had it turn out badly?

PROSPECT: Quite a few times, in fact. Seems like this summer I was always overestimating the range of my Rolliflex.

SALESMAN: Look at this attachment. By unscrewing the lens, like this, and screwing in this longer lens, you can bring those long-distance shots right up close for the kind of pictures you haven't been able to take before. Or you can put in this wide-angle lens, for shooting a group or a wide landscape. Do you think you would like these features?

PROSPECT: Oh, no doubt about it. How much does all this cost?

PROBLEMS

1. Why is the interest step also called the exploration step?

2. Why is product analysis so important to the interest step?

3. Is it possible for the customer to decide upon a specific product *before* making a need decision? Relate your answer to the interest step.

4. Of the salesmen with whom you have been in contact the past year, how many have effectively used the interest step?

5. When we say that building on strengths throughout life is creative, in what manner do you feel this can be helpful to you as a professional salesperson and specifically to your product?

6. How would you relate the interest step to attitudes, motives, and knowledge in developing need awareness?

7. List five strengths of a particular product and write five interest questions which will develop need awareness toward these strengths.

8. Write three exploratory questions. State the product you are directing your questions toward.

9. Write three general benefit questions you might ask this prospect during the interest step in order to get the information you wish. Following each question, list other useful information which the prospect might volunteer while answering it.

10. As a new car salesman for the ABC Dodge Company, give three interest questions you would direct toward a college graduate, single, twenty-six years of age, with an income of $9,000 per year. List three interest questions for a customer who is a regional sales manager, fifty-four years of age, income $23,000 per year.

See pages 256–258 for an additional case study.

SAMPLE ASSIGNMENT 1

Write in the product or service you might sell: Mobilgas and Mobiloil

List ten things you might wish to find out about a possible prospect during the interest step. Please list specific facts (such as age) rather than general terms (such as benefits desired).

1. Consumption of gasoline per month

2. Number of vehicles

3. Age of vehicles

4. Importance of economy

5. Importance of preventative maintenance

6. Desire for quality to prospect

7. What specific use vehicles are to the firm

8. Are engines of truck subjected to temperature change?

Write three general benefit questions you might ask this prospect during the interest step in order to get the information you wish. Following each question list other useful information which the prospect might volunteer while answering it.

Question: Would increasing the life of these engines by 30 percent be a considerable saving to your business?

Information in answer: Yes, due to heavy loads our trucks carry engine replacement as an important cost item.

Question: Would allowing your trucks just 5,000 miles per month more on the road give you a competitive advantage?

Information in answer: By all means. We have lost business because trucks were in the shop when moving loads were available to us.

Question: Would your capital investment be put to better use if these trucks would last six years instead of the present five?

Information in answer: If this were possible, we could consider the use of this money saved to begin construction of our new plant in Portland.

ASSIGNMENT 1

Write in the product or service you sell: _____

List ten or more things you might wish to find out about a possible prospect during the interest step. Please list specific facts (such as age) rather than general terms (such as benefits desired).

1.   7.

2.   8.

3.   9.

4.   10.

5.   11.

6.   12.

Write three general benefit questions you might ask this prospect during the interest step in order to get the information you wish. Following each question, list the other useful information which the prospect might volunteer while answering it.

Question:

Information in answer:

Question:

Information in answer:

Question:

Information in answer:

Chapter Seven
Formulating a Strategy
to Sell Your Product

Most untrained salesmen begin their sales activity with a discussion of the product they are selling. With the first six chapters of this book as a background, you are now aware of the important fact that the professional salesman does not begin to discuss what he is selling until he is fully aware of what the customer's needs are *and* that the customer is also aware of these needs. The selling system is used as a device through which the professional salesman can mentally evaluate the reaction of his customer to the selling situation and thereby use this understanding in a purposeful manner. This is why the term "strategy" is used in the title of this chapter: to suggest that you will utilize a rational approach in planning a course of action. This strategy becomes a linking process, a particular linking of customer needs to specific benefits. The selling system is not presented as an inflexible, rigid approach to selling; instead, it provides the guidelines a professional salesman must follow continually to "read" what is taking place in a selling situation. Of particular significance is the relationship between the salesman and his customer. As you develop more experience in selling you will react quite naturally to a situation because your mental process tells you how to respond as a professional salesman. The selling system does not "box you in," but allows you to adjust to any selling situation.

APPLYING THE STEP CLOSE TO THE CONVICTION STEP

The concept of the step close will be discussed throughout this book in connection with the selling system, because it has relevant inputs for all parts of the system. The linking of needs to benefits is continually taking place, either by the customer himself or with the aid of the salesman. To use an analogy, the human body is also a system and functions in particular ways as determined by the particular linking of the component parts. Yet running throughout the entire human system is a vital flow of blood which penetrates the entire body and is an important element to all parts of the system. So it is with the step close: the linking process takes place in all areas of the selling process and is inherent to every portion of the system.

When the conviction step is charted on the step-close diagram (see Figure 7-2), it is seen as a process of linking,[1] of supplying benefits to fulfill each need (or enough needs to complete the buying decision, since no product is perfect). Each need/benefit link is one plateau of the step close. In referring to the conviction step and how it is handled, we will use the term "product" to indicate both the

---

[1] This is another significant use of the term "process," denoting a flow of activity within the boundaries of the selling system.

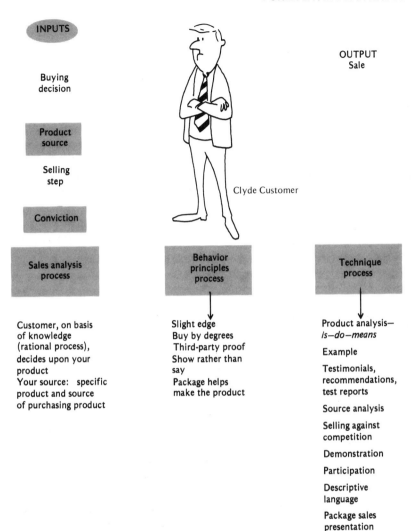

INPUTS

Buying
decision

Product
source

Selling
step

Conviction

OUTPUT
Sale

Clyde Customer

Sales analysis process	Behavior principles process	Technique process
Customer, on basis of knowledge (rational process), decides upon your product Your source: specific product and source of purchasing product	Slight edge Buy by degrees Third-party proof Show rather than say Package helps make the product	Product analysis—*is—do—means* Example Testimonials, recommendations, test reports Source analysis Selling against competition Demonstration Participation Descriptive language Package sales presentation

Fig. 7-1   The conviction step.

product and the source. This is done to avoid constant repetition. Please keep in mind that the same principles and techniques apply with equal force and effectiveness to both the product and the source.

ANALYSIS PROCESS

The strategy developed in the conviction step, or knowledge step, becomes the heartbeat of the selling system, because it is not until a knowledgeable linking of needs to benefits takes place that the selling process really lives. On the basis of specific needs developed in the interest step the strategy is born. From this

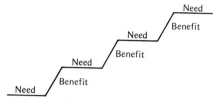

Fig. 7-2 Needs linked to benefits.

conception the salesman will find it much easier to proceed to the final growth stage, the sale. In the conviction step the salesman gives information about his product to show how it will fulfill the buyer's needs. Again, *remember the vow.* To show how needs will be fulfilled the salesman must first know the needs; to be aware that his needs will be fulfilled, the buyer must know his needs. The purpose of the conviction step is to help the buyer make two of the five buying decisions. The salesman helps him decide that

This is the *product* to fulfill his needs.

This is the *source* to supply the product.

Usually one of the two decisions is more important than the other. For example, in buying a used car a customer might visit many dealers to find the car he wishes, in which case the product is more important than the source. However, in buying a particular make of new car, the major choice, at that point in time, would be which of several dealers to buy from. The *source decision* would be of particular importance.

Once the salesman has determined and developed the need for his product by talking with the buyer and asking benefit questions, he is ready to seek the second buying decision: to secure the buyer's agreement that the product offered is the proper one to fulfill his needs. Too many salesmen try to jump to this decision without the proper preparation. Since they are excited or enthusiastic about the product, or eager to sell it, they assume that the buyer is automatically interested. That is why we make the vow *never* to proceed beyond the interest step unless we have definitely established the need in the buyer's mind. This one idea of selling will save you countless hours of selling time. It will make your sales efforts far more productive. It will make a drastic reduction in the number of objections that buyers raise, for most objections arise because need has not been established.

This vow applies to all types of selling, whether it is selling machinery to a manufacturer, stock to a retailer, insurance to a family, carpets to a homemaker, or shoelaces over the counter. It literally opens the door to increased sales, for in determining the needs of the buyer, you often discover that the buyer needs far more than you might have expected. When the salesman begins to obtain the second buying decision (the product), he is involved in the conviction or knowledge step, where he explains to the customer that his product will fit and fulfill the customer's needs.

Most products are purchased for one of two reasons: to be used or consumed by the purchaser or to be resold. If the customer is buying for use, selling points and benefits are aimed at the buying motives of economy, safety, comfort, convenience, pride, prestige, and affection. If the customer is buying for resale, his objective is nearly always profit, in the form of reduced costs, faster turnover, greater volume, or increased income. When the salesman is developing source as a buying decision, he is also involved in the conviction step. From the buyer's point of view the source may be any or all of the following:

Individual salesman

Retailer

Wholesaler

Local office

National office

Manufacturer

The first and most important source is the salesman himself. His company or store is second. The manufacturer is third. There are two reasons why the salesman is most important. First, all selling is a personal thing. The salesman is the person the buyer sees and reacts to. Living, person-to-person contact makes a tremendous impression on the buyer. Second, the sale is made by overcoming the three buying fears, one of which is the fear that the product will not do what the *salesman* says it will do. Buying is an act of trust; it takes place because the buyer feels he can believe the salesman. We sell the source the same as we sell the product, by presenting selling points, telling what they *are*, telling what they will *do*, telling what they will *mean* to the buyer, *supporting* them with examples, and tying them directly to the buyer's needs.

USE OF THE IS-DO-MEANS SALES APPROACH

In helping the buyer make the product and source decisions, there is a definite pattern the salesman can follow in presenting sales features and showing how they will produce the benefits desired or how they will fulfill the prospect's needs. The salesman follows the is-do-means formula:

The sales point of feature

What is is specifically

What it will do for the buyer

What it will mean to the buyer

At this point one other vital element is added — the *example*, or illustrations of the sales point and its benefits. The example is one of the key principles and techniques of all effective communication. It gives what the salesman says life, variety, human interest, meaning, and, most important of all, *believability*. It is the key technique for using the principle of putting the burden of proof on the shoulders of a third party. People must be sold two ways before they buy. First, they must be convinced mentally or intellectually, for buying is partially a process of logic, of considering the facts and their meaning. Chapter Four, relating to motives, attitudes, and knowledge, introduced the manner in which learning, or knowledge, takes place. Second, people must be moved emotionally, for buying is an emotional experience. People buy as much on the basis of feelings and beliefs as they do on the basis of facts. Even the most analytical, logical buyer will buy on both foundations: he will buy because he *knows* what the product offers and because he *desires* what it offers. In the conviction or knowledge step the salesman is directing his efforts toward creating in the buyer's mind intellectual conviction on the basis of facts and logic. In the desire step, which will be studied in Chapter Eight, the salesman learns to extend this intellectual conviction into a parallel emotional conviction.

PRINCIPLES OF THE CONVICTION STEP

Success Is Usually a Matter of the "Slight Edge"

Accomplishment, success, advancement, or greatness is almost always the result of being "just a little bit better." This is true throughout life; you see the proof everywhere you look. There is only a subtle difference between a good pianist and a great one, a fine painting and a masterpiece, an ordinary baseball player and an all-star. Sometimes the difference is all-important: a few seconds can make the difference between catching and missing an airplane, and a tiny bit more selling effort or skill can rescue the lost sale. Sometimes the difference is so slight as to be unnoticed until a crucial time. When several qualified men are being considered for a promotion, management often searches for a "slight edge," a minor point that shows one man to be a little better, so that a decision can be made. We said earlier that differences make sales. When you buy among products that are nearly identical, you buy the one that you feel will give you just a little more of something you want. Your prospects buy the same way; they usually buy the slight edge.

To stand out from the crowd, to be successful and make the products we sell and the services we render successful, all we need to do is have a slight edge — a *strength* — in the right direction and then capitalize on it. We do not have to be ten times better than our competitors, or even 10 percent better. All we need is to be 1 percent better, and that can be easy. And we do not have to be better in every way. All we need is to be better in *one significant way*. That too can be easy. Every product is different, and each has its strengths that can become the slight edge that means success. Even identical products are different, for the difference can come from the salesman himself, the source, or the salesman's skill in determining needs and presenting benefits. For example, examine critically the characteristics of two major-brand color television sets, RCA and Zenith. First, determine the characteristics which are relatively equal. Each has a quality wood console; each has a color picture tube, tuning knobs, quality sound, remote-control tuning, and some kind of a guarantee. What, then, is the difference between these two quality products if all these characteristics are reasonably similar? It is the slight edge — the difference in shading of the facial colors, or the *trueness* of color, or possibly a device called "electronic tuning." In their TV advertising commercials you will note that both of these television marketers will concentrate on those features which illustrate the slight edge, because that is what distinguishes them from their competition.

People Buy by Degrees

This principle shows itself in many ways. It shows itself in the five buying decisions and the six steps of selling. It shows itself in the step close, the step-by-step linking of benefits with needs. In the same way, conviction is one step of a process. First comes conviction through knowledge, the logical or intellectual reasoning process. Second comes desire, the emotional belief and wanting. Third comes decision, the result of conviction and desire and the trigger of action. These three elements are paralleled by the last three steps of the sale: knowledge (conviction), desire, and action (close). The prospect says first, "It's reasonable; it makes sense; I should." (For example, most people know that they should have safety belts in their cars.) Next he says, "It appeals to me; I want to." This can be true whether or not the proposition is reasonable or makes sense. (That is why many buyers are more interested in the styling of a car than in its safety features.) Third, the prospect says, "I will." He makes a decision and puts it into action.

The difference between conviction and desire is much the same as the difference between knowledge and realization. It is the difference between theory and actuality. A child can know that fire will burn; he will know the theory because he has been told it repeatedly. He may still not *realize* that fire burns, until he touches the flame. Suddenly, abstract knowledge will become living realization. It is the same way with buyers. Facts must be turned into living, understandable, powerful, realization.

The Principle of Third-party Proof

Related to the difference between theory and reality is the fact that people may hesitate to believe what a salesman tells them his product will do, but they will believe what he reports as the experience of others. They will believe the experience of someone they have never met or heard of, before they will take the word of the salesman who is standing before them. In the same way, children will believe a friend of the family; they will hail him as a sage for saying exactly the same things their parents have been trying to get across to them for years. We all put more credence on the outside expert, the person we feel is the voice of experience. In selling, this principle of putting the burden of proof on the shoulders of a third party is used primarily by providing examples and following the "example-reason-point" formula of organization, to be discussed below.

It Is More Effective to Show than to Say

This is more understandable when it is recalled that it is through the senses that we attain most of our knowledge and *all* the knowledge that relates to a particular selling situation. Related to the difference between theory and reality is the fact that people will more easily believe what they see or experience than what they are told, and they will believe what they hear most readily when it is told in vivid visual terms, terms that bring a picture to their minds. As the conviction step is studied, this principle will become particularly applicable when related to the use of demonstration, participation, and description.

The Package Helps Make the Product

People judge anything by its surroundings, by the way it is presented. They judge the package as well as the product itself and as a guide to the worth of the product. In professional selling this principle is applied using "package" in its widest sense, to mean everything surrounding the sale, including the salesman's appearance and manner. Very few people would buy gems from a tattered peddlar who carried them in a grocery bag. Very few businessmen will buy products or services to contribute to business success from a salesman who does not look and act successful himself. The way you package your sales presentation helps contribute to its success.

TECHNIQUES OF THE CONVICTION STEP

The Example

The most common and one of the most effective methods of using the principle of third-party proof is through providing examples. An example is nothing more or less than a story, a true story, about the experience of someone. It is an incident, an illustration, a "hunk of life." It is a living evidence that helps build true conviction. It is a human experience that generates interest and attention. It can give your sales presentation strength, life, variety, and suspense.

An *example-reason-point* formula is followed when we use an example. It is the essence of organizing a presentation. This formula has been used, accidentally or intentionally, throughout the history of language and communication. It is found in the parables of the Bible, for a parable is an example. It is found in Aesop's fables, for a fable or story is an example, and the moral is the *point* the story illustrates. This formula is a powerful technique of communication, for it makes each point come to life and meaning. The formula is flexible. The elements can be used in any order. The example can come first, for attention and suspense, building to the point. The point can come first, supported and illustrated by the example. The reason can come anywhere, for it is the link between the example, the point, and the listener; it is the reason the example is told. The *example-reason-point* formula can be used throughout the selling system.

An example can be used in the attention step to create immediate interest while presenting an important point related to your product. Examples can be used in the interest step to make your points clear and to ask questions in a tactful, impersonal way. Examples are used extensively in the conviction step. They can be used in special ways in the desire step. They can be used repeatedly in answering objections and in effective closing.

Product Analysis

The conviction step diagramed in Figure 7-3, is the first step in which you develop a knowledgeable relationship between the consumer's need and your product's benefits. The important thing to know is how to talk about your product — what to say and how to present it. We know, of course, that we talk in terms of the buyer's needs and interests, the benefits he wants as determined in the interest step. To apply this technique the salesman must return to product analysis. He must know how to determine the sales points of his product and how to translate them into living benefits. The procedure is the same one studied earlier, is-do-means:

First, we determine the product's *selling points*, or its significant features and abilities, whether they are exclusive or not.

Next, for each selling point the salesman tells briefly and specifically what it is, or how it works.

Ordinarily salesmen do an excellent job on these two parts, but stop there. This is particularly true of much "selling assistance" prepared by manufacturers for their products. Such material may list dozens of good sales points but leave it

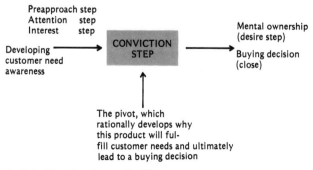

Fig. 7-3 The pivotal step of selling.

entirely up to the salesman, or the customer, to translate these into living bene-fits. For effective, professional selling, the salesman proceeds to translate points into benefits:

Tell what this feature, or selling point, will *do* for the buyer and how or why it will do it.

Tell what this feature will *mean* to the buyer, or what personal benefits it will bring him.

Then we add one other step, that of building *believability* and *conviction* by developing knowledge of need satisfaction. Examples can be used in the follow-ing manner:

In talking about what the selling point *is*, use examples to tell how and why it was developed or made and how it works.

In talking about the *do* benefits, tell what the product or feature has done for others as evidence of what it can do for your prospect.

In talking about the *means* benefits, tell what the product has meant to others as living evidence of what it will mean to this prospect.

The objective is to tie statements and claims to human experience, living evi-dence. Place the burden of proof on the shoulders of a third party, a true experi-ence, a living example.

Testimonials, Recommendations, Test Reports, Approvals, Sales Reports

The testimonial or recommendation is another application of the principle of third-party proof. It is a variation of the example. Every example is, in effect, a testimonial, and every testimonial is an example. Testimonials are particularly useful in overcoming the three fears of buying. If others have bought the product, the prospect has evidence that the salesman is representing it honestly, that it is worth the money, and that his purchase of it will be approved by others. Recom-mendations, laboratory reports, test reports, approvals, and sales reports are all further variations of third-party proof.

Source Analysis

Analyzing the source of the product and translating its sales features into bene-fits follow the same procedure as analyzing the product itself. Special attention is given to source analysis here because it is part of selling which many salesmen neglect or ignore and it is often of great importance, especially in selling stan-dardized products, competitive selling, and selling in price or bid situations. It is a fertile area for the slight edge that can mean success. The source may be any or all of the following:

Individual salesman

Retailer or company he represents, the local office

Wholesaler

National office

Manufacturer

For each of these, the source can include such things as the policies and concepts, background and experience, facilities, and staff.

The first and most important element of the source is usually the salesman himself. Selling is a personal thing. The salesman is the person with whom the buyer deals. The salesman is the person the buyer must believe and trust before he buys. The salesman is the company's representative to the buyer and also the buyer's representative to the company. In importance, the salesman is usually followed by the store or the company and then by the manufacturer. The nearest thing is most important; remote things are less important. The salesman, and each of the other elements of the source, must be sold the same as the product is sold, with sales points translated into benefits. The source must be sold without false modesty, for the source, like the product, has its benefits that are important to the buyer. It has its is-do-means that help fulfill the buyer's needs. Too often companies sell the source the same as they sell their products, with *untranslated selling points*, such as: "Seven plants to serve you. Plenty of free parking. World's largest manufacturer of plastic hinge pins. Established 1886. Supplier to leading firms. The quality name in dried mud." As in talking about their products, such companies neglect to translate facts into benefits. They fail to tell the buyer what the facts mean to him.

Each sales point of the source can be sold the same way as the sales points of the product, by telling what it is, what it does, what it means to the buyer, *and* by supporting the benefits with examples. To illustrate, this is *part* of what was said about parking in promoting a new office building: "The building will be set back 150 feet to provide privacy, quietness, and seventy-five parking spaces for your clients. They can keep appointments easily and promptly; you'll cut wasted waiting time."

How to Sell against Competition

Any time you sell, you face competition. In some cases, it is indirect competition, the general competition for the buyer's money, the pressure against buying your product exerted by all the other things in the world which the prospect could buy if he did not buy from you. Indirect competition is the factor that determines the *cost* of the product to the buyer, what he may have to give up which is more important than the dollar-and-cents price. In studying the desire step you will learn how to sell against this indirect competition.

The other, more obvious type of competition is *direct* competition from similar products or products offering to fulfill the same needs of the buyer. Here are suggestions on how to handle it. As much as possible, ignore your competition. Refuse to talk about it. You do not wish to inform or remind the prospect that there may be another product or source to fulfill his needs. Concentrate attention on your product. Keep in mind that the existence of competitors might be called a weakness of your product. Rather than trying to correct this weakness, build upon strengths — the benefits offered to the buyer. Be sure of your own confidence and selflessness. You and your product have strengths, definite benefits to offer. If these are foremost in your mind, you will not have time or energy to waste thinking or worrying about competition.

You are seeing this buyer to bring him benefits, to help him buy, and the best way to help him is to assist him in choosing the product that offers him the most — *your product*. Never knock, criticize, or condemn a competitive product. It focuses attention on the competitor, rather than on your product. It may cause the prospect to come to the competitor's defense, openly or in his own mind. If the prospect has previously bought the other product, or has been seriously considering it, he may take your criticism personally, as a criticism of his intelligence. Criticism shows a lack of confidence. It is an attempt to sell by making others look bad instead of showing how good your own product is. If you must discuss a competitor, you should lean over backwards to be fair. Acknowledge a reasonable quality for the other product, admit that it offers some benefits, but place emphasis on your own product: its benefits, including those the competitor offers, its slight edge, and its superior ability to fulfill the prospect's needs. Show the prospect that, although the other product might be a good choice, yours is a far better one. If you ever must compare your product with another, do it on the basis of your strengths rather than the other's weaknesses. Use the method of factual analysis rather than criticism. Whenever possible, put the burden of proof on a third party.

How to Show and Demonstrate

Demonstration and showmanship are both based on the same idea, that of using physical means (actions) as well as verbal means (words) to get a point across to the buyer. They help the buyer to understand and feel what the salesman is talking about. They add physical interest and life to the sales presentation, plus providing tangible evidence that what is said is true. Demonstrations and showmanship must have an element of the dramatic, yet they must be logical and natural. The key is to do something that will help the buyer see and feel the impact of what you are saying — something that will emphasize the point. Demonstration or showmanship is best when it is a natural extension of what you say.

For example, if you say a pencil writes smoothly, write a few lines with it so that the prospect can *see* that it writes smoothly. Ask him to write a few lines so that he can *experience* it writing smoothly. If you say something is as quiet as a whisper, you whisper. If you say something is exciting, speak with life, animation, and excitement; speak with actions as well as words.

To plan your actions to emphasize your words, try this system:

When I say . . . (the point you wish to make)

This is what I do . . . (the action to emphasize or illustrate the point)

A logical demonstration or logical showmanship adds selling power to what you say, for it adds emphasis and proof. It is far more effective than "gimmick" showmanship, the illogical or overdone demonstration, and the trite or tricky play on words, which are intended to get attention and little else.

Participation

Everyone has seen magicians — people who do what seems impossible and make it look easy. We all have seen salesmen glibly do a demonstration that looks easy while we continued to doubt that we could duplicate what he has done. But if a salesman shows us how and we do the demonstration for ourselves, we know we can do it. We know that it is as easy as it looks, that there is not a trick to it. This is part of the idea behind getting the customer into the act or getting him to participate. It builds conviction because facts have been translated from theory into *experience* and *reality*. Here is one suggested method of organizing demonstration-participation:

1. You say something, make a claim for your product or how it works. ("This sharpener gives pencils a perfect point.")

2. You demonstrate what you mean, show your claim in action. (You sharpen a pencil.)

3. You ask the prospect to do something, so he can feel and experience for himself. ("Here, you try it. Now look at the point, you can see how it is perfectly sharp and even.")

4. You confirm what the buyer has done or felt, usually by using a question to get his acknowledgement or his reaction. ("Isn't this the kind of point you want on all your pencils all the time for clear, easy writing?")

Here is another excellent method:

1. You ask the prospect to do something. ("Just swing this handle down to the lower position, if you would.")

2. You explain what has happened and the benefits. ("Now see how quickly and easily that brought the drum roller out where it is easy to check and clean. This one feature alone boosts average daily production by about 14 percent. This means this machine can turn out more than 9 hours of work in less than 8 hours; it will help you do a full 6 days of work in a regular 5-day week, helping to cut out those problems of scheduling, overtime pay, and deadlines.")

Notice how easily and naturally benefits can be incorporated into the demonstration. Demonstrations and participation are usually concerned with the product or sales feature itself — what it is and what it does. As always, it pays to translate, showing the value of what you have demonstrated by telling what it will do and mean to the prospect. It was mentioned that part of the reason for participation is to transfer theory into reality and build realization and belief. Another part of the reason for participation is that having the product in his hands, using it, and making it work makes it easier for the buyer to visualize (desire step) himself possessing it. Such participation helps build ownership in his mind. This will be discussed more fully in Chapter Eight in connection with the desire step.

Verbal Demonstrations through Descriptive Language

Not all demonstrations are actual. Sometimes a salesman can present a demonstration entirely in the buyer's mind by helping him build a visual image. This is done through dramatic language that is specific, visual, and descriptive enough to help the customer form a mental picture of what the salesman means. To illustrate, there is little visual imagery in the statement, "This carpeting is especially built for hard use. It has an abrasion resistance factor of 173 and a resilience factor of 991." Compare this statement with the following:

> When we first developed this carpeting, our testing division decided to see how good it really was. They took a length of it from regular production and laid it across the road to our parking lot. It was there for 3 months, with the sun and the rain beating on it. Every kind of traffic went over it — pedestrians, heavy trucks, cars — about 800 cars every working day. Any ordinary carpeting would have been in shreds and tatters, damaged beyond salvage by the wear and by the grease, mud, and sand ground into it. After 3 months of this punishment, they had the rug cleaned the regular way, with a commercial carpet cleaner. When it came back, it showed some results of the wear, of course, but it was still in reasonably good condition. After taking more wear and abuse than any carpet would get in 50 years of heavy-duty use, it still looked better than many heavy-duty carpets look after 2 or 3 years of use.

You can "see" that demonstration. You can see it because it has action. You can see it because it has visual words: "rain beating on it," "shreds and tatters," "sand ground into it." But you cannot "see" the carpet after it was cleaned because that part of the example was written without action, without visual words. You cannot see what is meant by "reasonably good condition" or "better than many carpets look." This demonstration could have been given much more impact by following it with actual samples of the carpet — one sample new, the other taken from the piece tested — so the buyer could compare them for himself.

Note one thing in particular: how easy it is to combine several techniques to give more power to your selling. The example above has *visual* words, a *living example*, and a *test report* (third-party proof) all in one. Each reinforces the others. Even small changes in language, changes from vague, general words to specific, visual words, can build the power of your sales presentation. If something is brown in color, what shade of brown is it? How do you help the buyer visualize the brown you mean? Is it the brown of a honey-colored cocker spaniel; the brown of a good, mellow cigar; the brown of a hand-rubbed leather saddle; the brown of parched, dead grass? When we use a word, each person has his *own* image of what we mean, unless we are specific. When you say something is "big" or "blue" or "strong," put it in words the prospect can "see" so that he forms the image you want him to have in his mind.

Packaging Your Sales Presentation

Appearance is part of the package. It makes the important first impression that can set the mood and attitude of the buyer. It can contribute to the sale — or detract from it. Appearance can mean the appearance of the salesman, of his sales aids and material, of the product or merchandise, or of the store or outlet. A hangdog look, a wrinkled suit, a shopworn product, a dog-eared sales folder or stained price tag, a dusty front window or unswept floor — these give one impression. They set a shoddy stage for selling, a poor "corporate image."

Manner is part of the package, and so are manners. When a salesman sells with life, energy, confidence, and enthusiasm, it shows in his sales records. He transmits these same qualities to his prospects. He sells with a sincere desire to help the prospect trade money for valuable benefits. It shows in the buyer's attitude, reactions, and decisions. There are many things that help build the right package for a salesman and his sales presentation. Most of them are obvious, including respect for the buyer, simple courtesy, good English, and the avoidance of profanity and off-color stories. The impression you give by how you act reflects its image on whatever you are selling.

Showmanship and dramatics are part of the package. They emphasize the points you want to get across; they are methods of putting energy and attention value into your sales story. Power words are part of the package. Words are one of the important elements that help deliver your sales message. They can deliver it alive and stimulating, or they can deliver it as a lifeless, meaningless recital of facts. The following are some word techniques:

Use fresh, lively, out-of-the-rut words — words with impact and mind-tickling power. Some words have been worn out, rubbed smooth by too much use.

Practice replacing them with words that still have flavor, words that have sharp edges that can nick the buyer's consciousness, words that catch the light and sparkle.

Use comparisons — the fresher the better. Use similes and metaphors (look them up!). Use analogies (look it up, too!). Throw out the old ones, such as "stuck out like a sore thumb." Replace them with fresh coinage of your own: "as out of place as tennis shoes at a formal dance."

Use visual words that appeal to the senses, that bring a picture to the buyer's mind: "This table is so strong that ten men could stand on it with perfect safety." "This finish is so tough that you could scrub it with sandpaper and not even dull the shine."

Watch the mood of a word, as well as its meaning. Every word has a denotation, its *exact* meaning. It also has a connotation — its mood or the impression it brings to a person's mind. Both must be watched. For example, in each of the sets below, the words have similar meanings but completely different connotations:

Imported	Foreign	Un-American
Cheap	Economical	Thrifty
Homemade	Handmade	Hand-crafted
Stranger	Newcomer	New blood

Watch the point of view of your words. Keep thinking and talking from the buyer's point of view, staying on his side of the fence. The second of each of the following pairs illustrates what I mean.

"You'll have to go to the other window,"
versus
"Would you mind stepping to the other window? Miss Jones is the person who can help you best."

"I have something I want to show you,"
versus
"Here is something you'll probably want to see."

"Take a look at the facts,"
versus
"Let's review the facts."

"Send your dollar for a copy of this book,"
versus
"Send a dollar for your copy of this book."

"This is completely fair; no one could argue with it,"
versus
"Does this sound completely fair to you?"

Use words that carry conviction with them:

"If you want a (product) that will do (such and so), this feature is a *must*."

"This service can give you *real* help."

"This is the truth."

"This works."

"The important thing is . . . ."

Use words and phrases that get the customer into the act:

"What is your opinion?"

"What do you think?"

"Have I stated that correctly?"

"Would you mind letting me know why you say that?"

"Why would you say that is so?"

Use words that trigger the mind, that suggest something new, different, or unusual:

"Have you seen this (or tried this) *lately*?"

"Have you had a chance to *test* this?"

"How *long* has it been since you had a *complete* demonstration?"

Watch for individuality in order to stand out from the crowd. Standing out from the crowd, having some identifying or individual characteristic, is part of packaging. It is a type of slight edge — a trademark that makes you or your product easier to remember.

CONCLUSION

The conviction step of salesmanship is the pivotal step of the selling system, for it symbolizes the activity that develops through conscious awareness a knowledgeable relationship between customer needs and an ultimate decision to purchase a product. It is important that you be aware of two things the conviction step is *not*. It is *not* the only step of salesmanship, as many salesmen consider it to be. This chapter indicates that the salesman cannot begin seriously to influence the decision to buy until there is a conscious awareness of needs. Furthermore, the conviction step is *not* the conclusion to a sales presentation, but it intellectually prepares the customer ultimately to make a favorable buying decision.

Perhaps now it is easier to see why the conviction step is called the "pivotal step." It connects through effective communication need awareness to a final buying decision. In order to develop effectively a logical, comprehensive linking of needs to benefits, it is important that you become familiar with all the techniques discussed throughout this chapter. As you have learned in studying the selling system, nothing is constant in selling. If you learn all the inputs of the system, you will be capable of evaluating a particular selling situation in a valid manner and consequently of using the particular method that will be of greatest assistance.

An example of this point involves the sales manager of a firm selling cough syrup to retail drugstores. His immediate problem was simple — how to increase his salesmen's sales within the territory. Recognizing that the marketing environment was characteristically competitive, he investigated the possibility of developing his sales strategy around testimonials. He made a tour of his entire sales area to determine which pharmacists were successfully selling his company's brand of cough syrup. Each time he found such a store, he wrote up the sales results on a piece of paper and included the pharmacist's "sticker" to prove that he really visited the drugstore. When he returned to the home office, he made copies of these successful sales results for each salesman to place in a leather binder. Each salesman then had a series of testimonials he could use to show the customer in the conviction step (through knowledge) why he should buy that specific brand of cough syrup.

This sales manager viewed the situation from the systems approach. He viewed the total situation in terms of the related inputs: competition, drugstores, salesmen, customers, brand of cough syrup, use of sensory perception. On the basis of this evaluation he utilized one technique (testimonials) which proved particularly significant to the selling system at this point in time. It can be stated with assurance that product analysis (is-do-means) will always be used at some point in the conviction step, for this is the means of developing a rational understanding of what the product is, what it does, and what it means to the customer in terms of values.

CASE STUDY USING THE INPUTS OF ATTENTION, INTEREST, AND CONVICTION

Salesman John Martin is calling on Sam Smith, a general contractor. Martin knows that Smith has just been awarded a state highway construction project.

MARTIN: Congratulations, Sam, I just heard you were awarded that Cedar Creek cutoff job.

SMITH: Yeah. I was afraid that Warwick's bid might be under ours.

MARTIN: Well, it was pretty close. I noticed there was very little difference in your bids. It looks like a good job. If you don't have too much trouble with your equipment, you should make some money on it.

SMITH: Well, it ought to be a profitable job, but you never know what'll happen.

MARTIN: As you know, Sam, anticipating the breakdown often means the difference in the profit on any job. When do you plan on starting?

SMITH: We're going to move some of our equipment over right away.

MARTIN: That's a big job, Sam, and you'll have to hustle to meet the September first deadline.

SMITH: Yes, it looks like I'll have to move in eight road gangs and all my local equipment.

MARTIN: In view of that deadline and the size of the job, isn't there a possibility that you might get into trouble with some of the old equipment you have here?

SMITH: Oh, I don't know. We take pretty good care of it. Most of it runs okay.

MARTIN: No doubt it does, Sam. You do take good care of it. But aren't a couple of those old bulldozers pretty well worn out?

SMITH: I do have some that are getting pretty old.

MARTIN: It could cost you plenty in time and money if those babies broke down! I'd like to fix you up with a couple of new models to help protect you on this job.

SMITH: That's darned nice of you, John. But I've always used Consolidateds, and they've been pretty satisfactory. If I do replace those two, I'll probably get two more Consolidateds.

MARTIN: Consolidateds are good scrapers, Sam, but this new model of ours has some improvements I think you'll want to see.

SMITH: How did they improve that thing?

MARTIN: They've improved many things to give you better operation — and at a lower cost than other bulldozers.

SMITH: What kind of improvements did they make?

MARTIN: Let's take the starting system, for one. That's always been a headache to you, and you've got some cold weather coming up soon. (*Martin takes out a folder which he shows to Smith, using the cutaway drawings to explain the new starting system and how it operates.*) And another advantage, Sam, is that the pistons and cylinders are warmed with gasoline heat at an idling speed. Then, when you switch it to diesel, it's ready to go. With this system, it's impossible to have half-burned fuel forming carbon around the rings. Would you say that might save you some repair costs and downtime?

SMITH: Yes, it looks pretty good — and I'm a little worried about time on this job.

MARTIN: Sam, in addition to saving you time and money on repairs, this starting system will save you time on the job. It makes getting the 'dozer on the job as quick and simple as starting your car. You just step in and hit the starter — it's all warmed and working in less than a minute. That could help you make that deadline for sure, and save you money too, because no one will be sitting around waiting for the machine to warm up. Doesn't that sound like the way you want this job to run, Sam?

SMITH: It sounds like it might be pretty valuable, especially in cold weather.

MARTIN: You bet it will, Sam. It will make your operators happier too; they'll like a machine that starts right up and works right. Sam, how about . . .

SMITH: Now just a minute — put away that order blank! I'm not going to buy a machine just because it starts better; there's more to construction work than that.

MARTIN: You bet there is! That's why I'm sure you'll appreciate the other improvements in our machine — like the new drawbar arrangement.

SMITH: What did they do to that?

MARTIN: Here, take a look at this folder. (*Martin uses a folder with drawings that show the old and new drawbar design. He shows the improvements and explains the advantages and benefits, including the advantages over the Consolidated design.*) So you see, Sam, this gives you the proper balance between weight and power. This means you can move dirt in a shorter time with less fuel cost. That's important to you, isn't it?

SMITH: It certainly is.

MARTIN: And you can see how this new drawbar arrangement makes this possible?

SMITH: It looks like it could — but I'd have to see it working to be sure.

MARTIN: That's the only way to tell, so I'll bring a machine out for you to try. Which would be better for you, Sam, this afternoon or tomorrow?

SMITH: Better make it in the morning. I'm tied up this afternoon.

MARTIN: Okay. How would nine o'clock be — on the Central grading job? I noticed you're doing both rough and finish grading there, so you can give the machine a real workout and see how it does on different types of work. How does that sound?

SMITH: Sounds pretty good. I'll see you there.

MARTIN: Fine, Sam. And I know one thing, the harder you work this machine, the more you'll like it. See you at nine on the Central job.

PROBLEMS

1. The terms "conviction" and "knowledge" are used to identify that step of salesmanship which formulates a strategy to sell the product. Why are these terms interchangeable? Use the systems approach in arriving at your answer.

2. Discuss the importance of the slight-edge concept.

3. Why do we say that the conviction step is the pivotal step of salesmanship?

4. Bring to class an object and demonstrate its use to the class. See if you can use the demonstration to gain participation by other members of the class.

5. Bring to class a newspaper advertisement which you feel uses fresh, descriptive words. Discuss with the class the impact of this style of advertising in terms of how the style could be applied to salesmanship.

6. Clip another advertisement from the newspaper and use your creativity in preparing a sales analysis of the product, using the is-do-means approach.

7. Clip a "hunk of life" from something you have read recently and apply it to a sales presentation as an *example*.

See pages 259–261 for an additional case study.

SAMPLE ASSIGNMENT 1

List five selling points of the *source* — yourself, as the salesman; your company; or the manufacturer — and tell in paragraph form what you say about each selling point.

Selling point: As your salesman I have always attempted to make available products by which you will make a profit, rather than merely trying to increase my sales.

Selling point: Our branch office has consistently given you prompt service, even at an inconvenience to ourselves.

Selling point: The Mobil Oil Corporation has based its sales policy on the premise that if we give you professional counsel, your increased sales will justify our time as well spent.

Selling point: Our credit department will make convenient credit terms when ready capital is not available.

Selling point: Although there are numerous accounts handled with each service station, our accounting department has done an excellent job of keeping each account clear and separate from others.

ASSIGNMENT 1

List five selling points of the *source* — yourself, as the salesman; your company; or the manufacturer — and tell in paragraph form what you say about each selling point.

Selling point:

Selling point:

Selling point:

Selling point:

Selling point:

SAMPLE ASSIGNMENT 2

List five selling points of the *product*, using the is-do-means technique.

PRODUCT: whitewall tire

Selling point: The *cord* of this tire is constructed of many nylon strands, which gives you complete protection against blowouts. This means that you will be able to travel those treacherous winding roads with complete confidence; once more you'll *enjoy* driving.

Selling point: Because of its *spliced tread*, this tire has greater traction. It will give you control of your car whether you are driving on ice, snow, or rainy surfaces. This means you will be able to travel at greater speeds this summer, making more calls and increasing your commission.

Selling point: Due to *specially compounded wax imbedded in the sidewall*, the whitewall is everlastingly white. No matter how many times you scuff the tire, it will always be a snowy white. This means that the beauty of your car will be continually enhanced as long as you have these tires.

Selling point: *This tire has 25 percent more tread than the average tire*, thus giving you many more driving miles at less cost. You will save enough money over one year to buy those water skis you've wanted for some time.

Selling point: *Our safety bead construction will not allow any air to escape through the rim*. This means your wife will not have to worry about changing tires, as was the case when she was taking the children to school yesterday.

ASSIGNMENT 2

List five selling points of the *product*, using the is-do-means technique.

PRODUCT:

Selling point:

Selling point:

Selling point:

Selling point:

Selling point:

Chapter Eight
Creating Mental Ownership

ANALYSIS PROCESS

The desire step is the step in which the sale is actually made. The sale is made when the buyer *assumes ownership* of the product in his mind — when he can visualize himself owning the product and enjoying the benefits it offers. This is the step in which the facts about the product, the theoretical benefits, are fully translated into living awareness of their meaning.

This step is also called the visualization or ownership step. Just as visualization, or imagination, is not the same as seeing, ownership is not the same as possession. You can own things which you do not possess; you can possess things which you do not own. For example, if you loan your car to a friend, you still own it, but he possesses it at the moment.

For many things, a strong feeling of ownership can develop through use or possession, even though legal ownership may belong to someone else. It is human nature to assume this emotional ownership, of tangibles and intangibles alike. We will discuss this more fully as one of the first principles of the desire step.

In the desire step, we are working to help the buyer make the price or value decision: to decide that the product offers value at least equal to what the cost will be to him. We call it "taking the ice out of price."

As we have discussed, price and cost are not the same. The price is the dollar-and-cents tag on a product being sold. It is usually the same for all buyers. The cost is what the individual buyer will have to sacrifice to buy a particular thing. It is whatever he will have to give up. The cost of a product is different for every buyer.

In the desire step, diagramed in Figure 8-1, we work to help the buyer visualize ownership of the product we sell. We make ownership of the product and its benefits as real as anything else in the world — in the buyer's mind. We talk about the past: his needs and the benefits he has been missing. We talk about the present: the benefits he is offered. And we move him into the future: we help him visualize owning the product. We help him *feel himself owning* the product and receiving the benefits. In this step, we can repeat the essence of our sales presentation as many as three times.

The result is that the product joins the ranks of items that the prospect owns. It moves beyond merely being something it would be nice to own. It becomes a part of his life which he must give up, do without, unless he buys it and takes possession. Because he *feels* its value, he does not want to lose it. He becomes willing to pay the price.

It is fortunate that many prospects arouse their own desire to possess, for the majority of salespeople neglect the desire step. They leave this most important final translation entirely up to the buyer, not realizing that this is the point at which the sale is actually made.

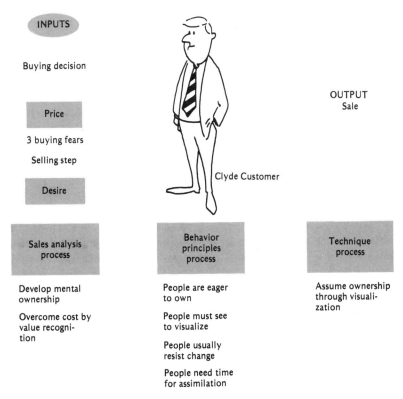

INPUTS

Buying decision

Price

3 buying fears

Selling step

Desire

Clyde Customer

OUTPUT
Sale

Sales analysis process	Behavior principles process	Technique process
Develop mental ownership	People are eager to own	Assume ownership through visuali-zation
Overcome cost by value recogni-tion	People must see to visualize	
	People usually resist change	
	People need time for assimilation	

Fig. 8-1 The desire step.

Most salespeople neglect the desire step for another reason. They do not know the techniques of helping the buyer assume ownership, of helping him visualize. Yet the techniques are easy to learn and so simple and natural to use that you will use them automatically once you learn them.

It is also possible that some salespeople hesitate to use the desire step because they do not believe in persuasion in selling. They may look upon the desire tech-niques as "playing on the buyer's emotions," unfitted to professional selling. They forget that professional selling is an honest attempt to help the buyer ful-fill his needs and realize the benefits he wants, and that every honest technique of helping the buyer has a valid and valuable place in professional selling.

The desire step *does* deal with emotions. It is part of translating the intellectual meaning of what you say into its emotional meaning, its human meaning. The purpose of the step is *not* to twist the buyer's emotions, not to tug on his heart-strings, not to make emotions override logic and sense. Its purpose is to *enlist* the emotions — to help the buyer realize the meaning of the facts presented and to build an emotional attitude from a foundation of logic and sense.

There are two chapters on this important step of selling. The first, this chapter, will concentrate on the principles and techniques of helping the buyer visualize, helping him assume ownership. The second, Chapter Ten, will cover how to handle objections and resistance. It will use the same principles presented in this chapter, with additional analysis and specific techniques.

On the step-close diagram, the desire step is charted as in Figure 8-2. Linking benefits to the buyer's needs has built the value of the product to the point where it is greater than the cost (as well as the price). Visualization, which helps the buyer assume ownership, leads him to realize the value and takes the sale over the cost hurdle.

PRINCIPLES OF THE DESIRE STEP

People Are Eager to Assume Ownership

Throughout life, people continually assume ownership — emotional ownership of the things they see or use. They do it almost automatically. They say, "This is *mine*," regardless of who may have legal ownership at the moment: This is *my* seat in the classroom, *my* typewriter and desk at the office, *my* bench and tools in the factory, *my* parking space on the street, *my* bus I catch to go home, *my* company, *my* club, *my* political party or candidate, *my* idea.

This emotional ownership is built through possession, use, participation, and identification. It is one of the most powerful principles underlying human behavior, actions, and reactions. Its power can be applied to selling, with predictable, gratifying results. In the buyer's eyes, it is not your sale, but *my* purchase; not your persuasion, but *my* decision; not just possible benefits, but *my* benefits to fulfill *my* needs. It is not just a product, but *my* product. The buyer assumes ownership in his mind, and to fulfill what he feels, he generates the desire to take possession by buying.

People Must See in Order to Visualize

Visualization is the process of taking facts and translating them into meaning, of building a mental picture that enables one to see and feel what the future could be. It is the process of transcending time and space; it is the basis of imagination and creative thinking.

Visualization takes the things we have experienced, or seen or felt, and mentally puts them into new arrangements. They are extended, projected, combined

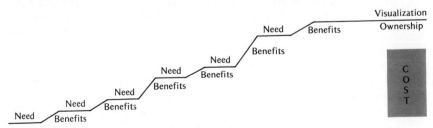

Fig. 8-2 Linked needs/benefits to overcome cost.

and recombined, related and contrasted, viewed from different directions. And it is all done in the mind.

The key to visualization is to experience, in your mind, what you wish to visualize. You must mentally see and feel, using your past experience as the building blocks. You must mentally *live* what you are attempting to see and feel in your mind.

The ability to visualize is a human characteristic. Nearly every child can do it — by "pretending." Many adults do it as part of their jobs. The architect visualizes a building in order to draw the plans; another architect can look at the blueprints and visualize the building. The economist visualizes future conditions in order to make his predictions. The salesman visualizes the sale being made in order to plan it properly in the preapproach. People have the ability to visualize, but only a few have developed it to any extent.

In salesmanship, and particularly in the desire step, we want the buyer to visualize himself owning the product and receiving its benefits, so that he can assume ownership. We must help him visualize by visualizing for him and then telling him what we see so that he can build the same mental picture. It is another part of the continual process of helping the buyer translate.

People Usually Resist Change

People are fundamentally conservative. They are wary of new ideas, new courses of action, any change in the status quo. They fear that change may take place for its own sake only, that it will create more problems than it solves, worse problems than the ones they have learned to live with. And even if the problems it creates are no worse than the present ones, they will still take effort to get used to. This fear of change, of the unknown or unfamiliar, is part of the reason why so many people procrastinate and hesitate to make decisions.

But people are willing to accept change, even to seek it, under the right conditions. They will accept it when they can see that it means progress. A man will change jobs, careers, or cities if he feels the opportunity for progress is there. People will accept change when they can see it as a relatively minor change that will help prevent or forestall a more serious, major change. A man will buy life insurance because he wants to prevent the possibility of too great a change in the way his family lives.

In sales, every purchase represents a change. It will be resisted because it is change and because it calls for a decision.

People Need Time for Assimilation

When we encounter something new and strange, it takes time for us to understand and react to it. It must register on our minds. It must be absorbed. It must be interpreted in terms of its meaning. Then, and only then, can we decide whether to accept or reject it or what our reaction should be.

Two things can contribute to this process of assimilation. One is adequate time. In selling, we cannot go too fast, or we may leave the buyer far behind. The other thing that can help the process is assistance in absorbing the fact and in interpreting its meaning. In selling, we can assist and speed the process of assimilation by helping the buyer translate facts into benefits and by helping him visualize.

TECHNIQUES OF THE DESIRE STEP

Help the Buyer Assume Ownership through Visualization

In the desire step, we talk about past benefits missed, present benefits offered, and future benefits being enjoyed.

When we talk about past benefits missed, we talk in the *past* tense:

> Mr. Benson, you mentioned that last summer your office staff had a slump in efficiency and production every time the temperature went up. You said you wished there was some way to solve the problem of heat-wave letdown and absenteeism, some way to keep your staff as efficient in summer as it is during the rest of the year.

When we talk about the present benefits offered, we talk in the *future* tense. We tell what the product *will* do and mean:

> Now, Mr. Benson, with your offices air-conditioned, you will have the conditions for peak efficiency and productivity throughout the year, whatever the weather may be. Your employees will feel good; they will feel alive and energetic; they will automatically turn out more work, better work, with less effort and fatigue. And the problem of absenteeism will be solved, because when the temperature soars, your offices will be the most comfortable place your employees can think of to be.

When we talk about future benefits being enjoyed, we talk in the *present* tense. This is the key — the present tense. We visualize the prospect enjoying the benefits. We describe what we see. We help the prospect visualize himself enjoying the benefits. In effect, by talking in the present tense and helping the prospect visualize, we are transporting him into the future:

> Mr. Benson, I can see you this summer. You're on your way to the office, and you can see that it will be another scorching day. The air is already hot; the breeze is like a blowtorch. You open the door to your office and step in. It's like stepping into springtime, into a perfect day that makes a man glad to be alive. And, as a businessman, you have reason to be glad. Your employees are at their desks. They all look alert, cheerful, comfortable. Their minds are on their work, not on the heat. They're producing at their best. The door opens, and a customer comes in — a man you know could be a top account if you could only get a half hour of his time. He's sweltering and carrying his coat. He sits down and relaxes. He talks about

how unbearable the heat is outside, and how pleasant it is in your office. For the first time, he is in no hurry to leave. You have your chance to talk to him at length, to discuss how your company can serve him, to sell him the service you know he wants and needs. And when he leaves, you have the first of a series of big orders from him. You look at the order. You look at your staff and the work they are doing. And you ask yourself why you waited so long to get the benefits of office air conditioning.

This particular technique, visualization, is one of the most important in selling. It makes the future part of the desire step one of the most powerful parts of your sales presentation. Here is why: By putting the buyer into the future in his imagination, by helping him visualize himself experiencing the benefits your product offers, you have given him a living experience. And you have, for a moment, given him ownership and possession. You have given him a mental picture he can look at and say, "This is mine." You have given him an *example*, with himself in the starring role.

You have helped the buyer realize and experience the joys of ownership. You have given him something he wants to possess and experience in reality as well as in imagination. If the visualization has been strong enough, if it has been tied to his needs, he will want to possess your product much more strongly than he will want to possess cold, meaningless money. Your product's value will outweigh price and cost.

You may be wondering why, contrary to what seems logical, present benefits offered are described in the future tense and future benefits are described in the present tense. The reason is simple: When we talk about present benefits, we are talking about what *could* be, so we talk in the future tense. When we talk about future benefits, we talk in the present tense to describe what we visualize *at the instant we see it*. We are not talking *about* the future, but transporting the buyer *into* it, so he can assume ownership.

Help the Buyer Assume Ownership in Other Ways

Let him participate, as much as possible, in the sale. If a column of figures is to be added up, let him add it or check your addition — the total becomes *his* total. Encourage him to take part, as much as you can, in working out the sale. Let him be able to say, "This is my sale, my decision, my facts and figures, my idea."

Let him feel, handle, and try the product. Get it into his hands. Let him do the demonstration for himself and show others how it works. Let him experience possession with his senses, to help him in the process of assuming ownership.

Assume ownership for him, and reflect it in what you say: "Your air-conditioner can fit in that window"; "When you park your new car in front of your house"; "As you can see, you'll have a fine view of the city when you live here." Talk as if he already owned the product, or undoubtedly will. At the same time, pull ownership away from the money involved — make it impersonal, mathematics, a medium of exchange: "If you have *a* dollar, it will confirm *your* purchase";

"a check"; "the down payment"; "the price is . . ." (*not*, "This will cost you . . .").

SALESMANSHIP: CASE STUDY "M" VISUALIZATION

Many, many times, Blade had taken his prospects to the "Top of the Mountain." Just for example, there had been that prosperous, sturdy, AAA-1 meat packing business in Brooklyn, an old family concern with nice distribution throughout metropolitan New York, Long Island, nearby Connecticut and Jersey. A sweet little business, a going concern. What does a salesman [for an advertising agency] do with such a prospect?

Why, he takes him on a walk to the Top of the Mountain. Shows him — from there — the wonders and glories of national, no, international distribution. Bedazzles him with visions of color spreads in the *Post*, network television, branches in Chicago, Denver, Los Angeles and Atlanta. Convinces the little provincial tradesman that he can be as big as Swift or Armour, only in a higher class way. The salesman, after getting his prospect to the Top of the Mountain, says, in effect, "See it? See it from up here, little man? See your small family business growing, growing, growing into a big, big commercial empire? See the money, the power, the glory? Look, little man! Look."[1]

CONCLUSION

The conviction step and the desire step have a particular relatedness within the selling system. The strength of the selling system is in allowing the salesman to evaluate the particular relatedness of a sale and to thereby utilize the technique most effective for *that* sale. Within the system concept, the conviction step allows the salesman to present product knowledge in a manner which motivates the customer to use his mental process to favorably assimilate this knowledge. This assimilation is diagramed in the step close, where the customer links needs to benefits. In the desire step, knowledge is the basis for a mental decision to accept ownership. This acceptance can take place only when the mental evaluation presents value gained (benefits understood and assimilated in the conviction step) as greater than cost. This could be diagramed as in Figure 8-3.

PROBLEMS

1. Why do most salesmen fail to incorporate the concept of mental ownership into their selling activity?

2. How can the salesman use the techniques of the desire step to support other areas of the marketing system?

[1] From John G. Schneider, *The Golden Kazoo*, Dell Publishing Co., Inc., New York, 1956.

Product Knowledge

1. *Sense awareness:*
   sight
   hearing
   smell
   taste
   touch

2. *Selective perception:*
   The brain accepts
   what it
   chooses to
   accept

Conviction step

3. *Cognition occurs:*
   Interpretative analysis
   by which the customer
   becomes aware

4. *Decision making:*
   On the basis of this
   interpretative analysis,
   the customer becomes aware
   of the value of the product

Desire step

Fig. 8-3 The decision-making process.

3. Discuss the difference between price and cost.

4. Write a one-page essay regarding a salesman you have had contact with who made use of the desire techniques discussed in this chapter.

5. Clip an advertisement from the newspaper which you feel uses the techniques of the desire step. In what way does this advertisement utilize the concepts of this selling step?

6. Use the desire step to sell a pleasure boat to a family with five children, ages four, six, nine years and eleven months, thirteen, and nineteen.

7. Describe a television commercial you feel uses the techniques of the desire step. In what way does this commercial utilize the concepts of the desire step?

See pages 262–263 for an additional case study.

Chapter Nine
Tying Down the Sale

ANALYSIS PROCESS

To the average person engaged in selling, the close is the most important and dificult part of the sale. The typical salesman feels as one salesman stated, "I can sell people, but I can't close them." He is eager to learn how to close, to pick up some tricks and gimmicks he can use to get buyers to sign on the dotted line.

To the professional salesman also, the close is important, for it is the final step of the sale, the point at which the egg is hatched and the chicken can be counted. But the professional salesman does not consider the close any more difficult than the other steps of selling. To him it is another simple, logical step. He closes after the buyer has already assumed ownership. The buying decisions of need, product, source, and price have already been made, and all that remains is to help the buyer decide the time to buy and to work out the details of the purchase.

This is one of the big differences between the typical salesman and the professional salesman. The typical salesman may try to get three or more buying decisions (product, price, and time) made in the close. He finds it difficult and so feels he must resort to tricks. The professional salesman has actually made the sale; the only decision left for the close is the time decision, which often is the easiest to help the buyer make.

The close, then, is not when we "make the sale." The close is when we wind up the details of the payment and arrange the details of delivery.

We Close, as We Sell, on Benefits

One important thing to remember about closing is that we talk benefits, just as we have in the other steps of selling. Benefits are what people buy. When we close on benefits, it is often a fact that the buyer cannot remember the close, because it was an easy, automatic decision, and his mind was on the benefits the product offered rather than on the technique the salesman used to make the deal final.

On the step-close diagram, the action or close step is shown this way:

Visualization
Ownership
Decision
Possession

The Trial Close, or Step Close

As we discovered in studying the desire step, the sale actually is made the instant that the buyer assumes ownership in his own mind. This can take place anywhere during the selling process. The buyer may have assumed ownership before we walked into his place of business or he walked into ours. Or he may assume ownership in the interest step or in the conviction step.

We have described this process of assuming ownership in a number of ways. One way it might be described is that the buyer has mentally linked his needs with the benefits our product offers him. This may be a firm and dominant linking. If it shows him that the product will fulfill his dominant needs, that the benefits offered outweigh the cost, he assumes ownership. Or it may be a tentative, minor linking. The needs he sees fulfilled may be minor ones. His dominant needs may still remain to be fulfilled. He sees the value of the benefits, but it does not yet outweigh the cost. In this case, he is not so much assuming ownership as "trying it on for size." The sale is progressing, but it has not been made.

Each time a need is linked with a benefit, we have the opportunity for a trial close. The trial close, or step close, is nothing more or less than an attempt to find the answers to two questions:

Has one of the buyer's needs been linked with a benefit in his own mind?

How important is the linked need/benefit to the buyer?

We are trying to see where the sale stands, to what degree the buyer has assumed ownership. If he has assumed ownership sufficiently in his own mind, we

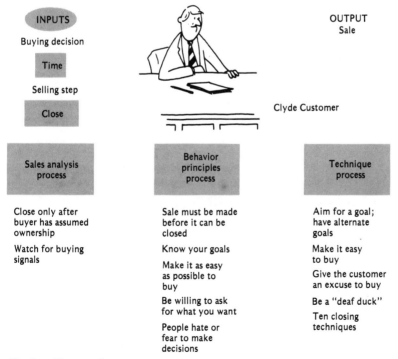

Fig. 9-1 The step close.

know that the sale had been made and that we can proceed to the close, wrapping up the details of the purchase. If he has assumed only partial ownership, we frequently get some idea of the direction to take to complete the sale.

The term "step close" is actually more descriptive of what we are doing than the traditional term "trial close." "Trial close" has connotations of an attempt to close, an attempt to short-cut the selling process. "Step close" has more the feeling that we are determining how many steps the buyer has taken toward assuming ownership. We are not trying to determine if the sale *can* be closed, but if it *should* be closed at this time.

The techniques of the step close are similar to those of the regular close. In particular, we use the techniques of choice close, example close, and weighing close, to be discussed more fully later in this chapter. As in all closing, we close on benefits.

In selling, every time you link a benefit with one of the buyer's needs you are a step nearer to the sale. You have applied the principle of step closing — supplying a benefit to satisfy a need. Pause briefly; give the buyer time to assimilate the information and to react. He may say or do something. He may give you a buying signal, requesting you to close the deal. When you attempt to close, he may resist or object, which merely means that one or more additional step closes may be needed.

Buying Signals

A buying signal is anything the buyer says or does which shows us that he has assumed ownership or a degree of ownership.

A buying signal may be given in words. A buyer might start drawing a word picture in which he sees himself enjoying a benefit. Or he might ask a question or make a statement which shows he is already in the close step.

Or a buying signal may be given in actions. A buyer who has been relaxed may suddenly lean forward to give you his avid attention. He may reach out to touch the product or to pick it up, or start examining a particular feature. Or he may react to the way you handle it.

A buying signal means you have accomplished a step close. You have supplied a benefit to satisfy a need. It may be only an indication that you are coming nearer to the sale, or it may be the buyer's way of requesting you to close. The following are examples of buying signals:

What the buyer *says* to give a buying signal: "Could I get this blue?" What the salesman says and does: "Yes, we have this dark blue and this light blue." Shows sample. "Which one would you like better in this room?"

What the buyer *does* to give a buying signal: Picks up the product to examine a particular feature. What the salesman says and does: "Notice how securely that fremistan is bolted on. That means you'll never have to worry about it working loose. You can just turn on the machine and forget it, sure that it will work properly for years and years. Since this is what you've told me you want, shall we have your machine installed Tuesday morning?"

PRINCIPLES OF THE CLOSE STEP

The Sale Must Be Made Before It Can Be Closed

We have discussed this earlier, but it is particularly important for a full understanding of the action or close step. A decision must be made before a course of action can be started. The buyer must assume ownership in his mind, he must feel the value a product offers, before he is willing to part with his money to take possession.

Know Your Goal(s)

In the early days of the West, one method that was used to tame wild horses was this: The bronco would be tied to a gentle, patient, stubborn burro with a line rope and then released from the corral. He would usually take off for the horizon, dragging the burro along. He could run and buck and kick all he wanted to; the burro would be there at the end of the rope. And every time the bronco rested for a moment, every time the burro could get his feet squarely on the ground, the burro would take a few steps back toward the corral and his food. Within a few days, the burro would come trotting in, leading a tired, gentle horse.

The reason this worked was that the bronco was merely spending energy, while the burro had a firm idea of where he wanted to go. It is the same in selling: When the salesman has a firm idea of where he wants to go, and knows he will get there eventually, he can afford to let the buyer spend energy. Eventually, he will be able gently to lead the buyer where he wants him to go.

For another point of view, slightly different but related, consider this statement: One reason that people will follow a leader is that he is going somewhere, and seems to know how to get there. Your own sense of purpose, your own confidence in the decision you want the buyer to make, helps build his confidence.

Make It as Easy as Possible for the Buyer to Buy

People have a great capacity for protecting themselves. They are lazy in that they do not want to spend any energy that they do not have to spend. They are often insecure in that they will not admit that they do not know how to do something.

These concepts apply directly to salesmanship. It is the salesman who should spend the energy to make the sale simple and easy for the buyer. It is the salesman who should work out all the details, so all the buyer has to do is say "yes." It is the salesman who should figure out how something can or should be done, so the buyer does not have to figure it out.

Be Willing to Ask for What You Want

One of the first men I ever worked for had this philosophy regarding raises: "If you ever want a raise around here, be willing to ask for it. That's probably the only way you'll get it, for I don't believe in paying more money to anyone who is already satisfied with what he is getting."

I have treasured that advice for two reasons. The first is the principle of life it contains: Be willing to ask for what you want; it will help you get it. And, in getting ready to ask, you are forced to organize your reasons for your request. The second reason is equally important: That employer was willing to tell me what he wanted, what was expected, and it is good to know what is expected.

Buyers, too, like to know exactly what is expected, what you want them to do. And they appreciate being asked.

People Hate or Fear to Make Decisions

As we have discussed, people resist change. They would rather not make decisions, for each decision usually means a change. They would rather delay and procrastinate, hoping a decision will not have to be made.

It is the salesman's job to help the buyer make his decision, the right decision at the right time. And it is the salesman's job to make decision making easy for buyers.

TECHNIQUES OF THE CLOSE STEP

Aim for a Goal and Have Alternative Goals

Based on your preapproach, or upon what you determine in the interest step, have a clear idea of what you want to accomplish: what you want the prospect to do and how you feel it should be done. This enables you to keep directing your efforts toward the goal. And it enables you to make a definite, confident recommendation for specific action.

It is wise to have a major goal and a series of possible alternative goals you can aim for in case your primary goal is blocked. With alternative goals, you are prepared to get the maximum value from even an "unsuccessful" sales interview. For example, in a call upon an industrial purchasing agent, these might be your goals:

1. Sale of 400 units recommended

2. Trial purchase of ten units

3. Placement of one unit for testing by engineering department

4. Arrangement of appointment with chief engineer to discuss possible testing of unit

5. Repeat appointment set up with purchasing agent, for further discussion and revised proposal

6. Door left open for return call on purchasing agent

Make It Easy for the Customer to Buy

Whenever you wish to ask for action, there are three checkpoints that help you achieve maximum success. What you ask must be

1. *Possible* — within the power of the other person to do

2. *Specific* — so he knows exactly what to do

3. *Easy as possible* — so he will be more likely to do it

All these apply to salesmanship and the proposal or recommendation you make to the buyer. What you ask must be possible; the prospect must have the means and authority to make the decision or purchase. What you ask must be specific; the buyer must know the facts and details of the purchase. And your request for action should be as easy as possible for the buyer to follow. As the salesman, you should do the work of arranging the details and mechanics of the purchase, so that all the buyer must do is chose or approve.

Give the Customer an Excuse to Buy

At times, it is possible to get an affirmative answer to all five buying decisions, yet still have the customer hesitate about buying. Often the cause lies in the third fear of buying, the fear of what others may say or think. This fear may have a real basis, or it may be all in the customer's mind.

When this fear is the stumbling block to the sale, we know that the customer is ready to buy. In his own mind he has a reason to buy. But he also needs an *excuse* to buy — a reason he can give to others to justify his actions. For example, a man may buy a new car to show his friends and neighbors, and himself, that he is a success, but he will say to them, and to himself, that he bought it because, "It was a good investment; the old bus was about ready to fall apart" or because, "It was too good a deal to pass up."

Self-justification is a fact of human nature. It is not our place to criticize it or look down upon it. But, as salesmen, we must be aware of its existence.

Be a "Deaf Duck"

Some salesmen panic at the word "no," just as they panic at objections and at the thought of "having to close."

If you are married, and if you have ever had your wife put on a campaign for something she really wanted, you know how unimportant the word "no" really is. The first time she asked for that new hat or dress, you said a very firm *"No!"* The same thing happened each time she asked, but she kept asking in different ways. No matter how strongly and definitely you said "no," she kept on asking. Then one day, in a weak moment, you probably said something that was not quite a "no" — and she suddenly had the hat or dress. No matter how many times you said "no," she could not hear you. All she could hear was your "yes."

It is the same way in selling. Be deaf to the word "no" — let it roll off your back. All it means is that the buyer has told you another of the millions of things that he is not ready to buy at the moment, and you are interested only in finding out what he *does* want to buy. Be deaf to the word "no," even though it is shouted, but have perfect hearing for even the whispered "yes."

Ten Closing Techniques

Closing, like all salesmanship, is helping the buyer to buy what he wants to buy in the way he wants to buy it. The following ten closing techniques are methods of doing this, making it easy and pleasant for the buyer to buy and helping him make the time decision. They are tools of the trade, not gimmicks or tricks to put the sale over "before the buyer knew what hit him."

1. *Ask him to buy.* This is the simplest and most fundamental method of closing, yet it is often ignored or neglected. When you are selling, the buyer often expects you to take the initiative; he expects you to ask him to buy. Do it.

2. *Give him a choice.* In this close, we give the buyer a choice between two things, not between something and nothing. We give him a little choice (a little decision) instead of a big one. In offering the buyer a choice, attach benefits to each side, to give him a choice of benefits. There are five basic types of choices we can give him:
   a. *Which* does he want?
   b. *Where* does he want it?
   c. *When* does he want it?
   d. *How* does he want it handled?
   e. *What* specific thing does he want included?

3. *Physical technique close.* In this, you do something the buyer must stop you from doing, or he has automatically consented to the purchase. This technique is especially useful with the buyer who will not say anything.

4. *Assumptive close.* In this, you assume that the buyer has bought and proceed on that basis. If he did not say "no," he must mean "yes." This is especially valuable with the buyer who seems unable to make decisions.

5. *Example close.* You put the close, the final decision, on the shoulders of a third party by using an example showing how someone else made the decision to buy.

6. *Weighing or contrast close.* Help the buyer compare the advantages and disadvantages of buying with the advantages and disadvantages of not buying. This can be done in words or on paper.

7. *Single objection close.* Talk with the buyer to isolate the one thing that is standing in the way of the sale. Get him to agree that this point is his only objection to buying. Then proceed to answer that objection.

8. *Impending event close.* This close is keyed directly to the time decision, by showing the advantage of buying before a certain time or coming event. The event, of course, must be one which is actually impending or definitely possible.

9. *Added benefit close.* Offer a benefit or extra which you have kept in reserve in order to tip the scales in favor of buying. If you do not need to use the extra for the close, give it to the buyer after the sale is made — as a little extra frosting on the cake.

10. *Pull back close.* Do not push too hard; do not be too eager. Instead, let off the pressure and pull away. Make the buyer figuratively reach for what you are selling. Make him chase it. Put the ownership in his mind to work for you, translating his desire into action. It is the same as catching a kitten by pulling a string for it to capture. Or the same as the old definition of courtship: A girl lets a man chase her until she catches him. Somehow, the thing that seems to be just out of reach looks the most desirable, far more desirable than if someone is trying to force it upon us.

TYPES OF BUYER SITUATIONS

In selling, you will run into various types of buyers, people with emotional attitudes or personality characteristics that call for special techniques. For example, you cannot sell the buyer who is angry about something in exactly the same way you would sell the buyer who is extremely pleased about everything. You cannot sell the buyer who is self-assured and aggressive in the same way you would the buyer who is hesitant and seeks assurance. You cannot use the same techniques on the buyer who is too talkative (often about every subject under the sun) and the buyer who sits like a bump on a log without even blinking to let you know if you are reaching him.

One caution: Although it is possible and helpful to classify the way a particular buyer is *at the moment*, do not attempt to pigeonhole him. Do not expect him to be consistent, because people are not consistent. The man who is busy and abrupt one time you call may have all the time in the world the next call; the man who is angry one time may be sitting on top of the world the next. Or a buyer can change his emotional attitude abruptly during a sales call. Take your buyer the way he is *at the moment*, and treat him accordingly. And that means treat him the way he wishes to be treated; his behavior is your clue.

Among the common buyer situations you may encounter are these:

1. The too talkative, too friendly consumer. This customer is pleasant to deal with, but difficult to sell. He keeps sliding out from under the sale, slipping off the subject to another. One answer is to keep bringing him back to the topic, politely and firmly. Another is to keep concentrating on needs and benefits and particularly those which lead toward the strengths of your product.

2. The silent customer. This customer has a reputation as one of the hardest to handle, but he may be one of the easiest to sell. First determine the reason for his silence. These are common reasons, assuming the customer is interested.

    a. He may be slow and deliberate — silent because he is letting the idea sink in and taking time to consider it carefully. He may want all the information you can give him before he decides.

    b. He may be reserved or shy — the type of person who normally does not talk much. He is similar to the deliberate customer, but there is one difference. Suddenly, when his interest is aroused and his reserve is overcome, he may break out of his shell and become talkative.

    c. He may want to be *sold*. He may be ready to buy but waiting for you to take the initiative. The assumptive and the physical technique closes are particularly useful with this type. He will either buy or open up and talk.

3. The customer who decides for himself. You cannot push him. He is very proud of the fact that he makes up his own mind. But you can sometimes lead him gently or probe to see if there is more information you can supply to assist his process of decision. He may react violently to an assumptive close or a choice close, but often welcomes the logical analysis of a weighing close, especially when you let him work it out for himself.

4. The customer who wants help deciding. Some people hate to make decisions. This is often related to the buying fears and the fear of making a mistake. This customer will hesitate and vacillate. He will lead you around and around the barn. He may welcome having the burden of deciding taken off his shoulders with an assumptive close. He may welcome the mathematical certainty of a weighing close. He may welcome the ease of a little decision instead of a big one, in the choice close. He may want the reassurance of an example close. Or he may have to be pinned down with a single objection close.

5. The angry customer. The way to handle the angry customer depends on the source of his anger. He may be angry at someone else, or he may be angry at you or your company or your product. When a customer is angry at someone else, the only thing to do is sidestep the anger. You may want to turn his attention from the source of his anger to his needs and the benefits you offer. You may wish to say, "I see you're upset about something. I'll come

back when you're feeling better." This may be the best thing to do, and it sometimes shocks a buyer into turning off his anger and directing his attention to your sales presentation.

When a customer is angry at you, your company, or your product, there are two things to remember. The first is "be a duck"; let the anger roll off your back. Do not let it affect you personally. The second is to remember that anger is an effect and to deal with it you must find the cause. So let the buyer talk. Encourage him to talk. He may have a justifiable cause for anger, and it may be one which you are able to correct. Or he may merely want an attentive audience for his gripe, a chance to blow off steam.

6. The customer who is "too busy to talk" to you. This may be true; it sometimes is. When it is true, plan to come back later. Try to find what time may be convenient, inside or outside office hours. For example, one wholesale grocery salesman found 7 A.M. an excellent time for appointments, and many salesmen found a new market waiting in last night's calls.

When the too-busy-to-talk attitude is a stall, sincere though it may be, remember that few men are too busy to talk about things that are of interest to them or about things that they can see will be of value to them. Your key is your own selflessness — and the customer's interest. With a customer of this type, perhaps more than with any other, the value of the needs/benefits approach to selling becomes evident. Even a busy man is willing to spend time talking about his needs, his desires, his problems, and his aspirations, and finding out about benefits he may be able to receive. These are things of importance to him. If you help him realize their importance, he will take time to discuss them.

In a Nutshell

The problem of handling various types of buyers is not a complex one. They are all people with needs to be fulfilled and benefits to be enjoyed. Their emotional attitudes or personality characteristics of the moment are not necessarily something to be "overcome" or "used," but merely another factor to be recognized in making the sale.

Handling any type of customer correctly boils down to this:

1. An understanding of the selling process and how people buy. This includes the six steps of selling, the five buying decisions, and the needs/benefits concept.

2. An awareness of your goal. If you know where you wish to go, it does not matter where the buyer may lead you. Each step you are able to take will tend to take you and the buyer closer to the sale.

3. Selflessness — with three different interpretations:
    a. Be a "duck." View what the customer does and says professionally rather than personally. Let things roll off your back.

   b. Empathy. This is the psychologist's term for being able to see and understand things from the other person's point of view. It might be called the
golden rule in action — or the golden rule stated as, "Do unto others as
you know they want you to do unto them." It is developing your insight
into how the customer wants to be handled, and handling him that way.

   c. Think in terms of the customer's interests. This is attitude, which is
coupled with the understanding of empathy. It comes back to the same
roots as enthusiasm and self-confidence: knowledge of your product and
knowledge of the benefits it offers. When you concentrate on linking the
customer's needs with the benefits you can offer, you are automatically
thinking in his interest.

CONCLUSION

To the average person engaged in selling, the close is the most difficult part of
the sale. The typical salesman tries to get three or more buying decisions into the
close. He finds it difficult and so feels he must resort to tricks. The professional
salesman does not consider the close any more difficult than the other steps of
selling. To him it is another simple, logical step. He closes after the buyer has already assumed ownership. The close is not when the sale is made, but rather
when the salesman winds up the details. An understanding of the step close, or
trial close, is important to the salesman because it answers two questions for
him: Has one of the buyer's needs been linked with a benefit in his own mind?
How important is the linked need/benefit to the buyer — a linking of dominant
needs to benefits, or a minor linking? It is also important for the salesman to
look for buying signals, which are something the customer says or does which indicates that he has assumed ownership or a degree of ownership. Buying signals
may be given in words, actions, or signs. For example, a buyer who has relaxed
may suddenly lean forward to give the salesman his avid attention. He may reach
out to touch the product or to pick it up or start examining a particular
feature.

   In determining which closing technique to use, the salesman must be aware of
the types of buying situations. For example, the salesman cannot sell the buyer
who is angry about something in exactly the same way he would sell the buyer
who is extremely pleased about everything. The salesman cannot use the same
techniques on the buyer who is too talkative as he uses on the buyer who sits like
a bump on a log. Always remember that although it is possible and helpful to
classify the way a particular buyer is at the moment, you must not attempt to
pigeonhole him. Do not expect him to be consistent, because people are not consistent. The common buyer situations include the following: the too talkative,
too friendly customer; the silent customer; the customer who decides for himself; the customer who wants help deciding; the angry customer; and the customer who is too busy to talk to you. Handling various types of buyers is not a
complex problem, for they are all people with needs to be fulfilled and benefits

to be enjoyed. Their emotional attitudes or personality characteristics of the moment are merely another input factor within the selling system.

The reason that the average salesman fears this step is that he has no basis upon which to make a determination of how the sale is progressing. Because of this, he usually resorts to one of two tactics: he crams as many of the selling activities as he can into the close "just to make sure" he achieves the sale, or he fails to ask for the close because he is fearful the customer will give him a negative response. When the professional salesman closes, he is sure that the interrelated activities between the salesman and the customer, which have taken place prior to the close, lead logically to the close step. This sale occurs because the salesman properly evaluates what is happening in the selling situation and because within the boundaries of the selling system he responds to that situation. The fact that the selling system represents a device through which facts and activities are significantly interrelated cannot be emphasized too many times.

PROBLEMS

1. The selling system attempts to relate in a meaningful way all factors affecting the sales of products. Why do you suppose that the customer's time buying decision is directly related to the close step?

2. Why is the close step often the step feared most by the average salesman?

3. Why do you feel that the principle of behavior "know your goal" is related to the close step?

4. Contact your life insurance agent and ask him what methods of closing he prefers. Ask him if he looks for buying signals.

5. Recount your last purchase of an automobile. How did the salesman close the sale?

6. List five closing methods you would use as a real estate salesman.

7. If you were selling washing machines and dryers for a major department store, what kind of close would you use? What kind of buying signals would you expect?

8 Present five closing techniques you could use in selling a color television set.

9. How is the step close related to the close step of the selling system?

10. If a professional salesman had properly used the closing techniques presented in this chapter, is it possible that the customer might not be aware that the close step had taken place? Explain your answer.

See page 264 for some case studies.

Chapter Ten
Overcoming the Nonbuy Blues

There is probably no stronger force in destroying the confidence, enthusiasm, and potential success of a budding salesman than the threat of customer opposition to the sale. To overcome this situation some salesmen are determined to monopolize the conversation in hopes that the customer will not be able to utter the least indication of sales resistance. This approach never really works, because ultimately the customer will either voice his objection or give an excuse for not buying. This chapter will show how the salesman can use the forces which give rise to consumer resistance in developing a *more* effective sales effort and thereby increasing his sale success.

The selling system plays a predominant role in allowing the salesman to react correctly to the opposition, or apparent opposition, of the customer. Possibly the handling of objections utilizes the selling system more completely than other areas of the selling system; certainly it maximizes the use of the selling system. Utilizing the systems approach, the salesman is equipped to evaluate words, actions, gestures, and expressions of the customer in a meaningful manner. The result is that the salesman confidently takes the proper action to overcome the specific objections. A keen awareness of how this is accomplished is one of the major steps toward developing a professional sales approach. This is true for two reasons. One, with this technique the salesman acquires a confident attitude. He has no need to be anxiously concerned or defensive, because he knows that at all times he controls the flow of events within the selling system. As the doctor adroitly examines the patient and the lawyer questions a witness, the professional salesman knows how to relate *all* the inputs within the selling system. Even though an objection may never arise, the salesman has confidence in his ability to handle the potential resistance. This positive attitude is of value since it permits the salesman the mental agility to respond readily with a positive course of action. Since selling is fundamentally a mental process of establishing need within the consumer's mind, the ability to approach all sales activity in the affirmative frame of mind is an ingredient of success. Two, in being able to recognize the relatedness of the objection to other inputs of the selling system, the salesman approaches the objections with an effective course of action.

ANALYSIS PROCESS

In an earlier chapter we mentioned the coins of selling and particularly the needs/benefits coin. We showed how the two sides are merely two views of what is essentially the same factor. The second important coin of selling is the objection/reason to buy coin. Every objection contains within itself the key to overcoming that objection. Whenever we encounter an objection, we can flip it over and see the other side — the related reason why the prospect should and will buy.

In most cases that which links the two sides is the buying decision involved. And most often, it is the need decision. For example, suppose you are trying to sell me an elephant — fine gray color, 10 feet tall, lives on peanuts, something sure to cause many active conversations with my neighbors, truly an unusual and distinctive possession. I object to buying, because I have no need for an elephant. You cannot sell me by expounding on the virtues of this particular elephant, by telling me how your company is the leading elephant importer, by offering me a special reduced price, or by proving that this is the best time to buy an elephant. You can sell me only by showing me how and why I need an elephant. The reason to buy must be linked to the reason for the objection. On the other hand, if you can prove to me that I really need an elephant immediately, my need can override the other buying decisions. To fulfill a sufficiently strong need, I might buy the elephant because you had it available, regardless of its quality, your company, or the price.

Here is why the buying decision involved is the link: it is the cause, the reason the objection exists. As one effect, one side of the coin, we have the objection. As the other effect, the other side of the coin, we can discover the reason the buying decision should be made favorably, the reason to buy. Objections and resistance are often one of these things:

1. An excuse for not buying because the need is not felt strongly enough

2. An attempt to buy — but conviction, desire, or decision is being held back by one unsettled factor

3. An attempt to get as much as possible — while paying no more than necessary

Many Things Masquerade as Objections

All salesmen meet resistance from buyers. Some buyers offer resistance because they feel it is expected of them; they do not want to appear "easy marks" or "pushovers." Or the buyer may offer resistance because he does not know enough about his needs or about the product and the benefits it offers him. Or he may have a fear of buying. Or he may wish justification for the purchase. It is important to recognize that many of the objections that buyers may seem to have are not really objections. The first thing to do when faced with an objection is to determine what it really is:

1. It may be a delay, an attempt to keep the sale from going too fast. People need time to accept a new idea, including the idea of buying something. They need time for mental digestion.

2. It may be an excuse, an objection wearing a mask. A man may say, "I'm waiting for the price to come down," when he means, "I'll have to ask my partner." Overcoming an excuse is futile; another will pop up in its place. You must probe for the root, the objection behind the excuse, and overcome it.

3. It may be a request for information, a question rather than an objection. The buyer may have tentatively assumed ownership in his mind, and may now want to get a better look at what he is buying. He may want information to clear up questions in his mind, to bolster his decision to buy, or merely to learn more about what he has already decided to buy.

4. It may be a buying signal. The buyer may be telling you, perhaps in a round-about way, that he has assumed ownership. He may even have jumped ahead to the close step and be telling you how he wants the details of the deal arranged.

5. It may be price resistance, an attempt to be sure that the price is as low as possible.

6. Or it may be an objection. The buyer is telling you, in effect, "I don't like it because . . ." or "I like it, but . . . ."

Buyers offer valid objections for many reasons, but the most common and most important reason they object is because they lack information. When a salesman tells a clear and complete sales story, tailored directly to the individual buyer's needs and wants, he reduces the number of objections that the buyer can or will offer. And the easiest way to handle objections is to prevent them from arising in the buyer's mind. When you do encounter objections, it is valuable to keep in mind the fact that, as a professional salesman, you should welcome objections instead of fearing them. An objection is an *expression of interest*; the prospect who is not interested seldom bothers to object. And every time a buyer objects, he is telling you something more about what he wants, how he wants to buy, and the buying decision he is trying to make. By objecting, he helps you know more about how to sell him.

Basic Causes of Objections and Resistance

Every objection, all buyer resistance, can be traced back to one of the causes listed below. What you do about the objection or resistance depends upon the cause. Buyers object or resist because:

1. They need additional time for assimilation.

2. They fear to buy.
   a. They fear the product is not worth the money.
   b. They fear the product will not do what the salesman says it will do.
   c. They fear some third party's opinion.

3. One of the buying decisions has not been made.
   a. They are not convinced of their *need* for the product.
   b. They are not convinced the *product* will fulfill their needs.
   c. They are not convinced this is a satisfactory *source*.
   d. They are not convinced this is a satisfactory *price*.
   e. They are not convinced this is the *time* to buy.

TECHNIQUES IN HANDLING OBJECTIONS

Identify

Is it an objection, resistance, delay, excuse, information question, or buying signal? What you do depends on what it is.

Determine the Cause

Then apply the proper technique.

When the cause is:	*Here is what you can do:*
1. Lack of assimilation	Stop talking; give the buyer time to think. Repeat the essence of your sales presentation, emphasizing needs and benefits. Put additional attention on helping the buyer visualize enjoying the benefits.
2. Fear that the product is not worth the price.	Emphasize needs and benefits. Use testimonials to show the worth.
3. Fear that the product will not do what you say it will do.	Use additional examples, testimonials, more third-party proof. Use additional demonstrations and participation; let the buyer see for himself. Use additional visualization.
4. Fear of someone's opinion of the purchase.	Use testimonials, third-party proof. Help the buyer rationalize or justify the purchase; give him excuses to buy as well as reasons. (Note: Buyers can have a good reason to buy, such as, "I want it," but they also want a good excuse to buy, something that sounds logical and sensible.)
5. The need decision has not been made.	Return to or review the interest step. Return to the desire step, particularly past benefits missed (needs) and future benefits being enjoyed (visualization). Keep emphasizing two types of needs: dominant needs and slight-edge needs (extra benefits).
6. The product or source decision has not been made.	Return to the conviction step: the SP is-do-means example. Give facts plus their translation into benefits and life.

Use additional visualization of benefits. Use additional demonstration and participation.

7. The price decision has not been made.

In general, use additional emphasis on the desire step, and particularly on the visualization of future benefits.

   a. It is a value (need) objection.

Use additional emphasis on needs, with the interest step and "past" desire step.

   b. It is a value (benefit) objection.

Use additional emphasis on benefits, with the conviction step and "future" desire step and visualization.

   c. It is price resistance.

In general, emphasize needs, benefits, and visualization techniques.

      1. "Let's dicker."

If your price is firm, stand firm, emphasizing needs and benefits. If it is not firm play the game, while emphasizing needs and benefits.

      2. "Not the price I expected."

Price-line your product. Show value equal to the next lower price line. Sell the difference compared to the next lower price line. Prove the price, and give the buyer time to get used to the idea of it. Divide the price and show how it is price-lined merchandise with a plus feature.

      3. "Can't afford."

Work on the need decision. Help the buyer justify the purchase. Show how payment can be arranged to fit the way the buyer wants to pay.

8. The time decision has not been made.

Show the needs and benefits of buying without delay. Emphasize the needs, particularly the immediate needs, the benefits that will be lost by waiting. Use closing techniques to help the buyer make a decision or to make it for him, so that all he will have to do is allow the decision or arrangements to stand.

Prevent Objections from Arising

In professional selling, you will encounter far fewer objections than in any other type of selling, for your sales presentation will be fitted to your buyer. You will automatically be able to tell him what he wants to know about your product, what he considers important, what your product will do for him and mean to him. And you will help him realize and experience the meaning of what you say and offer. This is part of the reason why, in professional selling, we place particular emphasis on the three steps of selling that many salesmen ignore: The preapproach step and the interest step, to help you know and understand this particular buyer; and the desire step, to help him assimilate and visualize the meaning of your sales presentation.

When You Can, Remove the Cause of the Objection

1. If it is easy enough to do, change the product. If a buyer likes a hat except for the feather, remove the feather. If he likes a used car except for the color, include a paint job in the sale (but not necessarily in the original price).

2. Sell up; sell a better line. The American consumer is becoming more and more quality conscious. He is tired of being disappointed by skimpy, unsatisfactory products that have been built "to meet a price." Remember that what the buyer may be objecting to is lack of benefits — because *people buy to fulfill needs, not to save money.*

Work to Pin Down the Objection

1. Gently keep asking "why," just as in the interest step. Get the buyer to clarify and explain his objection, so you get a clear idea or what it is and why it exists.

2. Try to find out if it is really important to the buyer. If he keeps hopping from one objection to another, they are possibly all excuses. As soon as you answer one, another will appear. But if the buyer keeps coming back to the same point, or makes it with sincere intensity, he is probably really interested in an answer.

3. Find out if the objection is what the buyer really means. For example, some buyers will say, "I don't want to spend the money," when they really mean, "I don't want to spend all the money at once."

4. Look at it closely: Does it make sense? Does it seem to be true? Some prospects like to test a salesman, to play with him, or to make excuses that only seem logical. For an objection that does not make sense, sometimes the best answer is silence.

Listen

Sometimes all a buyer wants is a chance to talk, and someone willing to listen. Often a buyer does not really want an answer so much as some attention paid to what he thinks and feels. This is one time when it is a priceless advantage to "be a duck."

Remember These Two Underlying Principles

1. It is better to build on strengths than to correct weaknesses.

2. People can think about only one thing at a time.

As much as you can, keep attention on the strengths and benefits of your product, rather than on its shortcomings or weaknesses. Answer objections, but emphasize benefits.

Help the Buyer Save Face

Treat the buyer and his ideas with respect. This, along with the two principles above, is the basis of the overworked, but still good, advice to salesmen in handling objections: the "yes, but" system. You tell the buyer, "Yes (you are right), but (here is something to consider)." You should never argue with a customer or attempt to prove him wrong.

IMPLEMENTING THE SELLING SYSTEM TO OVERCOME OBJECTIONS

Recognizing the selling system as interacting inputs directed toward a specific objective, we are now in a position to directly apply inputs of the system so as to complete the desired objective (overcoming objections). As in the examples in Figures 10-1 through 10-5, we must begin with the most relevant input — the objection. From that point we use the analysis process to determine the specific buying decisions to which the objection refers. On the basis of that particular evaluation, we determine which of the selling steps must be rediscussed. Principles of behavior relative to that step are presented for evaluation, and finally, the technique process is defined. These examples are excellent training exercises because they develop an understanding of the related functioning of system components in overcoming objections. Once these are mastered, the process takes place within the salesman's mental process.

It is important for the salesman to identify and understand the hesitation, delays, and objections of potential customers. Rarely is a customer immediately sold on a purchase; if this is the case the customer was probably presold by effective advertising. It is the salesman who is able to identify and overcome objections who is called the professional. Being accurate in the evaluation of objections is not easy; accuracy reaches a higher degree of reliability when the salesman has had an opportunity to contact a large number of customers and thereby widen his experience. The important point is to reach some evaluation of the sales resistance and take action. If you are incorrect in your first assessment, simply reevaluate the cause of the objection and take another course of action. As sales experience accumulates it will become easier to accurately appraise the cause of sales resistance and take the proper steps to turn objections into a successful sales effort.

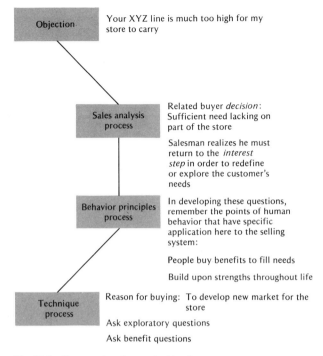

Fig. 10-1 Overcoming the need objection.

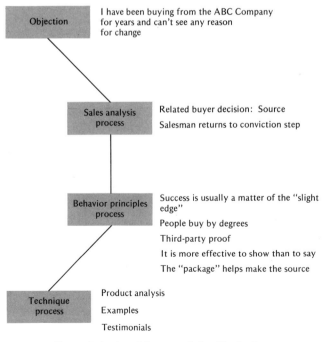

Fig. 10-2 Overcoming the source objection.

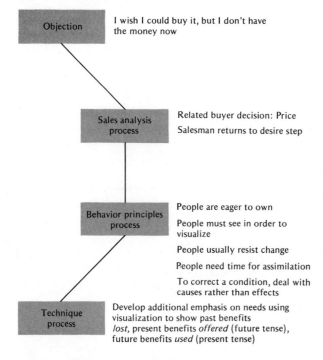

Objection	I wish I could buy it, but I don't have the money now
Sales analysis process	Related buyer decision: Price Salesman returns to desire step
Behavior principles process	People are eager to own People must see in order to visualize People usually resist change People need time for assimilation To correct a condition, deal with causes rather than effects
Technique process	Develop additional emphasis on needs using visualization to show past benefits *lost*, present benefits *offered* (future tense), future benefits *used* (present tense)

Reason for buying: The use of the product now will increase future earnings

Fig. 10-3 Overcoming the price objection.

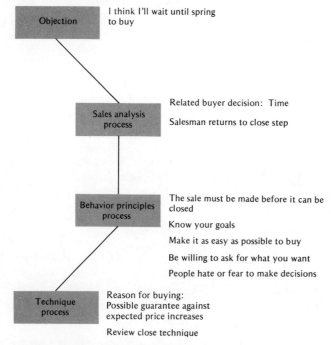

Objection	I think I'll wait until spring to buy
Sales analysis process	Related buyer decision: Time Salesman returns to close step
Behavior principles process	The sale must be made before it can be closed Know your goals Make it as easy as possible to buy Be willing to ask for what you want People hate or fear to make decisions
Technique process	Reason for buying: Possible guarantee against expected price increases Review close technique

Fig. 10-4 Overcoming the time objection.

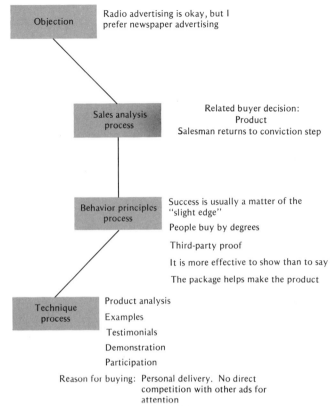

Objection — Radio advertising is okay, but I prefer newspaper advertising

Sales analysis process — Related buyer decision:
Product
Salesman returns to conviction step

Behavior principles process — Success is usually a matter of the "slight edge"

People buy by degrees

Third-party proof

It is more effective to show than to say

The package helps make the product

Technique process — Product analysis

Examples

Testimonials

Demonstration

Participation

Reason for buying: Personal delivery. No direct competition with other ads for attention

Fig. 10-5 Overcoming the product objection.

CONCLUSION

To correct a condition, deal with causes rather than effects. Many of the things in life we see are effects, the results of causes buried below the surface. In the same way, many of the things encountered in selling are effects, the results of hidden causes. When a doctor examines a patient, he sees symptoms, or effects. He can treat the symptoms, or he can treat the disease or condition that causes the symptoms. If a patient lacks energy, the doctor can give him stimulants, or he can determine and cure the cause of the lack of energy. If he treats the symptoms only, the cause will still remain and will probably produce other effects. If he cures the cause, the effects disappear automatically.

It is the same way in selling. Objections and resistance are effects. If we attempt to deal with them directly, if we work only with what we see on the surface, the cause will still remain. A cause is able to generate additional resistance and objections endlessly. But, if we can determine and correct the cause, we have eliminated the effects and the problem. To draw a parallel further, in medicine the symptoms carry the clue to the disease. The doctor is trained to use symptoms to treat it. In selling, objections and resistance carry the clue to their cause. The professional salesman can work from the symptoms to the cause and proceed to eliminate the cause. That is why we say this in professional selling: *Every objection contains the reason why the prospect should buy.* We also say that resistance is an indication of interest. It means that the prospect wants to buy, but that his desire is being blocked. If he had no interest in the product, no desire to buy, he would not resist. He would simply not buy; he would ignore the salesman and the sales presentation. He resists or objects only because he wants to buy — which is one of the many logical paradoxes of life. Related to the buying decisions is the fact that objections can come on any of three levels:

They may be on the *intellectual* level — the buyer may wish more facts and information in order to make a conviction decision.

They may be on the *emotional* level — the buyer may wish more visualization in order to make a desire decision.

They may be on the *decision* level itself — the buyer may wish help in the process of making a decision, of translating intent and desire into action, a process that is difficult for many people.

PROBLEMS

1. Why does the handling of objections utilize the entire selling system?

2. Why is the handling of objections so important to the salesman?

3. Explain how an objection can become the reason to buy. Why can we say that an objection is a reason to buy in *all* cases?

4. List four kinds of apparent objections that in actuality are not objections.

5. What are the basic causes of objections?

6. How can a professional salesman prevent objections from arising?

7. Discuss five ways a professional salesman can overcome objections.

8. To overcome an objection, does the professional salesman deal with causes or effects? Discuss.

9. Are objections causes or effects?

10. Why is resistance an indication of interest?

11. How does an understanding of the cause of a customer's objection free the salesman to be more effective in his selling effort? How is this related to the selling system?

See pages 265–266 for a case study.

ASSIGNMENT 1

Evaluate the following sales resistance or objection in terms of which buying decision it involves. Also prepare a specific sales strategy using the selling system as your frame of reference.

A customer is trying on suits for use in his business activities. He travels a great deal and sometimes entertains in the evening. At the moment he is appraising a double-breasted suit coat the salesman has just slipped on, and he makes this statement: "This coat feels quite comfortable, but you know, I haven't worn a double-breasted suit since 1947!"

Buying decision involved in the objection:

Selling step to which the salesman would return:

Specific action the salesman could take:

ASSIGNMENT 2

The business forms representative has just shown the purchasing agent a new form he has designed specifically for use in this firm. It has an extra copy for use by the accounting department in maintaining control of the check ledger. This requires preparing special information to be used on that particular sheet only and special carbon paper to block out other sections of the form. The purchasing agent can see the advantages of the form and compliments the salesman on his fine work. At the same time he says, "Are you sure that your firm can develop this rather complicated form to meet our specifications?"

Buying decision involved in sales resistance:

Selling step to which the salesman would return:

Specific action the salesman could take:

ASSIGNMENT 3

Through the interest step the salesman in a used car agency has determined that a prospective customer with a family of five young children is interested in a nine-passenger station wagon. The customer has informed him that the wagon will be not only a fine investment for traveling on camping trips, but a real asset on those fall hunting trips. The salesman shows his potential customer a late model, clean nine-passenger wagon; the customer appears pleased when he asks the price. Upon hearing it he exclaims, "2,500 dollars!"

Buying decision involved in this objection or sales resistance:

Selling step to which the salesman would return:

Specific action the salesman could take:

ASSIGNMENT 4

The salesman is discussing an additional mortgage insurance coverage which would assure complete payment of the outstanding mortgage if the husband were to die. Mr. Clayton, the husband, says, "I know that this coverage is very important to the family, but with Christmas just around the corner I should probably wait until I get my next year's tax refund."

Buying decision involved in this objection or sales resistance:

Selling step to which the salesman would return:

Specific action the salesman could take:

Chapter Eleven
Planning as Related to Selling

Planning is the analysis of information regarding the present and past and an evaluation of probable results based upon this information. Planning will be discussed both in this chapter and in Chapter Twelve; the emphasis here is on how to utilize the selling system *before* approaching the customer. This activity is called the preapproach step; it is the first selling step taken by the salesman. We are discussing it *after* the other steps of salesmanship because prior to this chapter you were not adequately equipped to plan the related areas of the selling system. You are now in a position meaningfully to understand the two broad areas of activity in the selling system: the sequential buying decisions of the customer and the particular action taken in the selling steps. For example, it does little good to prepare a detailed product analysis (selling step) unless it can be directly related to a particular buying need (buying decision).

The first step in successful selling is the planning accomplished in the preapproach. The salesman can think, talk, and act in terms of the customer's interest only after he has determined or reasoned that in which the customer is interested.

THE PURPOSE OF THE PLANNING

The key purpose of planning is to gather information about the prospect to help plan and give the sales presentation. The salesman knows that his product has been manufactured or created to satisfy needs and wants of his customers. He knows that, when a person makes a purchase, he buys not only the item but also the benefits which it will provide. In this step of salesmanship we attempt to find out the needs and wants of a certain prospect so that we can intelligently talk in terms of his interests. By analyzing the prospective customer, we can determine what we should say in our presentation.

In the preapproach we determine the customer's needs and wants. Then we can easily tell the customer how our product will satisfy those needs and wants. We can phrase our presentation to offer him benefits and appeal to buying motives. The preparation of the preapproach helps us uncover the dominant buying motive of our customer and will help immensely in the desire step of selling. In short, the preapproach has three parts: one, gathering information about the prospect; two, gathering information about our product; and three, preparing a selling plan by fitting information about our product to what we know about our prospect.

ANALYSIS PROCESS

The preapproach is the step of selling that takes place *before you see the prospect* on a particular sales call. It is the step of planning and preparation that helps

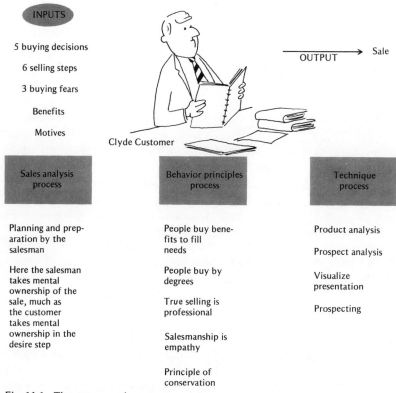

INPUTS

5 buying decisions

6 selling steps

3 buying fears

Benefits

Motives

OUTPUT → Sale

Clyde Customer

Sales analysis
process

Behavior principles
process

Technique
process

Planning and prep-
aration by the
salesman

Here the salesman
takes mental
ownership of the
sale, much as
the customer
takes mental
ownership in the
desire step

People buy bene-
fits to fill
needs

People buy by
degrees

True selling is
professional

Salesmanship is
empathy

Principle of
conservation

Product analysis

Prospect analysis

Visualize
presentation

Prospecting

Fig. 11-1   The preapproach step.

develop and assure more successful sales. The preapproach starts like the famous recipe for rabbit stew — "First, catch a rabbit." First, have a prospect. Once you have the prospect, you find out as much as you can about him. One of the first things to determine is whether or not he really is a prospect — you screen or qualify each possible prospect. Then, for a qualified prospect, you work to get the information that will help you sell him. In particular, you work to discover his needs, the benefits he wants.

Your information about the prospect is then combined with your product knowledge to plan your sales presentation. It is primarily a process of matching or linking his needs with the benefits you can offer. You plan the sales presentation by visualizing how and why this prospect will buy. In effect, you put yourself in the prospect's shoes — and buy the product for him. You do this on the basis of sound knowledge of his needs. Then all that remains is to go out on the sales call and tell him what he has bought and why.

During the preapproach you visualize the essence of your entire sales presentation, step by step. With this visualization you are able to plan and prepare for the sales points, demonstrations, and examples you wish to have ready to use and the benefits you will wish to emphasize to fulfill the needs you know exist.

The preapproach may be very brief, because that is all the planning that is needed for a particular prospect, or because only a brief time is available. Or it may take months or years, as you go around the prospect to get a view of him and his needs from different angles and as you investigate many avenues of approach to determine the best one. Sometimes, as in retail selling when a customer walks in, no preapproach is possible. You are immediately involved in the attention step — and quickly into the interest step.

As we discussed briefly, the preapproach and interest steps are parallel in many ways. Both concentrate on determining the prospect's needs. When a preapproach cannot be made, the interest step takes its place, and you mentally plan the sale as you talk with the buyer. When a preapproach has been made, you use the interest step to confirm what you learned in the preapproach, to expand upon it, and to adapt your sales plan accordingly.

PRINCIPLES OF THE PREAPPROACH STEP

People Buy Benefits to Fulfill Needs

This principle or concept underlines all professional salesmanship. It is the foundation of truly honest, effective selling. People do not buy products or services. They do not buy to save money. They buy benefits to fulfill the needs they feel.

Accepting this concept does not limit the opportunities for selling or reduce the potential market for any worthwhile product or service. Rather, it expands markets and opportunities — for people have millions of needs waiting to be fulfilled, and countless millions more needs that they are not even aware of.

One chain store executive once said there is no such thing as a satisfied customer, for even the most satisfied and loyal customer will desert his favorite product for a competitor that offers him more. People always have needs to be fulfilled; they always have more benefits they want to receive.

People Buy by Degrees

Very little of life, very little of decision making, progress, or development, is an all-at-once proposition. People need time to get used to things, to think things through, to absorb and accept change. In professional selling, with an understanding of the steps of buying and the fears of buying, we can speed the process. We can guide the buyer through the steps he must take in his mind and help him make his decision more intelligently and rapidly.

True Selling Is Professional

Salesmanship at its best is part science and part art. It is a service business, in the widest sense of the word "service." It calls for a professional attitude, professional understanding, professional skills and training. There are all degrees of salesmanship — your own salesmanship will be as base or as great as you make it.

Salesmanship Is Empathy

Empathy is the psychologist's word for the ability to put yourself in another person's shoes. The professional salesman works to develop this ability or attitude. He thinks with the buyer's mind; he acts in the buyer's interest; he understands the buyer.

Salesmanship Involves Conservation

The professional salesman continually fights waste. He develops the full potential of his time, his energy, and his prospects and customers. He seldom throws away anything of value until he has weighed its value and has decided to throw it away for something of more value. This principle may sound dull and preachy, but you will find that it has dynamic, exciting applications.

TECHNIQUES OF THE PREAPPROACH STEP

Product Analysis

Know your product and the benefits it offers. This is the process we discussed at length earlier, in Chapter Three — determining the selling points, or significant features, of your product and source, and building upon these strengths with the is-do-means approach.

Prospect Analysis

Know and understand the prospect. First, determine what you need or want to know about this individual prospect:

1. Is he a prospect? Does he have the ability to buy — the financial ability and the authority to make the decision? Does he have needs that relate to your product or service?

2. What are his needs and wants, as specifically and detailed as possible?

3. What else, specifically, do you need or want to know about this prospect? What else would help you in each of the steps of selling him?

Second, what are possible sources of the information you seek? For any prospect, they are numerous, ranging from friends, acquaintances, and other salesmen to public information such as the telephone book, city directory, newspaper, and public records, from observation to "inside" sources. The sources you will use will depend primarily on the type and amount of information you want.

Third, gather, organize, and analyze your information — to gain the needed understanding of this prospect and particularly of his needs.

Visualizing the Presentation

Combine what you know about your product with what you know about your prospect to plan and visualize your sales presentation, and to prepare for it.

Visualize your presentation in *essence* — boiled down to its essentials. And visualize it on the basis of realistic alternatives, just as you might a game of checkers or chess. When you do *A*, the other person will do *B*, or *C*. If he does *B*, you will do *D*; if he does *C*, you can do *F*. As you visualize, do not feel that he will automatically do *B* just because you do *A*. Try to visualize and plan for what he *might* do as well as for what you *hope* he will do.

This process of visualization in the preapproach is not an attempt to chart or determine exactly how the sales call will go. Rather, it is a technique to help you be prepared for the predictable things that might happen. Sometimes the buyer will suddenly skip huge segments of the sales call that might have taken place. Other times, the buyer will prove unpredictable and will go in a totally different direction than expected. Only very rarely will the buyer follow the pattern exactly. But whatever he does, you will be in a better position than you would have been without the preapproach.

Prospecting

There are three key techniques of prospecting:

1. *The endless chain.* On each sales call, and on each customer, try for names and information on additional possible prospects. The person who buys may well know someone else who would like the same or similar benefits. The person who does not buy may still know others who might buy.

2. *Looking about you.* Look for the need. Keep alert and aware for clues to needs that you have the benefits to fulfill. Whatever you sell, you are always surrounded by people with needs you can fulfill for mutual benefit.

3. *The snowplow or stockpile.* The "snowplow" is the one system that will guarantee you an almost endless supply of good prospects. If you use it faithfully, you will always find yourself with more prospects than you can possibly contact.

The snowplow technique of prospecting merits further discussion. The system is simple: You never throw away a prospect, or the work you did today. You save prospects and capitalize on today's efforts to build more sales tomorrow. It is called the "snowplow" system because prospects pile up before you just like snow piles up ahead of a snowplow — as the plow fills, the snow is pushed over to the place where it is wanted. As your sales snowplow fills, prospects keep moving into the "sold" column.

This system is also called the "stockpile" system because the salesman must have a stockpile of live prospects to sell, just as he must have a stock of merchandise or service. As he sells, and as he loses prospects, he must keep replenishing his stockpile. If he keeps his stockpile full enough, he always has a lavish supply of prospects that should be seen and an ample supply of people who are ready to be sold.

The average salesman has no stockpile. He lives hand to mouth. When he finds a prospect, he goes out to try to sell him. If he cannot make the sale, he throws the prospect away — immediately, or after a few tries. And if he can make the sale, he also throws the prospect away as soon as the sale is made. He feels that the customer is no longer a prospect, because he "just bought."

The professional salesman builds his stockpile this way: When he goes to see a prospect, if he cannot sell him, he stockpiles him. He knows that if this is a qualified prospect, he has needs to be fulfilled and he will fulfill them sooner or later. And if the salesman makes the sale, he again stockpiles the prospect, for he knows that the man who bought once will buy again. A man who buys a car this year will be needing and buying a car next year, or the year after, or some year. He is still a prospect, although not an immediate one.

On a sales call, whether the sale is made or not, we take a prospect off our list only when he is definitely no longer a present or future prospect — when he is completely away from our market, or when he does not, and will not, have needs to be fulfilled by our product.

As a guide to how much a salesman should push on his snowplow, or how big a stockpile of live (immediate) prospects he should have, we give this rule of thumb: At any moment, the salesman should have a list of live prospects, waiting to be seen, equal to the *amount of business he is aiming to sell for the entire year*. If you wish to gross $1 million in sales for the year, you should always have $1 million worth of potential business ready to be called upon. And as you call on each prospect and you sell and/or snowplow him, you should replace him with another live prospect, either a new prospect or a prospect who is on your snowplow already.

One other point: Keep in touch with the prospects on your snowplow, the immediate prospects and the long-term prospects alike. Keep them aware of your interest and of your desire and ability to fulfill their needs. Do not hound them, but do not let them slide off the wrong edge of the snowplow through lack of attention and interest. Take a moment now and then to contact them by mail or phone, to express your interest or to give them something they may find of interest or value.

THE THREE FEARS OF BUYING

Although the three fears of buying were discussed in Chapter Ten, they have particular significance to the selling system in the planning step. In the process of developing a sales strategy, it is necessary to visualize the product in specific relationship to *a* customer. A clearer understanding of the three fears of buying will help the salesman more fully understand why the customer may hesitate to buy and how to turn this hesitation into a positive force. This study of the three fears gives greater insight into human personality from a specific viewpoint, that of the customer.

FEAR THAT THE PRODUCT WILL NOT DO WHAT THE SALESMAN SAYS IT WILL DO

This fear is more obvious in selling situations where the salesman is making a sales call upon the potential customer. For example, the pharmaceutical representative makes a call upon a physician with the objective of presenting a recent drug discovery that has application to the doctor's field. Even though the salesman presents sales points that relate to specific needs of the doctor's patients, the doctor is not going to accept automatically the statements made in the sales presentation. A closer examination of the customer's background would be helpful. The doctor by virtue of his education and experience has a deeper understanding of how the chemical components could effect the types of patients he treats. As the salesman is talking, the doctor's mind is adjusting this compound to meet the specific needs of his patients. Although the sales representative is well trained in presenting the characteristics of his product, it would be unfair to expect him to answer satisfactorily all the questions the doctor might ask, particularly those of a technical nature. Therefore the salesman would be performing an effective sales function by (1) making the doctor aware of the significant feature of the product, (2) relating these features to the needs of his patients, and (3) gaining a favorable response to this relationship by securing the doctor's commitment to use samples of the product with his patients for a period of time, perhaps a month. During this month the doctor will have an opportunity to talk with his professional colleagues about the merits of the product. Also, he may find the opportunity to use the samples with his patients.

The conclusion here is that it may take a considerable period of time, and several calls, to establish the fact that the product really does do what the salesman says it will do. Many beginning salesmen jeopardize their opportunities for a long, successful sales future by allowing their natural enthusiasm to be crushed by this fear. After perhaps 6 months of training, the salesman feels a loyal commitment toward all the products sold by his firm. If he *assumes* that the customer shares this enthusiasm for the product, he will not be prepared to meet this fear properly, and possibly he will place unjustifiable blame upon himself for not immediately being successful in his selling career. This could lead to a feeling of pressure upon the salesman to prove his success and ultimately to a negative effect upon his sales career.

The following is an example of this point. A young sales representative for a petroleum firm was told in his training program of the importance of selling the firm's oil products at the service stations and of the importance of selling the service station dealers on the advantages of using the firm's brand of oil. Spurred by the enthusiasm of performing well, this trainee upon becoming a sales representative told each of his assigned service station outlets to remove all oil products other than those of the company. The result was twofold: One, the petroleum firm did not approve of this approach and had to take steps to dampen the new sales representative's enthusiasm. Two, the dealers became so angry with this approach that they would not allow the sales representative on their premises. He therefore became ineffective in that particular territory and had to be transferred to another.

Another example of the influence of this fear might be in the sale of advertising. In order to convince the customer that a particular ad will fulfill certain needs of the firm, the salesman must take every means available, primarily product knowledge and product analysis. Viewing the sales presentation from the customer's point of reference, the salesman readily sees that the advertiser has a natural reluctance to give a positive buying decision until he is ready to accept with confidence the idea that the *product* (advertising appearing in the future) will increase *sales* (needs — also expressed in the future). If the salesman recognizes the existence of this fear before making his presentation, he can then take measures adequately to prepare his approach. This might include market penetration of the newspaper, circulation figures, statistics concerning incomes of families reading the paper, and professional layout of the ad, to give the prospective customer a more perceptive impact.

To an insurance salesman this fear has a different kind of significance. The customer cannot question the fact that ultimately the product will do what the salesman says it will do — provide income upon the policy holder's demise. Thus the fear here involves the question of whether or not the need fulfilled — family financial protection at death — warrants a financial obligation at this time. Possibly there are other needs for the customer's income — a daughter needs teeth straightened, the wife's car needs new tires, the washer is beginning to make rumbles, etc. A professional insurance salesman recognizes this fear and overcomes it by projecting the customer into the future and showing what might occur specifically to his family at the time of his death if he does not plan adequately for their future. Statistical mortality tables can be of particular value to substantiate this projection.

FEAR THE PRODUCT IS NOT WORTH THE PRICE

Some salesmen will honestly and earnestly say that price objections are the only kind they ever encounter. Companies will say, "Sales are slipping, we'll have to cut prices." They will substitute "pricemanship" for salesmanship, because they think customers are objecting on price. But the more you study and understand professional salesmanship, the more you realize the truth of this statement: *There is no such thing as a price objection.* Rather, what exists is one of the following.

It may be an objection growing out of another buying decision, masquerading as a price objection. Most often, it is a need objection. The buyer is saying, "The price is too high *for me*; it is not worth that much to fulfill my needs." Sometimes it is a product objection. The buyer is saying, "The price is too high for the benefits your product offers." The buyer objects on the value of the product, in terms of needs and benefits, not on the dollar-and-cents price.

The apparent price objection may be, instead, price resistance, for one of these reasons:

1. The buyer is saying, "Do I really need to pay this much? If I put up a little fight, will he bring the price down?"

This is human nature — and good business. None of us wants to pay more than we must, for our money must stretch to cover so many things we need and want.

In some lines and types of business, this kind of resistance is nonexistent or not apparent. When we go into the usual retail store and see an item priced at 89 cents, we do not attempt to dicker with the clerk in the hope of bringing the price down. We know she does not have the authority to change the posted price. The most we might do is shop other stores for the same item, in hope of a lower price, or wait for the possibility of a clearance-sale reduction.

In other lines of business, and at times in the business cycle, this kind of price resistance is strongly encouraged by merchants and salespeople. They set prices with a margin for dickering or show a definite willingness to dicker. They encourage buyers to resist, to feel that the announced price will be cut to a lower selling price. We see this situation on most used car lots, in real estate, and in some types of industrial selling, when the market gets soft and inventories stop moving. We see it extend to the field of retail appliance selling when retailers vie with each other in offering "deals," "special trade-in offers," "discount prices," and the like.

The buyer is nobody's fool. He knows that one thing he should find out is whether the price is firm or whether he might be a sucker to pay the price asked. It is always worth a try to find out. If the price is firm, he will usually accept it. He will not have lost anything by trying, and neither will you by standing firm.

2. The buyer is saying, "This is not the price I *expected* to pay."

Price is largely a matter of habit. There are certain prices that people are accustomed to paying for particular items and services — "normal" prices where most sales are made. For any particular item, there are usually a number of these normal price levels. Merchandise at these prices will sell best; merchandise priced above or below these levels will not sell as well, regardless of relative quality and value. This is the theory of "price lining" — pricing your product at the price people *expect* to pay.

To illustrate: Three of the price lines for women's shoes are $8.95, $10.95, and $12.95. A particular pair of shoes should perhaps sell for $9.75, based on the costs of manufacturing and distribution, but $9.75 is not an *expected* price. The shoes will actually sell better at either $8.95 or $10.95 than they will at $9.75. At $9.75, the customer has trouble pegging their value in relation to what she is accustomed to buying.

When merchandise is not properly price-lined, the salesman has several alternatives. He can change the price to correspond to what people expect to pay. Or he can build the value up to the next higher level, to change his price from a misfit to a bargain. Or he can reinterpret his price: a $55 camera in a market with a $49.50 price line can be shown as a good $49.50 camera with a desirable $5.50 accessory.

3.   The buyer is saying, "I don't think I can afford it."

This is often a stall, an excuse. When it is sincere, it becomes a need decision, automatically and immediately. Actually, none of us can afford anything — and we can buy nearly anything, whether we can afford it or not. Every day, people buy millions of things they "can't afford," because the need is strong enough. They buy food, housing, medical and dental care — necessities — whether they can afford them or not. They buy power boats, bowling, dancing lessons, and perfume — things they *want* — whether they really can afford them or not. Anyone can buy nearly anything he really wants, if he wants it strongly enough. It is all a matter of how strong is his need and how big is the sacrifice he is willing to make.

When a buyer says, "I can't afford it," he is really saying, "The price may be right, but I don't know if I want to pay the cost. I don't know if it is worth (to me) the things I will have to give up or do without."

FEAR OF WHAT OTHERS MAY THINK

The influence of people upon each other has particular relevance to this fear, for a person reacts in some way to those with whom he associates. Goffman[1] explores this sociological phenomena, pointing out that human groupings are often so fleeting and informal as to be unrecognizable as social functions — a riding in an elevator, two strangers passing on the street. In contrast are such emphatic events as the cocktail party. All these gatherings, like the family group, have their own rules and laws. It is Goffman's contention that without the implicit obedience that these laws of behavior systematically command, the grander and more visible forms of human association would probably be unworkable. Goffman states that more than to any family or club, more than to any class or sex, more than to any nation, the individual belongs to gatherings, and he had best show that he is a member in good standing.

Goffman bases these conclusions on a fundamental assumption that all rational beings share, without necessarily knowing that they do, a desire for public order. Society is founded on an unspoken mutual trust. As Goffman points out, any social occasion takes on the aspects of a chess game, in which the moves vary widely but follow strict and unforgiving rules. For example, a potential customer in an office answers his phone. While he is talking, what should the salesman do?

[1] Irving Goffman, *Behavior in Public Places*, Free Press, Macmillan, New York, 1963.

The rules forbid listening. They also forbid just sitting there doing nothing, which could support the suspicion that he *is* listening. So the salesman exhibits "civil inattention." Unable to avoid overhearing one side of the phone conversation, the salesman feigns another activity — gazing out the window, ostentatiously lighting and puffing a cigarette — conveying or seeking to convey the impression that his attention is directed elsewhere.

The penalties for breaking the rules can be serious. Even minor infractions provoke them. A rainy day might be used as an example. A man wearing a trench coat will naturally pass muster. So will one who is coatless, as long as he suggests by his deportment — hunched shoulders, an improptu newspaper umbrella — that he is alive to his predicament. But someone who walks along unprotected and apparently unaware of the downpour is likely to evoke startled and uneasy response. The reason is that he offends the hidden code of behavior to which all "normal" people subscribe. The man oblivious to the rain is guilty not just of trivial impropriety but of the greater sin of social unpredictability. No one can guess with any assurance what ceremony he will next profane. People do react to social situations. In making a purchase, they are influenced not only by the gathering of that particular moment, but also by reference groups which form the basis of influential gatherings of the past. More importantly, they are influenced by the relationship of a particular purchase to gatherings with those reference groups in the future.

REFERENCE GROUPS: WHAT THEY ARE

The reference group comprises a restricted number of people, usually fewer than seven, who enjoy personal interaction over a fairly long span of time. People in this relationship show a degree of commonality of interest often expressed as a goal upon which there is mutual agreement.[2] There are two basic elements to a reference group, the group itself and the group norms, standards, or values.

Although the number of people in a typical reference group will range from three to seven, it may go as high as nine. Theoretically there is no particular number which comprises a reference group, but in order for its members to achieve the enjoyment of personal interaction, there must be participation by all members of the group. When the group reaches a particular numerical size, the opportunity for its members to play an active part becomes smaller. At this point the less active members tend to fragment from the original reference group and either form a group of their own or transfer to a new group.

We develop standards, norms, or values through a gradual accumulation of experiences with particular people, specifically those with whom we are actively involved in the cultivation of abilities, values, and outlook. Since the group serves as a point of reference in value determination, the source of the standards is directly related to the sentiments of the particular group. The family as a

[2] William G. Scott, *Organization Theory*, Richard D. Irwin, Inc., Homewood, Ill., 1967, p. 82.

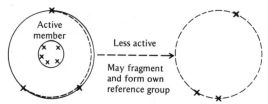

Fig. 11-2   Reference-group fragmentation.

reference group will develop its norms or values using the family background of the husband and wife as the overriding source, and thereby include religion, education, income, and social position as some of the determinants in arriving at the values of the reference group. A work group of salesmen would be another reference group having a particular set of values. The basis for these standards would be the work environment, but the personal background of each member would also be included in ultimately reaching a mutually acceptable set of norms.

Although the values of the family reference group and the work reference group are separate, it is unlikely that there would be serious conflict between the two. Since the family is a more basic reference group, it usually warrants a higher priority when there is a value conflict. If the family as a group determines that evenings are to be shared amongst all its members and the husband finds himself in a work group which spends its evening hours at the club, there is a conflict in values between the two groups. If the family reference group plays a dominant role in the husband's priority of values, he will risk membership in the work group by spending evenings with the other members of the family reference group.

If a salesman can develop needs/benefits which apply to several reference groups, he not only overcomes this buying fear, of what others may think, but presents supportive reasoning in helping a buyer reach a buying decision. A new nine-passenger station wagon may not only provide the means for more enjoyable family trips but also be quite acceptable to the sales work group in that the wagon is used for travel to sales clinics.

Also closely related to the fear of what others may think and reference group values is the fact that these values can serve as points of comparison in evaluating one's own status. In this respect the reference group acts as a motivator. The customer is aware of a particular social group and finds a need to become part of it. For example, the reference group of the socially ambitious is said to consist of people of higher strata whose status symbols are imitated.[3] A junior executive might purchase a Chrysler Crown Imperial because he is aspiring to someday achieve acceptance within a reference group of top-level executives. Although he is not in that particular reference group, the group serves as a standard or checkpoint in his decision to buy. Here motives, attitudes, and knowledge also interact with the dominant need to gain acceptance. Obviously the purchase of the

[3] H. H. Hyman, "The Psychology of Status," *Archives of Psychology*, vol. 38, p. 15, 1942.

automobile would not allow him to participate in the reference group, but it would bring the purchaser one step closer, for he now possesses something which is representative of the reference group to which acceptance is deemed a worthy goal.

The customer perceives, thinks, and forms buying decisions according to the fear of what others may think, or to express it another way, according to the frame of reference of the group in which he is participating. This could shift several times during the day. A man is influenced by the family while at home, the work group while at his profession, friends while at lunch, and a social club in the evening. Each of these reference groups are in a position to influence his preferences and consequently his buying decisions. If this man shops for a new suit during his lunch hour, it might be important to gain his wife's approval of his selection *before* he has the tailor measure for alterations. If this is the case, and the salesman knows the customer, it is good sales logic to allow the customer the privilege of taking the suit coat home for the needed approval. If the wife is present when the purchase is being made, her physical presence should be a significant sign to the salesman that she will have an influence upon the color and style that is best suited to her husband.

The work group could also play a significant part in the purchasing of a new suit. A rising young executive might choose to wear the style of his young associates, or he may also seek to emulate a senior member of the firm.

Even salesmen of products which hold obvious functional value will encounter this fear to a degree. A buying decision requires *justification by the purchaser* — always to himself, but in most cases also to someone else. The "someone else" refers to the reference group. To illustrate, if a salesman attempts to sell a $45 premier battery to a man with a stalled car, he would be wise to establish need which relates in some manner to his family reference group. The customer knows that his wife would show little concern if he were to purchase a medium-priced battery for $25, because the need for *some* battery is self-evident. However, the $20 difference between $45 and $25 could be used to purchase something else, possibly an evening out. The salesman who accepts the presence of this fear will make an effort to develop a particular need/benefit relationship directly pertaining to the wife's need to use a dependable car.

One tire manufacturer makes effective use of this fear in the television advertising of its puncture-proof tire. The scene depicts a desperate woman in the dark of night attempting to change a flat tire in a rainstorm. The concerned voice in the background asks if you would want your wife to subject herself to this predicament. "To prevent this situation from occurring, purchase ABC specially designed puncture-proof tires."

SPECIFIC APPLICATIONS TO THE SELLING SYSTEM

Firms have effectively utilized the fact of reference groups in promoting their products on television. Here we evaluate a few of these advertising promotions in terms of reference-group influence and then determine where they can best be related to the eye-to-eye selling situation, one-to-one relationship. This critical evaluation will strengthen your awareness of the influence of this buying fear.

Purchase of an American Motors Javelin

Automobiles are good examples of both the product and the brand being influenced by reference groups. The strategy of the American Motors Corporation is an appeal to attitudes and motives so as to associate purchase with a particular reference group. The Javelin is a sports car, which would attract a different market segment than, say, the Chrysler Imperial. The market potential for sports cars has increased in the last 5 years; it is now possible to own a representative sports car at a high or low price level. This market emphasizes the word "sport."

The objective of this television commercial is to attract the middle-age market, people in upper-middle income brackets ($9,000 to $12,000 per year). Reference groups would tend toward the conservative side. In the television commercial sequence, a Javelin owner who fits the above characteristics is sitting in his car waiting for the traffic light to turn green. As he is waiting a young lad on a motorbike admires the car and congratulates the owner on such a wise choice. At the next light a European "sport" driving an expensive foreign sports car suggests a race. The Javelin owner declines. This is followed by a driver in an expensive American sports car challenging the middle-aged Javelin owner by accelerating his engine. Again, the Javelin owner only smiles. In this advertising promotion a particular market group is depicted through reference, images, and symbols. The Javelin is symbolic of youth, adventure, and wealth, and at the same time it is portrayed as acceptable to the middle-aged owner's present reference group (in his refusal to race). From a motivational standpoint, the emphasis is upon the buyer's sense of belonging — gaining a stronger recognition by his reference group — and self-actualization, particularly the urge to strengthen his personal identity. He may spend his working hours behind a desk or performing routine tasks, but the sports car provides an opportunity to live a fuller life of excitement and adventure.

To apply this technique to a personal selling situation, the salesman would relate the customer's *needs* (desire to acquire the thrill of driving and the role of adventurer) to the reference group with whom he would enjoy the benefits in fulfilling these needs. The important factor here is for the salesman to employ the selling system in such a manner that the fear of what others may think can be used positively — to accentuate the benefits attached to a reference-group environment as well as those benefits attached to the satisfaction of personal needs.

Purchase of a Volkswagen

Volkswagen of America, Inc., has been highly successful in developing a market for its standard sedan. This has been achieved by emphasizing three features: a product of relatively low cost, recognizable economy, and quality workmanship. The reference groups which have accepted the Volkswagen include the young family concerned with the purchase of a car within its budget; the young single person who desires economic transportation; the family which desires an inexpensive second car; the sports car buff who cannot afford a more expensive mode.

Knowledge may be used as a means of relating the product to a new reference group, possibly the family neighborhood. The strategy here is to develop, through a rational process, a relationship between a Volkswagen as a family car and its acceptance by the neighborhood reference group. For example, a TV scene depicts two middle-class homes almost identical. In the driveway of one we see a new American-model automobile. At the driveway of the second home we see servicemen bringing in a new color TV, a washer-dryer, and a stereo console. The announcer summarizes the setting by stating: "Mr. Jones has just purchased a new color TV, washer-dryer, stereo console, *and* a Volkswagen." The conclusion drawn is that a family can have a new car plus the other items at the same price as the American model.

There is an attitude amongst a large segment of the populace that it is "patriotic" to "buy American." Without entering into a serious economic discussion, it can be stated that this is not necessarily true, for a favorable balance of trade can be achieved only if there is a percentage of goods purchased from abroad. Nonetheless, the preference for American-made goods appears to be well-accepted. Using a rational approach, Volkswagen does not attempt to dispel this preference. The strategy is to develop a rationale — a reason — which will become of greater importance than the particular preference. The rationale used is actually twofold. One, through the purchase of a Volkswagen the consumer is now in a position to purchase items which have broad appeal and acceptance to the family. Two, it infers that the consumer is now in a position to buy *more* American-made products. These two points would serve to reinforce the customer's position with the norms or standards of this reference group. The result of this strategy is to develop the Volkswagen as a typical family car.

The Purchase of Men's Suits

Since everyone in our society wears clothing, the product itself has no relationship to reference groups. However, the *type* or *brand* of clothing is influenced to a considerable extent by particular reference groups. The working environment is one area where this relationship is evidenced. Rising executives will develop certain standards of dress exemplifying an image of ability and success; this would involve a particular style, color, fitting, or brand. Students will accept particular styles often signifying their reference groups. From the focal point of needs satisfied, attitudes play a significant role. The type of clothing represents a particular image and symbolizes a commitment to a chosen reference group, or perhaps several. Motives might include the need for social acceptance and the need for self-esteem. Through an analysis of reference-group influence, the firm may direct its selling efforts toward a specific group.

A manufacturer of men's suits uses this approach in a TV commercial by suggesting that the successful young businessman need not spend $150 to $200 for a suit which will represent his success — he can reflect his success by purchasing XYZ brand for only $85. This firm analyzed consumer attitudes and then appealed directly to these attitudes through image and symbolism. The appeal is directed toward the youthful, successful businessman who is interested in good grooming not only to please his wife but to reflect the position of success he holds in his work group and the higher levels to which he is striving. The reference groups to which the appeal is made are the work group and the immediate family.

CONCLUSION

You have already learned that the desire step develops within the customer a mental image, a mental experience, which can lead to ownership within the mind. This is a most important step taken by the customer, because all physical ownership results from the development of mental possession. When the salesman prepares himself by properly planning his method of using the selling system to positively influence the customer, he must visualize the entire presentation, using information about the prospect combined with product knowledge so as to link or match the presumed needs/benefits with the prospective customer. During this preapproach the salesman uses his mental process to visualize the essence of his entire sales presentation, step by step. As this visualization begins to unfold, the salesman prepares for the sales points, demonstrations, and examples he wishes to use and the benefits he will wish to emphasize to fulfill the needs he feels now exist. In this process of preparation, the salesman *sells the customer in his mind*, just as the buyer, in the desire step, assumes mental ownership of the product.

PROBLEMS

1. How is the preapproach related to the five buying decisions and the other selling steps?

2. What is the primary purpose of planning?

3. What are the three parts of the preapproach?

4. Discuss how the preapproach and the interest step are similar.

5. Discuss the five principles of behavior of the planning process found in the preapproach.

6. Discuss three techniques of the planning process.

7. Discuss the three techniques of prospecting.

8. Why is the study of the three fears of buying important to the planning step?

9. How can a salesman's career be jeopardized by not properly understanding the impact of the buying fear relating to whether or not the product will do what the salesman says it will do?

10. Give an example of how a professional salesman can overcome the fear that the product is not worth the price.

11. What types of social groups influence the customer to fear what others may think?

12. How does understanding the influence of reference groups aid a professional salesman in his planning activities?

13. How can the needs developed in purchasing a station wagon be related to a reference group? In purchasing a suit? Tires?

14. Evaluate the following statement and explain your ideas concerning it: "The preapproach to the salesman is like the desire step to the customer."

15. If you were selling life insurance, how would you use the snowplow approach to prospecting?

16. Consider the car you or your family last purchased. Do you think that fear of what others may think had any influence upon the buying decision?

17. Describe a TV commercial which illustrates each of the three fears of buying (one commercial for each fear).

18. Discuss how you would overcome the fear that the price is too high when selling quality furniture.

19. Give a personal example of buying something where the price was higher than you expected to pay.

20. Give an example where the purchase of a product could break the rules of behavior that Goffman discusses. Give an example of a product purchase which would *support* the rules of behavior.

See pages 267–269 for an additional case study.

ASSIGNMENT 1

You are attempting to sell a Buick to the district sales manager of the ABC Aluminum Corporation. In your planning, what reference groups would you appeal to in overcoming the fear of what others may think?

ASSIGNMENT 2

You are developing a sales strategy to sell the Teamsters Union a retirement insurance program for the entire union membership of a particular local. In order to be successful in your sales efforts, you must convince the local union representative that your program is a good one. How would you develop the necessary background information to prepare your strategy?

ASSIGNMENT 3

You are planning a sales presentation for a doctor who is a general practitioner. He has purchased your products in the past, in a small rural town. The product is a new drug your firm has just developed to combat the common cold. Laboratory tests prove conclusively that the drug is effective in accomplishing this, and a test market was established in Denver, Colorado, to determine the feasibility of placing the product on the market. The overwhelming acceptance of the product by physicians in the Denver area influenced your firm to place the product on the general market. Prepare a sales plan on paper, utilizing the selling system.

CASE STUDY: PART ONE
WINTER BATTERY CAMPAIGN

John Carroll had just returned from a sales meeting of the American Petroleum Corporation, where he learned that his objective in the Winter Battery Campaign was $9,000. Based upon an average wholesale cost of $18 per battery, that amounted to a total of 500 batteries. Based upon the twenty-five service stations assigned John as sales representative, that averaged out to twenty batteries per station. John knew that some of his stations would buy only the minimum order of ten, while there were at least three accounts that were stocking Nickel-Cadmium batteries (their competitor) because they were placed in the service stations on consignment. With these thoughts in mind, John began planning the specific objectives he would set for each of his accounts.

"I'm glad that I took the time to transfer those yearly sales figures to my own record book," John thought. "It makes it much easier to check out what my stations purchased last year and how their monthly purchases are going this year."

John picked up the sales record for his first account — Stan and Paul's Service. Battery sales for last year were $750; thus far this year they had purchased $125 worth of batteries. John calculated that based upon $18 per battery Stan and Paul purchased about forty-two batteries last year. Subtracting the $125 in purchases this year, or seven batteries, meant that by using last year's purchases of forty-two as a base, there were approximately thirty-five to forty batteries yet to be purchased during the present year. Through experience John realized that 85 percent of these sales would be made during the colder months of November, December, January, and February. Because of this fact, he felt that setting a Winter Battery Campaign objective of thirty batteries would be in line with their previous sales.

"Actually," John thought, "since their gasoline purchases are up 18 percent from January until the present (ct.) and their lubricant grease purchases are up 35 percent, it's obvious that their pump island customers and service customers have increased to the point where they should sell more batteries than last year."

John also made a mental note of the pride which Stan and Paul have in their service work. John was at the station once when a customer whose car would not start phoned the station for assistance. Stan immediately went to the service car and put in an extra battery and jumper cables. John went along for the ride and found the customer to be quite appreciative of the time that Stan had taken to come to the house so quickly; he also saw in Stan personal satisfaction in being able to provide this kind of service for his customers. On the way back to the station, Stan remarked that they did not make any profit on this kind of a call, but it really made the customers loyal to their station, and the increased service work on their cars more than made up for these calls.

With these thoughts going through his mind, John took out a piece of paper and began jotting notes on the kinds of benefits which the battery sale could provide.

"Let's see," John thought, "the fact that the payments don't become due until February, March, and April means that they can stock these batteries at no cost and use the money for two months for other purposes at no interest. It also means that with a complete stock of batteries they will be in a position to increase their ability to give complete service during these winter months; when a customer needs a battery, either you have it in stock or miss the sale. With the variety of batteries required these days, this includes a sizable assortment. Another advantage of buying a large assortment would be that if they were to buy $900 in batteries this year, they could buy at a lower buying price the following year; this could mean increased profits from their battery sales. There's no reason why they couldn't sell a minimum of thirty batteries, and there is every reason that they could sell forty if they emphasized the sale of batteries in their winterized service promotion coming up next month."

The next morning John drove out to Stan and Paul's; he planned to arrive at the station around 8:45. Through experience he knew that Paul took his coffee break about that time, and this was a good time to discuss a battery promotion. He also realized that Paul had the greatest influence in the partnership; if he felt it to be a good program, the likelihood of Stan going along was very good. Fortunately Paul was free and readily accepted John's invitation for coffee.

"How's the service work coming along this month, Paul? Getting many winter tuneups yet?" John asked.

"You bet," replied Paul. "After our compaign of last year to maintain complete service records on all our accounts, all we have to do now is give them a call and make arrangements for an appointment."

"Appointment!" John exclaimed. "Do you mean to tell me that your customers will stand for that?"

Paul laughed. "Sounds funny, doesn't it? The fella across the street is giving away free lubrication certificates to attract customers, while we have to carefully arrange our daily work schedule."

"It certainly shows that customers will go out of their way to have their car cared for by experts in whom they know they can place their confidence," John commented. "Paul, from what I can see of competition in this area, you two appear to have the best reputation for outstanding service; wouldn't you agree?"

"Yes, I guess I would," Paul replied. "It hasn't come easy, though. It took two lean years to reach this point."

"How would you like to have the opportunity to develop a winter program which would strengthen your reputation as *the* station to take your car to for service in the valley?" John asked.

"Sounds like another one of your promotional programs," Paul replied. "Don't you fellas ever stop trying to work the angles?"

John laughed and said, "You know, we're always trying to develop new ideas, Paul; keeps our competition on their toes. Seriously though, Paul, with expenses running high this time of the year, wouldn't it be helpful if we could offer you a means of increasing your ready cash with no payment due until February?"

"Now I know you're putting me on!" Paul said. "Of course we can use money. What have you got in the back of your car, an extra bank? If so, that really will beat what your competition has to offer!"

John began to discuss the product with Paul. "As you know, Paul, Nickel-Cadmium has been selling its batteries to dealers on a consignment basis. This means that the station doesn't have to tie up cash in the purchase of batteries, but the margin of profit is reduced by 60 percent. In most cases the gross profit is only $2.75; hardly worth the time spent installing the battery. We have a program which allows you to purchase batteries in October at no initial cash outlay. Here's how it works. We ship the batteries out next week and you do not have to make a payment until February; one-third in February, one-third in March, and one-third in April. This means that if you were to purchase forty batteries, it could put around $1,000 in your till to use until your first payment comes due."

"Forty batteries!" Paul exclaimed. "We've never had that many batteries in the station at one time!"

"I know it sounds like a ridiculous amount, Paul, but do you realize how many batteries you sold last year?" John asked.

"No, I don't," Paul said with interest.

"Your total purchases amounted to $750, which averages out to about forty-three batteries for the year. Now, did you also know that you have purchased thus far this year 35 percent more lube grease? Now, at the rate you two are increasing your service work, your battery sales this year will show an increase if you can handle the necessary assortment.

"Paul, with an assortment of forty batteries in the display room, do you realize how that would impress your customers? Not only would it provide you with the kind of stock that your station really requires, but it would also begin to make your customers 'think batteries' when they are in the station. It also acts as a stimulant for yourself to check battery cells with your voltmeter when the cars drive in to the pump island."

"What happens when we stock too many RD-10s and run out of RD-25s? When you buy that many batteries, how do you know which ones will sell?" Paul asked.

"You don't have to worry about that, Paul," John replied. "If you find that you are long on a particular model, just let me know and I'll make arrangements for the plant to exchange it for other models."

John continued, "The fact that you ask that question tells me that you can see the potential sales, Paul. This winter when the temperature gets down below zero, your customers are going to want an immediate check on their antifreeze, spark plugs, fan belt, and battery. Next month when this lube bay is filled with cars, each of those owners is going to be interested in one thing: keeping his car running. Won't it be satisfying, Paul, to have a customer bring his car in and have the knowledge that you are in a position to give complete service? You check his battery before he takes the service car to work. The number three cell is way down; no doubt about it, the car needs a new battery. You show the reading to your customer, and take him out to the display room and help him select the model which is just right for his needs. He makes the selection, and thanks you for assuring him that his car will start tomorrow when the temperature is supposed to drop to five above."

"I guess that will work out OK," Paul said. "Why don't you drop around about noon when Stan comes to work? He knows more about what to order."

PROBLEMS

1. Evaluate John's preapproach technique.

2. Did John use his customer knowledge in an effective manner in preparing his preapproach? Discuss.

3. How does planning play an important role in John's selling activities?

4. Evaluate John's attention step. Was it effective?

5. Do you feel the questions John asked probed the customer's needs? Discuss.

6. What types of questions did John ask?

7. Upon what needs did John base his conviction step?

8. Did John make use of the desire step? How?

9. When did John realize the sale was closed?

10. Discuss how John used the selling system in effectively relating his activities with the needs of the customer.

PART TWO
DEVELOPMENT OF THE SALESMAN
WITHIN THE SALES ORGANIZATION

This section of the text deals with the involvement of the salesman within the sales organization, and discusses those activities which can be of value in the development of his capacity within the organizational structure. In Chapter Twelve the use of planning in terms of organization objectives is discussed. The reader, through study of specific examples, is presented with the opportunity to view how planning can be used effectively to reach sales objectives. Chapter Thirteen offers a procedure which the salesman may use in solving the many decisions with which he is faced. Frequently the salesman is placed in a position where a decision is required immediately or without the assistance of the sales manager. In these cases the "I-M-P" method of reaching decisions, discussed in Chapter Thirteen, can be of value.

Chapter Fourteen deals with the development of sales leadership; for those who have aspirations of rising within the organization this chapter has particular merit. For those who enjoy the thrill of sales activity and do not wish to relinquish this function, the discussion of leadership has application in influencing accounts to purchase their products. Chapter Fifteen discusses performance evaluation and allows the reader to become familiar with those factors which influence the manager's evaluation and how the evaluation may be accomplished. For those who desire to become managers, it offers valuable insight into how proper evaluation is accomplished.

The United Pharmaceutical Case is presented at the end of this section to give the reader an opportunity to apply these chapters to a sales situation. The questions focus on the related elements of all these chapters as they apply to the case.

Chapter Twelve
Planning: Its Relationship
to the Salesman's Success

In Chapter Eleven we discussed the activity of planning relative to the first step of professional salesmanship, that of planning the particular sales presentation. In this chapter the element of planning will be linked to the overall success of a salesman. Specifically, this chapter will deal with the two broad areas of planning and objectives. With an understanding of how these two important factors influence the effective use of the selling system, the salesman is in a position to (1) successfully plan his total sales activity and (2) develop the proper attitude and approach toward his sales activity. These are the two main reasons why planning is important. First, with proper planning, the salesman will know that he is taking the necessary steps in effectively planning his total sales activity. He will know that his efforts are justifiably sound, because his actions are based upon sound, rational judgment. Every salesman has the capacity to arrive at a logical action decision, but not every salesman takes the necessary steps to do so. Too often a salesman will make calls which are ineffectual, and he knows they are ineffectual. Yet he often feels that by the mere act of making calls the law of percentages is with him and he will find his fair share. This does not necessarily apply. Without proper planning, every call becomes a matter of chance—the chance that the customer is just waiting for a particular need to be fulfilled and the salesman just happens to have the product to fulfill the need. Usually this leads to a series of negative calls with the only result being a list of people contacted.

This leads into the second reason why planning is of particular importance. If the salesman is going to utilize his rational capacity to form positive judgments relating to sales activities, it is necessary that he have the proper approach and attitude toward his sales activity. When thorough planning is accomplished, everything that occurs between the salesman and his customer is viewed in a positive light. If the sale is not concluded, a professional salesman's attitude is not influenced by the often reached conclusion, "I have failed as a salesman," or "The customer lacks the capacity to understand what I have to offer." Rather, in all cases the salesman objectively evaluates the results in relation to his plan. Possibly his plan will be adjusted; if so it will be adjusted on the basis of a positive attitude to become a more effective salesman in the future.

This can have an impact upon a sales organization. For example, a large metropolitan newspaper was showing a decline in the advertising linage. After a weekly sales meeting during which this fact was discussed, a salesman was commenting upon this situation with a newly assigned salesman. The older salesman was offering the younger member of the firm his opinion regarding the drop in advertising. "Everyone knows," he said, "that the economics of the area are not good. There's no sense in attempting to pressure these accounts into placing more ads. Only make them mad. The best approach is to be sure that you are available when they wish to place advertising in the paper." The newer member of the organization fortunately did not apply this principle that his planning efforts were "locked in" or completely influenced by the economic environment. Instead he chose to plan how advertising could assist all his accounts in increasing their sales. He had a plan and a positive approach; if a particular account chose not to accept a particular sales plan, he evaluated the response and used the objection presented by the account as a basis for strengthening the reason why other accounts should buy. Within 18 months the new employee was promoted while the older salesman, who had suggested earlier that he bide his time with his accounts, was still waiting for a promotion.

THE IMPORTANCE OF OBJECTIVES IN PROPER PLANNING

Before any course of action is initiated, the objectives must be clearly determined, understood, and stated.[1] Objectives are the end results toward which the salesman directs his efforts. Therefore, in developing a plan of action, objectives offer two benefits: they offer direction toward the selling effort *and* act as motivators.

Objectives Provide Direction in the Sales Effort

The time buying decision is of significant importance in the sale of some products—for instance, lawn fertilizer. Most of the major brands make a serious effort to have fertilizer in the retail outlet by early February. With the intensive competition in the field, if Brand A is not well stocked in the stores during the winter months, the opportunity for Brand B to place its stock in the stores becomes a distinct possibility. This is further intensified when Brand B is a local brand and is not faced with logistical problems of shipping and storage. Direction in the sales effort begins with a specific plan inducing retail outlets to purchase in the early winter. An approach to attract early purchasing is a "spring dating" program. The plan involves three interacting features. One, the fertilizer will be shipped directly to the retailer well in advance of the fertilizer season, allowing the retailer to attract the "early dirt dobber." Two, assuming a minimum of 100 sacks, payment by the retailer is not made until May, June, and July, one-third paid each of these three months. With Brand A retailing for an average cost of $12.95 per sack, this means that (benefits) a retailer who purchases the product in February has use of the potential gross sale of $1,295 ($12.95 x 100 sacks) from February until May and a reduced amount until the total is paid in July. This means further that the retailer, when he sells the product prior to May, can utilize the manufacturer's money during a calendar period when expenses are high and business slow, without an interest charge. Three, a special allowance of $1 per sack is given on all dating purchases. This is

[1] John F. McGee, "Management for Professional Executives," *Business Horizons*, Bureau of Business Research, School of Business, Indiana University, Bloomington, December, 1956, pp. 5–11.

offered to stimulate early purchases by passing on the $1 reduction to the customer. Advertising by the manufacturer is assured, to attract early purchases in February and March. Typically a customer who buys any amount during this special early allowance period will continue to buy the product throughout the summer.

Direction becomes a reality when the salesman is given a specific objective to achieve. For example, let us assume that the salesman has a quota of $10,000. When he begins to determine how he will reach the objective, something happens. The objective given to him by the firm becomes the basis of a plan of action through which the salesman will assign himself personal objectives—direction in a sales effort. With this $10,000 quota, let us assign the sales representative twenty accounts; these include three local department store chains, one hardware chain with garden supply outlets, one national chain with local purchasing authority, five independently owned hardware outlets, and ten suburban all-purpose nurseries independently owned. The first step in planning is to review the total purchases by each account during the previous year. If the year prior to last year is also available, this would be helpful in determining trends by each account. For example, an increase in purchases of 15 percent over a 2-year span may be of value in projecting purchases during the current year.

On the basis of prior total purchases by year, the sales representative then determines specific account objectives for each of his twenty accounts. Probably he would include an extra $2,000 in potential sales to compensate for those accounts which will buy less than his preset objective. On the basis of these objectives, the salesman uses the techniques discussed in Chapter Eleven to reevaluate each of his accounts relative to his awareness of the customers' personal and business motives and how the benefits of this particular dating program can fulfill the needs suggested by these motives. Still using the pre-approach, the salesman now carefully plans how he will develop all phases of the selling system to most effectively accomplish the dating objectives projected by the firm. Although the account objectives he develops will typically be considerably less than the yearly sales of the retail outlets, the salesman does have a solid base in assuring the retailer that he will not be overstocking.

Another illustration of how planning and setting objectives provide direction in a sales effort involves newspaper advertising. The type of advertising presented here is of a specialized nature. Many large newspapers issue special editions at particular times of the year: in the spring, a "Boating Edition" and "Parade of Homes"; in the fall, a "Hunting Edition"; in January, a "Baby Album" and annual "Review Section," which includes feature articles about all the towns and cities within a 200-mile radius. The purpose of these special sections is to stimulate interest in a particular area and thereby develop additional advertising. For example, in the "Hunting Edition" there may be an article about the choice locations for duck hunters. On the opposite page would appear an advertisement depicting mobile trailers "just perfect for hunters" or motel accommodations for hunters. The "Review" section is the most comprehensive in content and entails considerable sales effort. In it each town within the 200-mile radius is given from two to four pages, depending upon size and importance, showing color pictures of major industries or recent community achievements—new library, historical monument, park, etc. Along with the informative write-up, at least a page of advertising is anticipated from each of these towns.

The salesman in this situation has no real opportunity to develop a working relationship with his "accounts"; he may spend one week at one location, and not return until the following year. Thus, when he approaches a town with the objective of selling a page of advertising, he must be well prepared and possess a clear sense of direction. The planning begins with a review of the accounts that purchased advertising space the previous year. Next a conference is held with the art department to establish a tentative layout for the advertising. For instance, if Boulder City is the gateway to the Grand Canyon, an artist might sketch a drawing of Grand Canyon depicting the proximity of Boulder City. The objective becomes one of depicting through advertising the geographical importance to tourists and potential business investors. Even though the salesman does not have an opportunity to research his prospects, he does have a well-defined plan to present to his accounts. Since this is a continual process of "cold selling," the development of a sense of direction through proper planning is essential. The clear understanding of objectives is the key.

Objectives Serve As Motivators

The act of meeting an objective becomes a motivator when the salesman recognizes that in its attainment something of personal value also results. Sales objectives inherently relate to the future achievements of the organization. In order to arrive at a positive attitude in striving to personally achieve these objectives, the achiever must clearly recognize the personal, as compared to organizational, value in achieving goals. In a sense the achieving of company goals is the means, or the motivator, leading toward the achievement of personal goals. A commission salesman may not possess this positive attitude if he is called away from his territory for a day to attend a sales meeting. He will become enthusiastic about the sales meeting only if during the course of the meeting it becomes evident that the material presented more than compensates for the lost selling opportunity.

Another example, in a different selling environment, concerns a retail specialist for a petroleum firm. He has the objective of increasing the profit of a training service station to the extent that it serves as a "living example" to future dealers as to what can be accomplished when a service station operates according to certain techniques and policies. In order to use objectives effectively, the retail specialist must relate his activity to personal achievement, possibly the next promotion, an increase in salary, or a feeling of personal accomplishment and self-actualization. He will develop means to increase the gallonage and service of the station because he realizes that, by showing the firm he is capable of successfully managing a training station, he will prove himself worthy of future promotions. Because of the close relationship between personal objectives and the objectives of the firm, the retail specialist becomes motivated to take whatever action is necessary to sell the service and products of the station to the motorist. This could range from neighborhood solicitation, offering free lubrication or oil changes, to maintaining superior windshield cleaning at the pump island. In this situation salesmanship occurs in developing an attention step which is further supported by outstanding service.

Another illustration showing the importance of congruency of interests is expressed in an article appearing in the *Wall Street Journal* entitled "Firing Up the Team."[2] The article discusses various approaches to develop enthusiasm and increased sales through the creation of meaningful individual objectives. One case involves Addressograph-Multigraph Corporation, a Cleveland maker of of business machines, which decided to give its top salesman a replica of a sword of El Cid, the Spanish hero. The company told its sales force that El Cid, sword in hand, signified "all the courage, skill, and persistence for successful combat" and that the image "in a very real sense is representative of the Addressograph-Multigraph salesman in his own quest for success."

Thomas Prinn, a Detroit salesman who had been meeting or slightly exceeding his quota, sold 456 percent of his quota to win the sword. Why? Partly because he had a run of good luck and partly because some orders that had been in the works for a long time suddenly materialized. But he also worked harder because he wanted the sword on his living-room wall. "It's really something to be proud of, and it goes on your record at the home office," he said.

These examples are presented to develop an awareness of the fact that specific action by the salesman becomes effective and relative only when the action clearly relates to the goals of the organization *and* the individual. The two must be mutually supportive. This concept attracts singular significance in view of the environment in which a salesman functions. Almost constantly he is confronted with the responsibility of making decisions—which account should he see today, should he "waste" another hour awaiting the return of a key client from a meeting, and so on. Judgments must be made by the salesman, for that is the inherent responsibility attached to the job function. In order to make sound evaluations, the salesman must always be able to relate his activities in a supportive attitude toward goal accomplishment. Some salesmen transact all their major business affairs over a cup of coffee or lunch. To the casual observer it might appear that the salesman is wasting valuable time, but a professional knows that there is no one place to sell a customer, and if a coffee shop offers the proper environment, the time spent sipping coffee becomes supportive to the firm's goals. One sales representative calling on distributors spends most of his time with a particular wholesaler traveling in the wholesaler's truck, for this is the only opportunity that he has to discuss specific business activities. It also gives the salesman an opportunity to call on retail accounts with the wholesaler and gain valuable feedback.

The selling system becomes most effective when the salesman relates the

[2] Greg Conderacci, "Firing Up the Team," *The Wall Street Journal*, Oct. 13, 1970, p. 1.

particular linking of the processes to the accomplishment of something specific—an objective—and as a result develops confidence that all his activities, although not directly related to a selling situation, are important to goal accomplishment. It may take several hours in the home sales office to obtain the necessary sales records of a particular account. To a professional, whose attention is focused upon sales activity, this nonselling activity is important in developing a proper sales presentation to realize objectives. The salesman who has a sense of direction and is motivated to achieve specific objectives develops a positive attitude and consequently finds a way to meet these objectives.

PERSONAL SALES MANAGEMENT

As a salesman, you must learn to be your own sales manager, for selling is one of the world's most independent professions. Most of the time your income is tied directly to your ability to manage yourself as well as to your ability to sell. We will discuss a number of key points of personal sales management. Each of these points will utilize planning and objectives as the basis for success.

Examples of the Use of Sales Reports in Planning Sales

A sales report becomes a valuable tool in good planning. Computerized reports are becoming more common and will find continued use in the future. The computer makes possible a more complete report in a shorter period of time; thus the information is highly relative to the present sales involvement.[3] A sales report for a petroleum firm, shown in Table 12-1, is our first example, because it offers a variety of items and may be easily understood and evaluated by any student of professional salesmanship. This service station account represents a new dealer who leased the station 9 months prior to this report. The high gallonage indicates that it is located in a large metropolitan area, in this case a suburb of a city with a population of 750,000. In evaluating the sales for the month, it is apparent by the increase in oil, lubrication grease, and tire sales that the present dealer is using a more effective means of selling his products and services than the previous dealer. The drop in gallonage may be due to a number of factors, some of which might be (1) the previous dealer taking a share of customers with him to a new location, (2) lack of proper staffing at the pump island, resulting in customers driving away because of a long wait, (3) shorter hours of operation, and (4) negative economic determinants of the area. The increase in all oil purchases indicates that there is a greater effort to service properly all facets of the motorist's needs. This could indicate to the sales representative that while the new dealer is more effectively selling his products than the previous dealer, he is not able to serve properly *all* the customers—thus the reduction in gallonage. The impressive increase in lubricants is a healthy

---

[3] Computer service bureaus equipped with the latest machinery are available in more areas, allowing even small firms to take advantage of this efficient record-keeping system.

TABLE 12-1 SERVICE STATION 16-130, SALES FOR JULY 19 ___

Product	Month's sales	Previous year	Total to date	Total to date, previous year	Percent over/under current year's objective
Premium gasoline (gal.)	20,000	27,000	170,000	210,000	−9
Regular gasoline (gal.)	35,000	40,000	490,000	520,000	−8.4
Canned oil 10/40 w (gal.)	60	50	320	265	+15
Canned oil 30 w (gal.)	30	20	180	145	+8
Canned oil 20 w (gal.)	45	40	200	175	+4
Canned oil 10 w (gal.)	24	20	85	80	+2
Lubrication grease (lb.)	240	240	1,440	1,200	+10
Transmission fluid (gal.)	30	24	150	138	+4

economic indicator of the overall financial position of this station. Oil and grease consumption are associated with service work performed in the lubrication bay; this is where the dealer makes the highest percentage of gross profit and where he must succeed to be financially sound.

This evaluation of the sales record becomes the basis of planning future activities. In this situation a special promotion involving a giveaway—possibly a free glass with 10 gallons of gasoline—could attract more customers to the pump island. This plan should also include an increase in personnel to assist in pumping the gasoline and giving under-the-hood service. At the beginning of each selling period, the professional salesman will make an appointment with his district manager in order to discuss his plans. From a communications viewpoint this allows the district manager to be fully aware of the action taken by the sales representative and thereby maintain a confident attitude in his official appraisal of the sales representative. This mutual trust is extremely important.

Another example of the use of sales records in future planning involves the sale of business forms. In this selling activity there is a need to maintain continuous records of all sales to the customers. The primary reason is that any one firm offers a sales potential of a variety of business forms, and thus accurate records must be maintained to determine the proper time for reordering and to determine potential sales of new forms. For a large hardware chain, we would find a need for the following forms:

Sales invoices

Purchase orders

Voucher checks

Payroll checks

Interoffice memorandums

Letterhead stationery

Envelopes

Statements

Inventory records

Sales records are maintained by individual items, by each account. Each salesman receives a copy of each sales invoice sold to his accounts and posts the information to the sales record card. This can best be illustrated with another example. The ABC Lumber Company has ordered 50,000 invoices, three copies each, snapout carbon, numbered 1 to 50,000. The salesman prepares the sales invoice and forwards it to his sales office; he keeps a copy to be used in posting to his sales record (see Table 12-2).

This type of sales record is helpful in several respects. It assists the salesman in providing a service for the account by showing a usage pattern for the particular form. In this example, usage is about 3,000 forms per month. When the form sequence number reaches 35,000, indicating a remainder of 15,000 invoices, the salesman should confer with the account as to possible changes that may be necessary on the next order. This could range from special artwork to additional copies to printing on the back of the form.

TABLE 12-2 SALES RECORD CARD

Item purchased: Sales invoice				
Person sold: Fred Carter, purchasing agent				
Date	Item	Price	Numerical sequence	Inventory status
8/16/19__	5 1/2 x 7 1/8 3 part stand. snapout, 1st p. white, 2nd p. yellow, 3rd p. pink, all 20 lb. paper	12.75/m	1–50,000	10/20 no. 5076 (used) 11/1 no. 8606 (used) 12/4 no. 11,076 (used)

In addition, accurate sales records at the salesman level provide a springboard for acquiring sales of those forms presently supplied by a competitor. If a unique art design can be developed for the invoice that was already sold to the account, it might be possible to recommend the artwork for all the forms, resulting in the salesman selling a "family of forms." An account respects the salesman's interest in a continual desire to improve the effectiveness of a form as well as maintain an inventory inspection. Because of this, the account is more willing to discuss how the other forms used in the various departments relate to the overall operation, allowing the salesman the opportunity of evaluating how he could improve the design of the form. This is another good example of price not being the primary basis of professional salesmanship. Once the customer is aware of the beneficial service provided, he is willing to pay a fair price and not shop for the least expensive.

Summary Sales reports have two main purposes. If you can keep these purposes in mind, your sales reports will be briefer, more meaningful, and more valuable. First, sales reports are made to help keep your sales manager and your company aware of how you are doing and to show the conditions you are encountering, the potential that exists, the work you are accomplishing, and the problems with which you may need help. Second, sales reports and records are made for your own use, to help you sell more and develop your market through better planning. To make your sales records and reports of the greatest value to you, make them accurate and reasonably detailed; on the things that matter, go below the surface to give more comprehensive evaluations. A sales report or sales record will vary with each organization. The examples used here are to show that in all selling activities the customer information, or benefit information, is utilized to increase the effectiveness of the salesman's involvement within the selling system. A point which cannot be overemphasized is that the use of this report in effective planning requires visualization with a positive attitude. If a sales challenge can be more effectively met with a different approach, it is no personal reflection upon the salesman to admit this possibility, for at the same time positive planning is initiated and consequently the salesman becomes motivated and directed to attain higher goals.

Call Reports

A call report that states that you called on a prospect and spent 30 pleasant minutes with him, but that he was not interested in buying at this time ("see again in 3 months") is practically valueless. If it gives the essence of what you talked about, the essence of what was accomplished, the factors that led the prospect to feel that he was not ready to buy yet—the how and why as well as the what—you have a record of what was accomplished. You have a springboard for planning the next sales call and making it more successful. Analyzing your call records and sales reports can help you direct your efforts where they will be most successful. Even your "lost" sales will not be wasted, for they will help contribute to making other sales. For example, you will know how many calls a prospect might be worth. If you find, as a salesman in one line did, that most of your sales are made on the second call, you will know that your good prospects are worth two calls and that staying with most prospects for six, seven, or more calls will be a waste of time. On the other hand, you may find that your line takes six or seven calls for success, so you will know that you should be willing to invest the effort and time to develop each prospect fully. Your call records and sales reports give you valuable clues to making the best, most profitable use of your time and effort.

Developing Your Abilities

As your own sales manager, you must work to develop your potential, just as you would work to develop the potential of each member of any sales staff you managed. Try to look at yourself as you would look at an employee working for you, to judge your abilities and potentials, to determine the training or study that might be needed to make you more productive, and to decide whether you are worth the investment in time and money needed. As a salesman, you are working for yourself; be sure you have the best employee you can develop.

Keep looking at the potential and making the most of it. To make the most income, concentrate your time and energy where it will do the most good. Many salesmen have found that it is just as easy to sell the large accounts, and they have become wealthy by concentrating their efforts on their best prospects. Successful life insurance salesmen sell a percentage of "the big ones." Doctors, for example, are prime prospects for large policies, particularly endowment programs that can be converted from life insurance to retirement after

20 or 30 years. The need for such policies is not hard to determine. An article in the *Wall Street Journal*[4] states that the average doctor's income is $32,000 per year; in the city it may amount to as much as $100,000 per year. These professional men need three specific classes of insurance: income protection for the family in the event of their death; financial protection for the family in the event of their death; retirement income suitable to their needs. For an insurance salesman, this is the type of sales potential which offers a reason for proper and thorough planning and should be included in his personal objectives.

Success is the progressive realization of worthy ideals; goals are ideals translated into specific accomplishments. There are three ways you can increase your income and volume: One, increase the number of calls you make, by working longer, harder, or faster. Two, increase the size of your average sale by selling more to each customer or by seeking customers who will buy more. Three, improve your closing rate through better selling or by doing a better job of selecting prospects to call upon.

CONCLUSION

Planning and objective development have a direct relationship to the salesman's success. Planning allows the salesman to work most effectively by basing his actions upon sound, rational judgment. Effective planning also permits the salesman to achieve a positive attitude; as a result all of his efforts, even those which result in no sales, have an impact upon potential sales by providing a basis for more successful future efforts. From the salesman's point of view, objectives offer two benefits. First, they direct the selling effort so that the salesman can make his plans supportive of the desires of the firm. Second, objectives serve as motivators; the challenge of meeting and establishing objectives becomes a motivator when the salesman recognizes that its accomplishment will result in fulfilling personal desires. Goals of the firm are more readily achieved when the salesman realizes that he will also achieve personal objectives, such as promotion, salary increase, or job security.

The sales report is useful in developing effective planning. It helps maintain an accurate record of past selling efforts and suggests how the salesman might use these facts to achieve future results. The call report provides a more detailed analysis of what has occurred with each account, what was discussed, and what was accomplished. Understanding planning and objectives and the role of sales records and call reports can help the salesman develop his true potential. It allows him to visualize sales potential and transform potential into goal achievement through completed sales.

PROBLEMS

1. From an organizational viewpoint, give two reasons why planning is important.

[4] Jonathan R. Laing, "Sitting Ducks," *The Wall Street Journal*, Aug. 17, 1970, p. 1.

2. Use an example to illustrate your answer to Problem 1.

3. What two functions do objectives provide in proper planning? Discuss.

4. Present an example which illustrates that specific action by the salesman becomes meaningful only when the salesman relates this activity to both organizational and personal goals.

5. How can we relate goal accomplishment to the selling system?

6. Give two uses of sales reports in sales planning.

7. How does having a clear set of objectives assist the salesman in developing a positive attitude toward selling?

8. How would the use of planning to achieve objectives affect the success of a life insurance salesman?

9. If you were the sales manager for a metropolitan newspaper with the responsibility to develop national advertising with accounts such as Mobil Oil Corporation, Ford Motor Company, and Coca-Cola Company at the local level, how would you suggest that your sales organization prepare themselves properly to plan their sales activity?

10. If you were a sales representative for RCA Corporation with an income based upon a monthly salary and you were asked by your sales manager to spend the next three Saturdays working with a large account in developing better selling techniques, how would you reconcile this time spent with your personal goals? Remember you will receive no overtime for these efforts.

11. Plan your college activities for the next 2 years on paper. Notice how these plans become meaningful only if they are related to a goal or goals.

12. Why do we say that salesmanship is primarily mental activity?

13. Why do you think the selling system is a useful device in effective incorporation of a selling plan of action?

See pages 270–271 for an additional case study.

Chapter Thirteen
Decision Making in Selling

As was pointed out in discussing the importance of objectives, the ability to make decisions is also a factor in a successful sales career. Decisions such as which call list to prepare the following day, which products to emphasize in a sales presentation, who to approach, and which sales techniques to use are made daily.

METHODS USED IN MAKING DECISIONS

Hunch: Trust to a guess, or to intuition; decide on impulse. Sometimes it works, often it does not.

Munch: Check the problem over hoping it will disappear. Try nibbling it to death, or worrying it away.

Punch: Try to substitute energy for direction; ride off in all directions at once. Overwhelm the problem out of existence.

Bunch: Turn it over to a committee, so things can become thoroughly delayed and confused with no one person to blame.

Lunch: Go to lunch and forget the problem, in the hope that it will disappear or solve itself if ignored.

Systematic: Use method and direction to analyze the problem, determine the solution, and proceed to a decision.

We all know the first five methods. We have seen others use them, and we may have used them ourselves at times. We know what the results can be, so let us look into the sixth, the systems approach.

THE SYSTEMATIC APPROACH

First, do you have a problem? In solving a problem, the only decision needed is to *select* a course of action. But many of the situations which people call "problems" are not problems. What needs to be done is known. The way it should be done is known. So it is not a problem, it is a *task*. The decision needed is merely one to *do* it.

Next, which kind of problem do you have? Problems are of two types: problems of *identification* and problems of *method*. The problem of identification is the most common. It exists when you know something is wrong but you do not really know why. It is any problem in which you see the effect but not the cause. The problem of method exists only when the cause or causes are absolutely clear. You know what needs to be corrected; the problem is *how* to do it.

THE I-M-P SYSTEM OF SOLVING PROBLEMS AND MAKING DECISIONS

Identify: Approach your problem as a problem of identification, and seek to identify its causes. Keep asking, "What is the cause? Why is this problem occurring?" When the why of the problem is absolutely clear and seems complete, it is possible to move on to the how of solving it. It has been transferred to a problem of method. To help solve your problem of identification, gather appropriate facts. Look for facts and information that will help you determine the nature and cause of the problem. State your information in clear, specific terms. Use number values rather than generalities: 76 or 28, 743 or 63 percent, rather than "many." Understandable comparisons help: "a man about John's size"; "a room twice as long as this one."

Method: Once the cause of a problem is clear, the method of correcting the cause may be self-evident, or it may take some digging. To help solve your problem of method, gather facts and information about the resources or methods you can use on your problem. Again, keep your information clear and specific. A problem of method is solved when you uncover or develop a technique or plan to overcome the obstacles to your reaching your goal.

Proceed: Make your decision and put it into effect. Once you know exactly where you are and the directions that are open to you, it is much easier to make your decision, to pick the direction that seems best. Make an *immediate* decision when there is nothing to be gained by waiting or when a decision, right or wrong, is needed immediately. *Delay* making a decision (decide to decide later) only when you need more time to gather essential facts, when more time is needed for consultation, checking, or considering; or when there is nothing at all to be gained by an immediate decision. To decide between a long-run and a short-run decision, spell out the probable consequences of each and decide which will do a better job of giving you what you want or need. Minimize the liabilities of each; do not assume you must necessarily sacrifice immediate benefits for later benefits, or vice versa. It may be possible to have both, merely by making another decision later.

You may be wondering how this systematic approach to problem solving and decision making corresponds to the conference-room technique, which is also concerned with solving problems. How are the two similar and how are they different? The answer is that the I-M-P system is built upon a broader concept, a more inclusive definition of "problems." The conference-room technique applies to specific problems, to situations that need correcting. The I-M-P system applies to these problems, actually incorporating the basic theme of the conference-room technique, and also applies to situations where there is no problem but a decision is necessary. It is a way of organizing your mind and effort, organizing your approach to a situation and your consideration of it, to yield organized results. For example, one frequent use of the I-M-P approach is in considering and defining objectives and working out the best methods of achieving them. The I-M-P approach makes it possible to take a general objective, such as to make more money, and narrow it down to a specific objective or objectives, and then develop a method of working in the needed direction. The I-M-P system makes it possible for you to turn either a *problem* or an *objective* into a *decision*.

THE CAUSES AND EFFECTS OF INDECISION

All action must start with a decision. Making decisions is one of the prime responsibilities of every executive or leader in any group, organization, or company. The major cause of indecision is the fear of making a wrong decision. The effects of indecision are invariably costly and time-consuming. Indecision (Hamlet's disease) is a cancer which is frequently fatal; no organization can produce, prosper, progress, or survive while stalled on dead center. The effects of indecision are usually far worse than the results of any decision that might have been made. Few decisions are ever 100 percent wrong—or 100 percent right. Few decisions are ever permanent; decisions can be changed or improved later. All it takes is another decision. Do not let the fear of making a wrong decision paralyze you. Make the best decision you can, at the time it should be made. You may not be 100 percent right, but you will be accomplishing something of value and that is what is important.

DECISION MAKING IN ACTION USING THE I-M-P SYSTEM

Identify

American Forms, Inc., a leading manufacturer of business forms, was unable to maintain an effective sales organization in the Los Angeles area. The sales organization is categorized in Table 13-1. It was apparent to the sales manager that the

TABLE 13-1 EVALUATION OF EMPLOYEE TENURE BY AGE

Age	Years with firm (average)	Yearly income (average)
25–30	1.25	$ 7,700
35–40	5	8,900
40–45	12	12,500
45–50	18	15,200
50–60	23	17,000
over	34	18,500

turnover was occurring among the younger members of the sales staff. In order to correct the problem, the company hired a consulting expert to determine and identify the cause of the problem. The conclusion reached was that the firm was not acquiring the quality of personnel suited for the sophisticated forms systems of the potential customers. Also, the firm was not properly selecting the sales personnel. The *cause* of the problem was therefore identified as one of *proper selection* and *setting adequate hiring standards.*

Method

The method selected to correct the problem utilized the services of the regional manager (who directs the West Coast territory, which includes the seven Western states), the district manager (whose territory includes the Los Angeles district, which comprises all of Orange County), and an area manager. Of the eight area managers in the Los Angeles district, two were particularly trained for this assignment: the Santa Monica area manager and the Westwood area manager. As a result of this decision there was an interviewing team of three at all times: the regional manager, the district manager, and one area manager. Each of these managers interviewed each applicant; no decision was made until the interviewers, as a committee, jointly evaluated their impressions. In order to gain a higher quality of personnel, they considered only applicants with 2 years of college.

Proceed

The system was initiated. Within one year under the new program, the rate of resignation of those salesmen between twenty-five and thirty years of age *increased* significantly. At this point American Forms, Inc., contracted another consulting firm to evaluate the problem.

Identify

The second consulting firm found the cause of the problem to rest not primarily with the sales organization, but with the method used in dividing the territories and training new personnel. There was no question that American Forms, Inc., was selecting qualified young men to the firm, but these men were becoming frustrated in not being able to develop *their* potential in the territories assigned them. It was the practice of the firm to give the older salesmen the territories with the highest potential and the newer members of the firm the territories with the lowest potential. Since the compensation was based primarily upon the commissions from sales, this left little opportunity for the newer members, and consequently they were leaving. In the area of training, this was accomplished under the supervision of the area manager. The newly hired salesmen would spend 4 weeks in the sales office learning the techniques of business forms design, pricing procedures, sales techniques, etc. Since the area manager was also assigned a number of accounts (his income was also closely related to commissions from sales), he spent little time with the new trainees; consequently the newer salesmen did not possess the proper background to sell effectively.

Method

The sales territories were reconstructed to allow the younger members of the sales organization a greater sales potential. The area manager was placed upon a direct salary plan with no accounts assigned directly to him. This gave him a greater incentive to develop the skills of his sales organization, particularly to work closely with the new personnel, both in training and in the field once the training was completed.

Proceed

American Forms, Inc., proceeded with this decision and to their satisfaction found a significant rise in the number of employees who were now remaining with the firm. This example illustrates not only the I-M-P system, but also the importance of an accurate appraisal of the cause of the problem. The best methodology will be of no value if it is used to solve the wrong problem.

Summary   On the managerial level, decision making is an important function, particularly in evaluating those problems which do not fall within the realm of existing policies. It is in this area that the sales manager must rely upon his past experience, training, and ability to relate the information in an objective and effective manner. The sales manager's ability to combine past experiences in such a way that they form a related network of information that can be used in solving a problem is one of the main reasons that emphasis is placed upon past experience in choosing a sales manager.

CONCLUSION

Daily the salesman is involved with making meaningful decisions. These could range from how much discount to offer a customer to which customers to contact during the day's activities. The method recommended in arriving at the right decision is the I-M-P approach. The salesman first identifies the problem in terms of its cause. In order to accomplish proper identification he must gather facts to help in determining the nature and cause of the problem. Next he chooses the proper *and* necessary method which will solve the problem. The function of method is fulfilled when the salesmen uncovers or develops a technique to overcome obstacles. Finally he proceeds. Once he knows exactly where the problem lies and the most effective method of solving that problem, he should take immediate action in arriving at a decision and implementing that decision. The salesman will delay making a decision only when he needs more time to gather essential facts.

The I-M-P system makes it possible for the salesman to turn either a problem or an objective into a decision for action. Since the action must start with a decision, making decisions is one of the prime responsibilities of every executive or leader in any group, organization, or company. The salesman should remember when making decisions and implementing them that he cannot be 100 percent right every time. However, he should also remember that in making a logical decision he is always accomplishing something of value.

Objections are also viewed in the light of cause and effect: the cause of objections is some lack of need fulfillment. As you learned in studying this area earlier, if the salesman evaluates an incorrect source or cause of the objections, he obviously will not take the proper action in solving the problem or overcoming the objections. In overcoming objections the salesman uses the I-M-P approach in the same sequence as in the decision-making process, identifying the objection, determining where within the selling system it falls, and returning to that specific selling step to reinforce the lack of needs displayed through the objection. This example illustrates the fact that this approach has value when planning any phase of selling activity, whether it be the evaluation of a sales territory, the performance of the sales organization, or one part of the selling activity in terms of one customer. The application becomes quite universal and can easily be implemented by the salesman as well as the sales manager.

PROBLEMS

1. Discuss the six methods people use in making decisions.

2. Why is problem identification so fundamental to problem solving?

3. Present the I-M-P approach to problem solving.

4. Describe a selling situation where the I-M-P approach could be used in reaching sound decisions.

5. Why are decisions so basic to sales activity?

6. As an inexperienced (6 months on the job) sales representative for a pharmaceutical firm, you find that you are able initially to gain admittance to the doctor's office, but are unable to consistently gain the doctor's confidence in committing himself to use your products. How would you attempt to solve this problem using the I-M-P approach?

7. How is the procedure for making effective decisions related to the area of the selling system where the salesman deals with objectives?

8. From the viewpoint of the professional salesman, how does the following statement affect his mode of operation: "Few decisions are ever permanent; decisions can be changed or improved later"?

9. From the local newspaper or the *Wall Street Journal* clip out an article which discusses sales problems for a firm or an industry. Bring it to class and dis-

cuss what you feel are the problems and how they can be solved using the I-M-P approach.

10. Write a one-page success story of a firm that overcame a sales problem.

11. Why do you think that "hunch, munch, punch, bunch, and lunch" are frequently used by the inexperienced salesman? Why do you think that the I-M-P approach can be a key to success?

12. Is there a relationship between a positive mental attitude and the I-M-P approach to solving problems? How?

See pages 272–273 for an additional case study.

Chapter Fourteen
Sales Leadership

The definitions of leadership are about as varied as the number of experts who wish to define it. From a salesman's viewpoint, the following definition has merit: Leadership is a characteristic or quality which signifies an ability to influence the actions and intentions of the sales organization in a positive manner.

In the sales function of influencing an account to purchase products, the quality of leadership is found in every successful salesman. However, this does not necessarily imply that every successful salesman will be a successful leader within the sales organization. Many firms make the mistake of seeking the most successful salesman and automatically giving him the position of sales manager. Often this individual lacks the desire, temperament, or mental discipline to be a sales leader. This chapter deals with those elements which specifically apply to leadership within a sales organization. The intent is to provide a frame of reference the reader may use in developing a harmonious relationship in the sales organization and in developing those qualities necessary for sales leadership.

TRAINING AND DEVELOPMENT

The ability to influence positively the behavior of salesmen depends upon the particular backgrounds of the salesmen interacting with the depth of understanding and perception of the sales manager. For example, the leadership approach of a sales manager would not be the same for a new member of the organization as for a 20-year veteran; for a young salesman of twenty-five as compared with a professional of fifty-seven; for a salesman who is not producing well because his son is seriously ill as compared with a salesman who is not producing well because of alcoholic problems. Certainly the I-M-P method of decision making can be of value, particularly in relating causes to implementation of training and development programs.

Even though the sales manager may not be directly involved with the training process of a new employee, he should take the time to discuss with the trainee his rate of progress. When a trainee makes the decision to work with a firm, he has no positive or negative attitudes regarding the firm apart from being positively motivated to succeed. If this positive attitude is strengthened during the first month of employment through proper training and development under the watchful eye of the sales leader, the probability that the trainee will remain with the firm *and* be successful rises.

The following example illustrates the relationship between the sales manager and a new sales representative with the ABC Petroleum Corporation. The sales representative was twenty-four years of age and was recently graduated from a 4-year university. Through *accurate observation*—a leadership trait—the sales manager determined that the young sales representative was performing below standard. The sales manager determined this by *properly relating*—another leadership trait—the following facts. The sales representative was spending a large amount of time in the district office, while his accounts were calling the district manager to ask for assistance with matters that should have been handled by the sales representative. The sales representative gave the outward appearance of low morale and apparently did not enjoy his work.

The sales manager first reviewed the sales representative's personnel file and discussed his personal characteristics with the personnel manager and other managers of the firm, such as the credit manager, who had some contact with the sales representative. The consensus was that this young man came to the firm with a good college background and a high degree of motivation to succeed. It became apparent that he was not accustomed to planning his work activity properly. He was constantly taking time from his accounts to return to the district office for something he needed and had forgotten. Being motivated to succeed, he soon became frustrated with himself for not performing as effectively as he would like, and ultimately he became discouraged.

When the sales manager was sure that he had all the knowledge available to evaluate the sales representative properly, he called the young man into his office and quickly communicated to him that the purpose of the meeting was to upgrade his performance to the level they *both* knew he could achieve. The sales manager asked the representative to come into the district office the following morning, write down *one* account he wished to call upon that day, and list the items of discussion and include all items necessary to be taken from the plant to the account. This could include a supply of sales invoices, battery guarantees, promotional information, road maps, credit-card application, etc. When the sales representative had completed the call, he was to *go home* and play golf or whatever he wished.

The next day the sales manager wanted to see the representative. He asked how the sales call was conducted and reviewed the areas of discussion with the account. Being satisfied that the sales call was an effective one, and therefore supportive to increased effectiveness of the sales representative, he told the salesman to plan *two* calls. He was not to leave the office until he was completely sure that all necessary items were in his car and that he had discussed matters of importance to the accounts with interested office staff. Once he had completed the two calls, he was to *go home*.

This approach was repeated until the sales representative became one of the most effective sales representatives in the Portland office. His newly found success was the result of two factors. First, the sales manager understood the characteristics of the sales representative in relationship to the job function and used this knowledge to develop a positive means of evaluating the salesman's capabilities. Second, the sales representative gained confidence when he realized that his leader was aware of his abilities and was sincerely interested in helping him find a way of developing these abilities.

In further developing professional salesmen who have been with a firm a number of years, the sales leader must show respect for the ability and skill of these men. This does not mean that the sales manager neglects the leadership function when dealing with these men. Rather, he utilizes *their* selling abilities and leadership capacities to influence the remainder of the sales organization to attain positive goals. From the personal development standpoint, the sales manager would probably have little success influencing the sales techniques of these men. However, his leadership could be very helpful in developing with these professionals knowledge and understanding of new products, new markets, or tactics of competitors.

Sales meetings provide another technique by which the leader can influence his organization to greater productive results. One word of caution: regularity of sales meetings is not necessarily indicative of their effectiveness. Research was done with one firm which held sales meetings promptly at 8:15 every Tuesday morning. At precisely 8:15 A.M. the secretary would read roll call; if someone was absent, an explanation was forthcoming. Over a span of years this type of sales meeting did not have a positive influence upon the sales organization in increasing their sales performance. Learning of a fine trip one of the managers took to San Francisco may have been interesting, but the sales meeting missed the important mark of being a valuable investment of time by the sales force. Consequently a negative attitude developed toward the weekly roll call.

Probably an outstanding example of a poorly conducted sales meeting involves a sales manager who holds a weekly Monday morning meeting. In the center of a round table which seats the entire sales organization is a hole cut out, allowing the sales manager to sit there with a 360-degree view of the sales force. He begins his meeting by loudly and "enthusiastically" asking the sales organization why XYZ thermons are the *best*. With a rash of outward enthusiasm, the entire sales force loudly gives their reasons for the obvious quality of the product. The sales manager (leader!) then points a finger at a salesman and asks him why the XYZ Company is the best company in the world. Quickly a salesman responds with an explanation of why the XYZ firm is the best. At the conclusion of the meeting, the men are at a high pitch of enthusiasm. They literally march to their cars waiting at the curb, and speed away—to the nearest coffee shop, where they gather again, this time to discuss the antics of the "leader."

To be successful, a sales meeting must utilize the capacity of the sales leader to organize, plan, and coordinate. The sales meeting must be carefully planned, possibly with an agenda given to the salesmen before they arrive at the meeting. Proper notice must be given to all salesmen far enough in advance for necessary arrangements to be made. The meeting must be of such a numerical size that all members feel free to participate and find it easy to do so. It must provide the kind of knowledge that influences the salesmen to take a positive viewpoint toward the sales meeting. The sales leader must be able to understand and analyze salesmanship and then communicate his knowledge to his people.

DECISION MAKING

The members of the sales organization rely upon the sales manager for important decisions. As already discussed, the I-M-P approach to solving problems and reaching decisions has particular importance to the sales leader. Any decision reached by a sales leader will have some impact upon other members of the organization. Sometimes it will involve other departments. The essential point is that when a decision is reached which does involve another department, that particular department must be notified of the decision. It might even be worthwhile to include members of that department in the decision-making process.

For example, the sales manager of the automotive section of a national retail store decides to sell tires to firms selling used trucks and highway construction equipment. Since these dealers usually place new tires on all their equipment before attempting to sell an item, there is a real market potential. The sale of one of these tires amounts to several hundred dollars; consequently the total sale to an account could vary between $1,000 and $10,000. The credit department should be notified of this decision so it has time to develop the necessary procedure to investigate the credit rating of these accounts. The credit department might even require that a financial statement be prepared before credit could be approved. Thus, when the negotiations are in progress with the potential customer, it could be helpful to include a member of the credit department so that the firm could hear firsthand what steps would be required in establishing proper credit procedures.

OPEN-DOOR POLICY

The necessity of making decisions is closely related to the degree of freedom the salesmen have of seeing their sales leader. It has already been established that to become a professional salesman there must be within the salesman the motivation to use his energies in an effective manner with a positive attitude to fulfill the needs of the customer. Since these ingredients are essential to the success of a salesman, it can be assumed that when this salesman discusses matters with his sales leader, he is doing so with the motive of furthering the goals of the sales organization. The leader who recognizes this will gain the trust of his organization. His salesmen will bring him the important feedback from the sales territories that he needs in order to maintain an accurate understanding of the marketing and sales environment for the firm's products. Consequently, an element of good sales leadership is that the leader always makes himself available to his salesmen. If he is in conference at the particular time a salesman wishes to see him, he will make arrangements for a convenient appointment.

WORKING WITH SUPERIORS

The confidence and respect of the leader's superiors is another essential ingredient of successful leadership. A good measure of that relationship is the result of leadership characteristics. A good leader must have the imaginative ability to construct first in an abstract form and ultimately in a concrete form how the past and the present of the sales organization are going to affect the future. When the manager develops plans and objectives for the future, this abstract ability takes place. Any time our thinking process deals with the future, we become concerned with the unknown; this is purely a mental process. Superiors are naturally dealing with concrete facts—sales figures for the month or year, rate of increase in sales over the previous year, percentage increase in the market as compared to last year. All these facts refer to happenings in the area of sales, and the sales leader's superiors become concerned with how these facts are going to relate to the future. Once a sale is made it becomes history; consequently a sales organization must constantly examine the *next* sale or the *future* sale. In working with his superiors, the sales leader should maintain a strong communications link with higher management involving all areas of activity—sales to cost ratio, development of the sales force, nature of the market, what competition is doing, recommended new products, concepts of reorganization, etc. The manner of accomplishing this is varied, including written reports, telephone conversations with superiors, and conferences, to name a few. Probably a combination works most satisfactorily. The important point is that the sales leader takes the initiative to maintain this line of communication. Once he establishes a working pattern with superiors, the superiors will tend to find time to discuss matters with him.

The concern for proper communications cannot be overlooked at any point in the selling system. The act of communicating is so fundamental that it occurs in every part of human interaction. To say that it becomes important in maintaining a strong position within the sales organization is simply placing special emphasis upon the broad subject of communications. It is an understandable and acceptable fact that upper management is going to make its decisions on the basis of facts communicated to it. If these facts do not include information from the sales leader, then upper management is going to base its judgments and decisions on the facts available or on whatever top management is able to develop. This does not necessarily mean that the decisions of upper management would be detrimental to the sales leader and his sales organization, but it does mean that the decisions are reached without the assistance and expertise of the sales leader and therefore offer no real substance from the organizational level of the sales group.

STYLES OF LEADERSHIP

From a traditional viewpoint, there are three styles of leadership: autocratic, democratic, and laissez faire. Autocratic refers to the leader who makes all the decisions. In this case there is but one decision maker in the organization; the remaining members of the organization carry out the results of the decision. The laissez faire approach occurs when the leader releases all his decision-making authority and responsibility to other members of the organization and allows them to reach their own decisions. The democratic approach probably works best for a sales organization. This takes place when the sales leader develops particular guidelines specifying the types of decisions which can be made freely by the salesmen and those which will be made by the sales manager. At the same time, the sales leader leaves the door open for the salesmen to consult with him if they feel that the sales manager can be of particular value in analyzing a problem or reaching a decision.

Much has been written about the democratic process of leadership. Despite the fact that it offers the greatest avenue leading toward a successful sales organization, this approach seldom functions properly. This is somewhat of a paradox, since the democratic leader almost without exception, assuming necessary ability and experience, is the more successful sales leader. The reason the democratic sales leader is successful is that professional salesmanship is a continual decision-making process in which the individual salesman must learn to plan and set objectives for himself. The sales leader who develops the competency within salesmen to make decisions *at the point of sale*, or closely related thereto, will have a more effective sales organization, one in which the salesmen will continue to grow in their ability.

The reason that the democratic style of leadership is the exception rather than the rule is because leaders find it difficult to relinquish the power they have acquired through their position of leadership. By allowing the salesman to develop his own decision-making process, the sales leader is also giving him the power and authority to make the decisions. For some leaders this is difficult to do. Also, this style of leadership requires faith and trust in the sales organization. If the leader lacks this faith and trust, the development of the democratic approach should not even be attempted. Again, the ability to influence positively the behavior of the sales organization depends upon the interaction of the particular backgrounds of the salesmen and the perceptive ability of the leader. The sales leader must be able to understand and then communicate his knowledge to his people.

CONCLUSION

A large part of a sales manager's job is management. He must be able to organize and delegate. He must plan. He must coordinate. As part of management, he must take a broad view of the sales department in relation to every other department of the business. The sales leader must be able to deal successfully with a wide range of people, on a continuing basis, which can be quite different from dealing with individual customers on a temporary or once-in-a-while basis. In a sense, this is much the same as the difference in the type of person you would choose to marry compared to the person that is a pleasant date. The sales leader must "wear" well with people, from his staff to other elements of company management to key accounts. Frequently a sales manager exists primarily to coordinate the efforts of the sales organization and to help each member of the team manage himself. The more you can understand and use personal sales management, the better you will be as a salesman and the better your potential for advancement will be.

PROBLEMS

1. Will a good salesman always make a good sales manager? Explain.

2. What factors affect a sales manager's approach to leading his sales organization?

3. How can a sales manager influence a new salesman to increase his sales performance?

4. How would you suggest a sales manager approach a salesman with 25 years of selling experience in attempting to influence his selling effectiveness?

5. What inputs are necessary for a profitable sales meeting?

6. How can the I-M-P approach to reaching decisions be of value to the sales manager in effectively leading the sales organization?

7. What does the open-door policy imply?

8. How does an efficient sales leader link the past and present with the future?

9. Discuss the relationship between effective communication and good leadership.

10. Discuss the three styles of leadership.

11. Why does the democratic approach to leadership often fail?

12. The district manager of the ABC Computer Corporation is reviewing the personnel files of his sales organization in order to determine who should be appointed to the newly developed post of area manager for the city of San Francisco. The position would entail responsibility for five salesmen and an office force of three. Since this is principally a selling activity, the district manager decides to make the sales records of each applicant the sole determinant of his choice. Evaluate this decision in terms of an effective sales organization in San Francisco.

13. The Denver sales manager for Developmental Forms, Inc., has been with the firm for 18 years. He is forty-six years of age and was graduated from the University of Michigan with a major in business administration. His sales force includes Bill Jayson, fifty-eight, who has been with the company since it was formed in 1938. Jayson has no college education, but was a printer before coming to Developmental Forms. Mark Langley, forty-two, recently joined the firm. He has an excellent sales background in the field of insurance, with 10 years of experience, but has spent only 18 months with Developmental Forms, Inc. He also has a degree in business administration from San Francisco State. Fred Peterson, twenty-three, recently returned from a 2-year military tour. Prior to that he spent 4 years at the University of Southern California and was graduated with a degree in business administration. He has been with the firm

6 months and is enthusiastic about his chances for advancement. Would the Denver sales manager develop and manage the ability of each salesman on this sales force in the same manner? Discuss your answer.

14. If you were the sales manager for the Independent Bottling Company, would you make it a point to tell your sales organization that you want them to come to you with all their problems and to always feel free to walk into your office? Discuss.

15. Interview a sales manager and report to the class his method of sales leadership.

16. Which style of leadership best suits your personal ability? Why?

17. Develop a sales training program, one month in length, for a firm of your choosing.

18. If you were a sales manager, what characteristic(s) would you seek to develop in your salesmen to prepare them for greater responsibilities?

See pages 274–277 for a case study.

Chapter Fifteen
Using Performance Evaluation
in Professional Selling

Chapter Fourteen discussed the characteristics essential to sales leadership. In this chapter sales leadership is applied in evaluating sales results and relating this evaluation to increased sales productivity. In order to understand the importance of performance evaluation it is necessary to coordinate this evaluation with the selling system. Since the primary function of a sales organization is to sell products, all activity of that organization must in some way be evaluated in terms of selling activity. Performance evaluation is a continuous process whereby the sales manager assists the employee in developing his human resources for attaining *increased* effectiveness in working toward corporate goals, at the same time satisfying more fully personal goals.

ELEMENTS NECESSARY FOR PROPER PERFORMANCE EVALUATION

Three specific elements are necessary in utilizing the evaluation process effectively. Since this area of activity will involve a considerable amount of the sales manager's time and consequently weigh heavily in evaluating his success as a manager, the importance of these points cannot be overemphasized. They are (1) establishing standards of performance, (2) measuring current performance in terms of established standards, and (3) taking positive action intended to bring performance in line with predetermined standards. Each of these will be discussed in detail.

ESTABLISHING STANDARDS OF PERFORMANCE

The importance of communication has been discussed through the earlier chapters, principally the basic communication of mutual awareness by salesman and customer that a product satisfied a need. Communication implies that the recipient of the communiqué through some outward manifestation—words, signs, or gestures—understands the meaning intended by the sender. *Effective communication occurs when the recipient takes the action suggested by the sender.* Effective communication plays a dominant role in the establishment of valid standards of performance. Both the salesman and the sales manager must clearly understand the standards of performance, or goals, and accept the fact that they can be accomplished.

These standards of performance, or goals, are most effective when they are developed mutually by the salesman and the sales manager. In order to do this, there must be basic trust on the part of the sales manager that his salesmen are of the caliber to offer an acceptable contribution to the sales organization. If this is not the case, the sales manager should evaluate his process of selection, training, or development, or himself. When the salesman becomes involved in the specific development of standards of achievement, he becomes an active agent in the appraisal process and shares responsibility for developing his potential. The proper role of the superior then is one which falls naturally to him: that of helping the salesman relate his career planning to the needs and realities of the sales organization.

The emphasis here is on the future rather than the past. The purpose of the performance standard is to establish realistic targets and to seek the most effective means to reach them. Appraisal thus becomes a means to a constructive end. The sales manager can take a giant step forward in developing a positive attitude within the salesman, for he helps the individual salesman integrate personal goals with the requirements of the organization so that both are served. The use of standards of performance in this manner will greatly enhance the use of the performance evaluation process to achieve greater motivation and more effective development of the individual salesman.

MEASURING PERFORMANCE IN TERMS OF ESTABLISHED STANDARDS

The sales manager utilizes standards as the foundation for his evaluation process. These standards can involve various aspects of the selling activity and may include profit, share of the market, cost per unit sold, and increased sales over the previous year. Probably a combination of these will be used. The degree to which a person can make accurate judgments about others is a function of his general ability to judge specific situations. The following factors influence the sales manager's ability to judge other salesmen.

Intelligence and perception: Understanding people is largely a matter of intelligence and of perceiving relations between past and present activities, between expressive behavior and inner traits, between cause and effect. There seems to be a positive relationship between intelligence and the ability to judge analytically.

Emotional stability: Poor judges tend to be poorly adjusted and more likely to allow personal biases to affect their judgments.

Social relations: Common sense would suggest that a person who possesses good ability to judge people is able to use this ability to advantage in situations requiring social skill, in leadership or salesmanship. Conversely, the person who possesses these social skills is likely to be a good judge of people.

The ability to judge others has been considered as a personality trait. The main attributes of the ability to judge others seem to lie in three areas: (1) appropriate judgmental norms, (2) judging ability, and (3) motivation. The relevant judging ability seems to be a combination of general intelligence and social intelligence. Probably the most important of all is motivation. If the sales manager is motivated to make accurate judgments about his salesmen, and if he feels himself free to be objective, then he has a good chance of achieving his aim.

There are two primary means of accomplishing the evaluation process. One is continuous observation and discussion with the employee at his work, with particular attention to activities demonstrating either unusual accomplishment or the need for assistance or training. This is done on an almost daily basis. The second is the formal evaluation process which involves performance over a period of time. Usually it is formal in nature in that an evaluation form or technique is used to relate the salesman's characteristics and achievements over the time span to specific areas. These areas might include product knowledge, enthusiasm, and ability to fulfill objectives, plan his sales program, preside at sales meetings, etc.

TAKING POSITIVE ACTION TO BRING PERFORMANCE IN LINE WITH PREDETERMINED STANDARDS

The major value of performance evaluation is that it improves the work performance of *both* the salesman and the sales manager. The personal characteristics of the sales manager necessary to proper performance evaluation again play a key role. Norman Maier discusses the following three approaches of utilizing performance evaluation to increase the effectiveness of the selling system.[1]

The Tell-and-Sell Method

In this approach the fairness of the evaluation by the sales manager is assumed. The sales manager seeks to let the salesman know how he is doing, to gain his acceptance of the evaluation, and to get him to follow the plan outline for his improvement.

It is not unusual for salesmen to regard their sales manager's expectations as unreasonable, their criticisms as unjustified, and the methods of work they suggest as inefficient. Frequently the problem is one of attitude rather than motivation. If the sales manager can influence the salesman's attitude in such a manner that the salesman adjusts to the criticism, *then* the salesman can be motivated to achieve more positively in the future. For example, if the sales manager openly points out that everyone in the organization is evaluated, or that everybody gets criticized, the salesman is more likely to take the evaluation in a positive light. Once this is achieved, the salesman is more likely to be motivated to change.

This approach has its greatest potential with young and new employees who are inexperienced and insecure and want the assurance of an authority figure. Since the tell-and-sell type of interview makes no provisions for *upward com-*

---

[1] Norman R. F. Maier, *The Appraisal Interview: Objectives, Methods, and Skills*, John Wiley & Sons, Inc., New York, 1958.

munication (from salesman to sales manager), it tends to perpetuate existing values. Although changes may occur effectively when initiated from the top, or when approved by the proper superiors, there is no means of stimulating new ideas. Insofar as conservatism rather than change is desired, the tell-and-sell method is effective.

Tell-and-Listen Method

The sales manager communicates the evaluation to the salesman and then lets him respond to it. The sales manager listens to objections without attempting to refute them. In fact, he encourages the employee to disagree, because the objective is not only to communicate the appraisal but also to drain off the negative feelings it arouses. To utilize this approach, the sales manager must be an active listener and possess the ability realistically to understand the feelings of the salesman. These characteristics do not imply that the sales manager either agrees or disagrees with the employee. Rather, they suggest the possibility that the evaluation may be unjust and even incorrect and that the employee should accept only ideas which may be helpful.

This type of interview provides an opportunity for the sales manager to learn of his individual salesmen's needs and thus allows the superior to profit from the interview from the standpoint of supervision, work methods, job assignments, and job expectations. A sales manager who listens *and* learns may encourage upward communication in deed as well as in word. Values are also developed on the part of the sales manager: tolerance and respect for the individual tend to make the sales manager "employee minded" rather than "production minded." This attitude generally stimulates higher morale and consequently greater objective achievement.

The Problem-solving Approach

This technique takes the interviewer out of the role of judge or sales manager and makes him a helper. In this approach it is recognized that the *development* of the employee often is the primary reason for conducting an appraisal interview. The goal of employee development immediately establishes a *mutual interest* for the interviewer and his subordinate. It is important to understand that mutual interest is present only as long as the salesman's merits are being praised; it ends when the interviewer indicates that he is somewhat less than satisfied. The sales manager's function is to discover the salesman's interest, respond to it, and help the employee examine himself and the job. Communication may be faulty unless each person tries to understand the background, attitude, and experience of the other.

When a salesman is faced with personal evaluation, he tries to hide his defects and to protect himself by defensive behavior. As long as he defends himself, he is not searching for new or better ways of performing. If the evaluation is very threatening, it may arouse hostile and stubborn reactions which further delay problem solving. The objective of the problem-solving interview is to go beyond an interest in the subordinate's feelings to a discussion of the *job*; once the job is analyzed in terms of the way it is done, some time can be spent discussing the ideal working conditions. If mutual understanding of the job has been reached in previous interviews, the salesman can be asked to review the year's progress and discuss his problems and satisfactions.

The problem-solving approach motivates original thinking because it stimulates curiosity. Curiosity is a strong drive as long as fear is not aroused; problems offer opportunities to explore, and their solutions lead to new personally supportive experiences. This approach lends itself to strengthening personal motivation of the salesman. This intrinsic motivation can be an important ingredient in making the work situation, and all its challenges, enjoyable.

The problem-solving approach, like the tell-and-listen method, stimulates upward communication. The sales manager places mutual interests above personal interest and respects the problem-solving ability of the subordinate. The attitude of mutual respect cuts across barriers of rank, focusing attention on *problems to be solved* rather than on prerogatives of status and personality clashes.

CONTINUOUS APPRAISAL PROCESS

The continuous appraisal process takes place on a daily basis and consequently involves a higher degree of interaction between the sales manager and the salesman than does the more formal approach discussed above. The two appraisal processes are complimentary to the degree that if the continuous evaluation is conducted properly, it becomes a positive foundation for conducting the formal evaluation. The value of the continuous evaluation process lies in its application to operational activities as they occur. It is a daily evaluation by the sales manager of the salesman in his relatedness to the specific tasks assigned him. Because of this relationship there is a higher degree of interrelatedness between the parties.

For the proper utilization of this process, certain inputs are required of the sales manager. One, he must be aware of the general economic conditions of the sales territory and properly evaluate these conditions in terms of their impact upon sales results and sales activities. Two, he must possess the ability to understand the potential of his sales personnel. Three, he must have technical competency for the particular sales functions. Only by being familiar with the sales activities can the manager hope to be able to offer meaningful suggestions or make accurate appraisals of the salesman's performance.

Two situations are presented to develop this point. The first involves the field of advertising. The sales manager is training a newly assigned salesman to sell feature advertising. It is the fall of the year and the newspaper will be running a special feature section for hunters—where to hunt, what to wear, campsites, etc. In order to evaluate positively the efforts of this newly assigned salesman, the sales manager initially makes sales calls with him. The purpose is for the sales manager to complete the sale and thus develop a standard of performance which is understandable to the sales manager *and* the salesman. In this situation the salesman, as an observer, is able to evaluate the efforts of the sales manager and to see what is expected of him in his sales efforts. When the sales manager becomes the observer and the salesman the performer, the salesman is more sensitive to the evaluations of the sales manager because he has respect for the sales manager's ability and has objectively experienced the development of performance standards.

The second example involves a sales manager with the United Forms Company. The territory of the salesman is 100 miles from the district office; the salesman rents a local office and resides in a city with a population of 35,000. Approximately once every 3 weeks the sales manager travels to the salesman's local office to spend the day with him. He arrives around 10 A.M. and leaves about 4 in the afternoon. The sales manager makes several calls with the salesman, as well as discussing problems that have arisen within the past 3 weeks. The evaluation of the salesman's sales efforts is based solely upon a gross sales formula (for every $1,000 total gross sales in the area, x amount of forms should be sold). A large paper mill account has been purchased by a national firm. Due to centralization of purchasing, all forms will be purchased by the home office in another area, resulting in a loss of $10,000 in sales. *Problem:* How to compensate for the $10,000 per year sales loss. *Answer:* The sales manager refers to his gross retail sales guide and states that there is a sufficient amount of gross sales in the area to indicate that the lost sales can be made up elsewhere in the area.

The difference between these two examples is that in the first the salesman was clear as to what standards of performance were expected of him; thus continuous evaluation became a positive device in effecting increased sales results. In the second example the device utilized was a ratio of personal sales to the gross retail sales for the area. In itself this is of little value in relating the salesman's activities to the problem. It becomes beneficial only when the salesman can clearly relate the quantitative criteria to his territory; this requires that the sales manager understand the particular sales activity and its relation to the specific territory.

Continuous evaluation is an important function in maintaining an efficient sales organization, for it becomes a means of controlling the sales activity. The situation is not unlike that of a ship which functions to transport a cargo of sugar from Honolulu to San Francisco. The *objective* is to deliver the cargo to a wharf in San Francisco at a particular date. One control device is the ship's compass. The captain of the ship frequently checks the ship's course to determine that it is in the proper sea lane to ultimately bring it to the predetermined point. If the captain, upon checking the course, determines that the ship is not on course (this now is the act of controlling), he will take specific steps. One will be immediately to adjust the ship's wheel to right the course. The second may be an interview with the first mate. Before doing this the captain may take the opportunity of reviewing the first mate's papers—what kind of ships he has sailed, years of experience, etc. He will then discuss with the first mate why he feels this ship was not on proper course. It may be that the seamen under the first mate were not sufficiently supervised by the first mate and became lax. If this is determined to be the problem, the captain and the first mate will reach some agreement that there will be closer supervision by the first mate, and the captain will continue to check to make sure that this is accomplished.

The sales manager must remain close to the "course" of his sales organization. The control measure of performance evaluation becomes an effective device to keep the organization functioning toward the goals of the firm when the sales manager possesses the foresight to evaluate his personnel in terms of the *total* environment, including the sales organization, the economic environment, and the competitive environment. For instance, the sales manager of the West Coast Petroleum Company may determine that the sales of industrial oils are down in the city of Phoenix. In evaluating the problem, he may find that the cause of the decline is the sales personnel's lack of product knowledge concerning industrial lubricants. The solution, therefore, is to evaluate the personnel relative to their capacity to sell this product. On the basis of an evaluation indicating the lack of product knowledge, a special sales clinic might be initiated to assist the personnel in becoming more competitive.

This evaluation process by the sales manager is one of the most critical activities he performs. He is daily confronted with information related to sales performance. The manner in which he utilizes this knowledge in his future planning will have a direct effect upon his success. His aim is to utilize this information in accurately appraising the efforts of the individual salesmen within the sales organization and consequently gain the salesmen's positive interest to use their sales efforts in a way that will achieve individual and company objectives. If this is attained by the sales manager, he achieves a high morale within the sales organization—a high degree of motivation to achieve the sales goals. This kind of motivation can be given only *willingly* by the salesmen. The power to decide is recognized as a management function, but the accomplishment of the decision requires the assent of the individual salesmen and their commitment to the decision.

CONCLUSION

A sales organization is deliberately organized for a specific goal and/or goals. These goals may be at variance with the individual goals of particular members of the organization. In order to obtain individual commitment toward the goals of the sales organization, the organization must offer potential satisfaction of personal goals. Performance evaluation is a particular process the sales manager uses to help the employee develop his human resources for attaining effectiveness in working toward corporate goals and at the same time satisfy more fully personal goals. Only when the goals of the sales organization are supportive to personal goals can the sales manager assume that the salesmen can be motivated to greater achievement.

PROBLEMS

1. How can a salesman use continuous evaluation to increase his sales efficiency?

2. How can a sales manager use continuous evaluation to increase sales efficiency?

3. If you were a salesman representing a major insurance firm, which formal evaluation procedure would you desire the sales manager to use in evaluating your sales efforts? Discuss.

4. Why is motivation so closely related to performance evaluation?

5. If you were to evaluate your own sales efforts, how would you apply the points discussed in this chapter?

6. Why is performance evaluation called a control device?

7. Discuss this statement: "To be effective, performance evaluation must result in more effective sales performance."

8. Discuss the three essential elements of performance evaluation.

9. Discuss the functional relationship of performance evaluation to the selling system.

10. What is the purpose of continuous evaluation? Why can it be of value to both the salesman and the sales manager?

11. If you were a sales manager, which approach would you prefer using in a performance evaluation discussion with one of your salesmen: tell and sell, tell and listen, or problem solving? Discuss your answer.

12. Discuss the concept of controls as related to sales evaluation.

13. Contact a local sales manager and determine which method of performance evaluation he uses.

14. Contact a local retail sales manager and determine what standards he has established for performance evaluation.

See pages 278–280 for an additional case study.

Bill Powers, area sales manager for the United Pharmaceutical Corporation, was viewing the beauty of Mount Rainier at 20,000 feet. He had traveled the jet route from Seattle to Spokane many times in the last 5 years and always enjoyed watching the pink rays of sun hit the "big ice cream cone." Bill was also quite satisfied with the performance of Clancy Jones, the new replacement in Spokane. Clancy had been with United for 18 months; he had come to the firm directly from Arizona State, where he had majored in business administration. "Good student," Bill thought. "Came out of Arizona with a 2.97 grade point average; almost made the honor roll. It sure took a lot of persuasion to convince him to leave the sunshine of Arizona for this part of the country. But Clancy's done a beautiful job of adjusting. Spent 6 months after his training course working in the Seattle office and apparently became quite attached to this part of the country. Guess that's what made me decide to give him the Spokane assignment—his ability to adjust to changing conditions without constant supervision. Wish all my men had that quality."

Bill opened his travel case and began again to review in his mind the issues that he must consider while spending this week with Clancy: development of a market for the company's new anti-flu serum; projected sales of concentrated B-10 vitamins below expectations in the Spokane area; sale of five basic standards 15 percent above objectives. "Not bad," Bill told himself, "for his first 6 months in the territory. Looks as though he needs an assist in making his physician calls more productive. The increase in sales of the standards shows he certainly has made inroads with the hospitals and pharmacies."

The following morning Bill and Clancy were having breakfast together. After the general conversation concerning the weather (cold) and economic conditions (good), Bill asked if there was any particular area of activity where he could be of help to Clancy.

"Yes, there is, Bill," Clancy stated. "Since I have been more or less on my own here in the Spokane area, I seem to have lost the touch of selling these specialized drugs. Can't figure out what I'm doing wrong."

"Fine, Clancy," Bill replied. "Let's spend the rest of the day seeing if we can't find some reasons. Probably the best place to start is calling upon doctors in the Medical-Dental Building."

As Bill entered the car he automatically began looking for "Indian signs"—indicators of how his salesmen responded to the total sales environment. The back seat, he noticed, had three boxes of display and promotional material. He was pleased to see that Clancy had taken the time to segregate by account the material which might be of value to each account.

As they entered the doctor's office, Bill again became cognizant of "Indian signs." Clancy showed an air of authority when he approached the receptionist's desk and asked to see Dr. Knowles, in spite of four patients who were also waiting to see the doctor. After 15 minutes Clancy again approached the receptionist's desk and asked how long it would be before he would be able to see the doctor. The receptionist smiled and said, "The doctor has an emergency. He will probably be another 15 minutes."

"Another Indian sign," Bill told himself.

Approximately 20 minutes later the receptionist nodded to Clancy and Bill that Dr. Knowles would now see them. Upon entering the doctor's office, Clancy introduced Bill to Dr. Knowles and immediately reached into his sample case for a bottle of the anti-flu serum. He handed it to Dr. Knowles.

"Here's our newest product, Doctor. Why don't you take five samples and give them to your patients if they wish flu shots?" Clancy asked as he handed Dr. Knowles the samples.

Dr. Knowles graciously accepted the five samples and asked Clancy if there were any allergies that he should look for when giving the serum to patients. Clancy said that he was not sure, but as far as he knew it had no side effects. As Clancy reached for another drug sample, Dr. Knowles stated that he had a large number of patients yet to see. He thanked Clancy and Bill for their interest.

Six other calls were made the same day, with similar results. That evening in Bill's hotel room, the two discussed the day's activities.

"Clancy," Bill began, "I was pleased to see that you have taken extra efforts to maintain a good file on your promotional material. That includes your sample case, which was well arranged. You would be surprised at the number of salesmen who don't take the time to arrange their samples in an orderly manner. It certainly doesn't leave a good impression with the doctor if you don't know where your samples are when reaching for them. Your approach with the receptionist was excellent; in fact, if you don't mind, I would like to pass along to other members of the sales staff your technique.

"I feel your major area of concern involves your discussion with the doctor," Bill continued. "There are two areas that you could develop more fully. First, take some time this evening and tomorrow morning to review your product knowledge regarding this anti-flu serum. The kinds of questions asked by the doctors today are covered in the company evaluation of this product. Remember this about a technical product, Clancy—the doctor expects you to be knowledgeable in this specific area. If he feels you are not familiar with the product, he probably will not feel confident in using it. Also remember one of the principles of behavior of the attention step of salesmanship, that confidence begets confidence. When you present the product for the doctor's inspection, begin the conversation in a manner that will immediately get his attention away from the patients in the waiting room. One important point to keep in mind is that the reason the doctor is taking the time from his schedule to see you is in hopes that you will provide some information or products which will prove beneficial to his patients. For example, 'Dr. Knowles, serious respiratory ailments occur most frequently in the fall and winter. One of the major causes of these chest illnesses is the flu bug. May I show you a United product which has proven to be 93 percent successful as a vaccine against winter flu? Do you find this to be an ailment with a number of your patients?'"

The following day Bill used the show-and-tell approach. He took the part of the salesman and showed Clancy the way to use the approach. On two calls Bill was not very successful; Clancy joked about these and Bill took the jokes good naturedly. The following day Clancy again accepted the role of salesman with Bill evaluating his new approach before the doctors. The third day was "contest day": Bill took one call, Clancy the next. A score was kept to determine who made the most effective calls according to the ground rules.

Friday afternoon, as he was jetting toward Seattle, Bill was feeling satisfied with the efforts of the week. Clancy was beginning to develop the confidence to squarely meet selling challenges without the fear of failure. Bill smiled to himself when he thought that he probably helped Clancy see that the sales manager does not always succeed in every call. "Actually," Bill thought, "who does succeed fully in everything he does?"

PROBLEMS

1. Give your evaluation of Bill's leadership qualities. What style of leadership would characterize Bill?

2. Discuss the step of planning and organizing taken by Bill before he took positive evaluation steps with Clancy.

3. How would you suggest Clancy more effectively plan and organize his sales activity?

4. Do you feel that Bill lost Clancy's respect as a sales manager when Bill failed to succeed in all his sales presentations?

5. Present the three elements of performance evaluation found in the case.

6. Do objectives serve as a motivator in developing a plan of action?

7. "To be influenced to produce more successfully, the salesman must first realize that his effort will be in harmony with his personal goals." How did Bill apply this concept in his activities with Clancy?

8. Is the fact that Clancy was willing to speak honestly with Bill a reflection upon Bill's leadership qualities? Explain.

9. List those "Indian signs" which suggest planning time spent by Clancy in his preapproach.

10. "It is always easier to accept criticism (even constructive criticism) when you realize that the person doing the evaluating first recognizes your strong points." How did Bill apply this concept in his evaluation of Clancy?

11. What do you think of Bill's show-and-tell approach to developing a means of implementing objectives?

12.   Do you feel that Bill's continuous evaluation procedure will have a positive effect upon Clancy's future efforts?

13.   Using the selling system as your basis, evaluate Clancy as a salesman.

14.   How was the I-M-P approach used by Bill to solve a particular sales problem?

15.   Does the ability to make a sound decision play an important role in Clancy's sales activities? Explain.

16.   Why did Bill find Clancy's ability to adjust to a new geographical location an important factor in evaluating his performance to date?

17.   Do you think that Bill forgot to discuss the fact that B-10 vitamins were selling below expectations? Discuss.

PART THREE
SALESMANSHIP IN ACTION

The selling system as represented in Part One can now be applied to specific areas of salesmanship. Essentially each selling organization possesses certain characteristics of a general nature; each is concerned with determining the needs of consumers and satisfying these needs. Once the reader grasps the relationships among the various components of the selling system, he is in a position to apply these factors to any sales organization.

In Part Three, emphasis is placed upon an understanding of particular sales activities so that the reader may become aware of how to apply the selling system specifically. Chapter Sixteen deals with the concerns of retail salesmanship, including a discussion of the store environment. Chapter Seventeen covers the broad areas of activity of the sales representative or distributor representative. The use of advertising and the telephone to increase selling effectiveness is discussed in Chapter Eighteen. Besides providing an insight into particular areas of salesmanship, Part Three also demonstrates the flexibility of the selling system. The variables which are comprised in the system are related in a separate and distinct manner within the framework of each selling activity, and yet the selling system, as a concept, can be used effectively in each activity.

Chapter Sixteen
Retail Salesmanship

In the functions of retail selling there is the basic assumption that anyone present in the store expresses some interest in making a purchase. This interest can range from the customer who has read the most recent clothing advertisement and has a specific item in mind to the husband browsing in the tie department while his wife finishes her shopping. The distinguishing characteristic of retail selling is that the customer comes to the salesman rather than the salesman going to the customer. In satisfying the needs of customers there are two basic thoughts to keep in mind. First, to develop need awareness, it is important to approach *every* customer who enters the department. Second, once needs are established, an effort should be made to determine related needs. For example, if the customer buys a camera, there is now a need for film, flashbulbs, and other associated items.

THE FIRST IMPRESSION COUNTS

The sale begins with the first impression the customer gets of the store, the department, and the salesperson.

The store: Is it clean, attractive, well lighted, in good repair?

The department: Is the department, and the merchandise, clean, well organized, neatly arranged?

The salesperson: Is he neat and well groomed, properly dressed for the occasion? Is his manner one of friendliness and efficiency? Is he alert, pleased to see the customer, eager to be of service?

WORDS CARRY THE SALES MESSAGE

Use correct English; slang may give the wrong impression. Try to keep your language fresh, colorful, and varied. Use descriptive, dramatic words and phrases to give life and meaning to what you say. Try to avoid the empty, overused words. Watch the emotional tone of your words. No one wants to buy something that is "cheap"; the customer does want something "inexpensive," "lower priced," "moderately priced," or "budget priced."

ESSENTIALS OF GOOD SALESMANSHIP

Charm

Be interested in the customer and in supplying his needs. Treat the customer with respect and courtesy. Show an attitude of helpfulness and cooperation.

Curiosity

Ask questions to determine the customer's needs and desires. This shows your interest in helping the customer and helps you satisfy him.

Knowledge of Your Store and Merchandise

Know your stock and its location. Know the merchandise itself—its selling points and the benefits it offers and how it compares with other merchandise. Know the store's practices and policies, such as credit or delivery information, and what it is doing, such as the items it is advertising, where they are, the price, etc. Be ready to help the customer as well as willing.

The Welcome Mat

Watch for and welcome the customer. Put him at ease immediately, and show your interest in serving him. Remember, a customer is not an interruption, but your reason for being there. Greet each customer immediately. Let him know you are glad he came in. If you are serving another customer, say, "I'll be with you in just a moment," "Would you like to look at these while you wait? I'll be with you soon," or something similar to show you wish to be of service.

Greeting the Customer with Friendliness

If the customer is examining merchandise, you might start by saying something about the merchandise: "These tea sets are imported. They just came in." "This new shade of brown is extremely popular." If the customer is in the department but not looking, you might say: "Good morning. What may I show you?" Try not to say, "May I help you?" It is overworked, and it is too easy for the customer to say, "No thanks, I'm just looking."

When a customer says, "I'm just looking," you might say: "Please do, and when you find something that interests you I'll be happy to assist you." "That's fine. May I show you something new that just came in this morning?" "Here is something you might like to look at before you decide." Such statements show your interest and spotlight the merchandise.

When a customer has had to wait, say, "I'm sorry you had to wait," or "Thank you for waiting." This is the same courtesy you would show a friend in your home.

Sell by offering benefits. You tell the customer what the product will do for him or mean to him. For example:

Men's shirts: "These button-down collars look neat even on the hottest days."

Curtains: "This yellow color will give a sunshine cheerfulness to your kitchen."

Gloves: "These gloves will go with the suit you are wearing."

Bread: "This wholewheat bread has a hearty flavor that gives a lift to breakfasts."

Good salesmanship consists of satisfying the customer, and that must begin with finding out what the customer needs and wants. A few moments spent on this will make the sale go faster and assure customer satisfaction. Be a good listener. Most customers in retail stores are eager to tell you what they want or what they have in mind. Ask questions to draw out the customer; every customer appreciates your interest. Offer benefits to fulfill needs.

Using Demonstrations and Showmanship

When you say something, illustrate it. Do something so the customer can visualize what you are talking about. For example:

When you say, "This oven is unusually big," put pie pans in it to show how big it is.

When you say, "This suitcase will support 500 pounds," put it on the floor and jump on it.

When you say, "This raincoat can be carried in your pocket," roll it up and put it in your pocket.

Put your merchandise in its proper setting. Show it with confidence and enthusiasm. Treat it with the respect it deserves. If possible, show it in use or as it is used:

A refrigerator should be shown running, so the customer can hear how quietly it runs and feel how cold it is.

A necktie should be shown knotted, or with a simulated knot, and in place on a shirt.

China or silver should be shown in a place setting. Help the customer see and visualize.

Increase the Sale

Trade up to a better line. Do not take it for granted that every customer wants the lowest price line. Start by showing the medium or top line; it is easier to move down than up. Remember that the buyer's needs and his means may be completely different from yours. Give him the chance to choose want he wants at the price he is willing to pay.

You trade up to a better line, or give a choice between lines, by comparing the prices and what each offers. For example: "This model at $3.95 has these features (a, b, c, d); this one at $5.95 also has these features (a, b, c, d) plus these others (e, f, g, h). They are both excellent values."

Sell a larger size. For example:

Refrigerators: 12 cubic foot instead of 10

Ranges: two-oven model instead of single-oven model

Sell in multiple units. Sometimes a customer is willing, even pleased, to buy several units instead of one. It is all a matter of benefits. For example:

Hosiery: Three pairs instead of one; get extra wear because "leftovers" can be matched into a pair.

Shoelaces: Two pairs instead of one; have a spare set handy for emergencies.

Sell related items. Make a tie-in sale. For example:

With a shirt, try to sell a tie or a handkerchief.

With shoes, sell a bag, or hosiery, or shoe polish. (One salesman even sold brown or black polish with white shoes. To protect the shoes that were being put away for the summer.)

Sell an extra item. Have a separate item you give a little extra push each day. Show it to each customer. It can be a small item that sells on an impulse basis, or a large item or special promotion. For example:

In a service station, ask each customer about antifreeze, snow tires, lubrication, or an accessory such as a rearview mirror or a first-aid kit.

In a department store promote umbrellas to each customer on rainy days, or tell customers about a special sale going on in your department or another department.

The sale may be made just because you brought the subject up. Or the idea of buying may have been planted to become a future sale.

Closing the Sale

It is suggested that you review Chapters Six and Nine, on the interest step and the close step, to have in mind the philosophy of closing. The same principles apply to all selling.

Choice close:

Which: "We have this chair in emerald green, coffee brown, desert sage, and summer rose. Which color do you prefer?"

When: "When would you like us to deliver?"

What: "What color suit do you usually wear?"

How: "How would you like to arrange your monthly payments?"

Where: "Where do you want us to install this air conditioner?"

Ask-for-action close: "I'm sure you'll be happy with this. Would you like to take it with you?"

Physical technique close: Do something which the buyer has to stop you from doing or he gives consent to the purchase.

Impending event close: "This is the last one we have of this model, and we may have difficulties getting more for awhile. Would you like me to reserve it for you now?"

Techniques in closing:

1. Narrow the choice; help the customer choose. Suggest the one or two choices you think might be best, and tell why.

2. Close on benefits; help the customer visualize what each item offered will do for him or mean to him.

3. Analyze your "misses." See if you can determine how and why the sale was not made and what can be done better the next time. We learn by knowing the progress we are making.

Building a Personal Following

The successful retail salesman builds his volume and income through repeat business. This is one application of the snowplow principle. You can build your personal following by service and by being sincerely interested in your customers. The key is to keep a record of your customers and what you know about them and use this record to serve them better. For example, what woman would not be flattered by a telephone call telling her that a style she has been seeking has just arrived at the dress shop? What mother would not appreciate getting a postcard reminder that it is time to let the shoe store check the fit of her child's shoes? What motorist would not like being reminded that it is time for an oil change to protect his car's motor?

PROBLEMS

1. Discuss the distinguishing characteristic between selling men's suits in a department store and selling life insurance in a prospect's home.

2. Discuss six essentials of good retail salesmanship. How can you develop them within yourself?

3. Discuss three techniques of increasing the size of the sale.

4. Give examples of the choice close, the ask-for-action close, the physical technique close, and the impending event close for retail selling in a furniture store.

5. How do you build a personal following in a women's shoe department?

6. You are the manager for the men's wear department of a large department store. Items found in your department include shirts, ties, socks, and hand-kerchiefs. In preparing for your Friday morning sales meeting, your primary concern is how to increase the sales efforts, principally in the area of multiple purchases. Develop a sales plan that would fulfill this objective and present it to the class (representing your sales organization).

7. As manager of the shoe department, you would like to employ some method of increasing the sale of accessories. You realize that this could increase the overall sales figure by as much as 8 percent. Yet, your sales organization appears to have little enthusiasm for extending the original sale to other products. To develop greater interest in other sales, you are convinced that if the salesmen would recognize the potential in creatively selling *one* more item to each purchaser, they would begin selling a variety of related items. To attain this enthusiasm, you have a special meeting with your salesmen and tell them that during the month of March there will be a $50 bonus to the person who sells the most shoe polish. You explain that possibly the best approach would be suggestive selling, something like: "Do you have the proper shoe polish to match your new shoes?" At this point a salesman says, "Yes, but isn't that pressure selling?" How would you respond to the question?

8. Describe the characteristics of a retail salesman who left a favorable impression with you when you made a recent purchase.

9. Choose a major retailing firm, such as Allied Stores or the J. C. Penney Company, and determine the various positions a trainee would follow through in becoming a vice-president (or comparable position).

10. What can a retail salesman do to develop his own select group of customers?

See pages 281–282 for a case study.

Chapter Seventeen
The Company Representative:
A Sales Consultant
Who Sells Ideas

Recently a major marketing organization held a series of meetings to reassess the role of the company representatives within their respective areas. The firm felt that these discussions were so important that an entire week was allotted for them. The second day of these sessions was spent evaluating how the representatives could go about influencing dealers to become more successful businessmen. The conversation continually returned to the central point that here was a major firm possessing literally millions of dollars in background information and proven ways in which the dealers could increase their profits, and yet there was a uniform feeling among the representatives that the dealers were not accepting the information in a positive way but rather were suspicious of the motives of the firm. To these men it was a frustrating experience to possess the personal background and the firm's expertise as backup and not realize the effective results they knew were possible. One of the men responded to the conversation by saying that this lack of positive attitude by the dealer signified that the job of the representative was not a selling function, but rather that of managerial consultant, whose activities involve developing with the dealers ways of improving their operations. Another picked up the point by stating that he felt his job was that of a salesman and his primary responsibility was to sell the company's products.

These observations are only two examples of the many ways a company representative is defined. It is interesting to note that many textbooks refer to this representative as a "missionary salesman," meaning that the salesman does not sell to the consumer, be it an individual or a firm, but rather "brings the message" to the wholesaler or retailer who does the selling. This is an accurate statement, but it does not really fully explore the activity, particularly in today's dynamic market, where competition adjusts swiftly, customers' preferences change, and technology makes possible a myriad of new products. In light of this, the primary function of a sales representative must always be that of a salesman. This involves the sale of products to the dealer, for ultimately his success as a company representative will be evaluated in this light. Along with this primary function is a coprimary function which involves the selling of ideas to the dealer—ideas that can become the objectives and plans by which the dealer can sell more of the salesman's, or company representative's, products.

It is important to understand the subtle distinction between this concept and that of the representative being a managerial consultant and "bringing the word" to the dealer. The company representative does not *assume* that promotional plans or sales tactics will be effective for each of his accounts; rather, he uses the selling system to determine whether or not an idea can fulfill needs with benefits. In this approach the company representative *and* the dealer, together, reach the conclusion that an idea, a plan, or a sales strategy will be beneficial. In this chapter you will learn how to use the selling system to sell your ideas to the dealer in a manner that will have favorable results.

THE ROLE OF A COMPANY REPRESENTATIVE

Basically a representative is assigned a geographical territory which includes a number of business firms that are presently purchasing his products. The company representative is held accountable for all the activities that occur within that area. Categorically this would include the following:

Sales performance by accounts: Results are measured in terms of set objectives or by comparison to previous years' sales.

Promotional activity: This could range from newspaper advertising to neighborhood solicitation.

Service given to customers: The service activities performed by the retailer reflect upon the parent firm. A regional manager for the Buick Division of General Motors Corporation once said that the reason that General Motors has been so successful is not due totally to their products. He felt that their success was closely related to their smoothly functioning sales organization, which makes extraordinary efforts to assure complete customer service. He felt that if there is any "weak link" in the process of manufacturing and selling cars, it reflects upon GMC. For this reason, the sales representative spends considerable time working with dealers in developing sound service practices.

A balanced sales effort: Most firms that utilize the sales representative have several products to sell. It becomes a responsibility of the company representative to (1) evaluate the sales results in terms of selling the complete product line and (2) transfer this evaluation into productive sales efforts by the retailers or wholesalers. For example, the ABC TV Corporation may have a line of color TV sets ranging in price from $350 to $795. If sales reports show that a dealer is making 60 percent of total sales with the $350 model, 20 percent of total sales with the $425 model, and 10 percent with the $795, $650, and $550 models, there is a possibility that the dealer is not utilizing the most effective sales program. Unless the market is homogeneous, more of the $550, $650, and $795 models should be selling. The reasons, or causes, for this lack of sales must be first understood by the company representative. Then a plan of action or idea is developed. The cause might be lack of meaningful advertising, poor floor display, a lack of product knowledge by the sales organization, or a lack of interest on the salesmen's part more realistically to sell a product to fit the buyer's needs. Many salesmen feel "safe" promoting the least expensive models.

Awareness of competitor's activities: One of the critical responsibilities of the sales representative is to become aware of the operational success of competitive firms. Using the example of the ABC TV Corporation, it is important to the central sales organization to know from the men in the field what trends competition is taking. To the sales representative, gathering this information might seem a waste of time, but when the home office evaluates this information from various geographical areas, it is possible to determine a pattern. A West Coast sales manager for a major petroleum firm was very much aware of the importance of this information. Whenever he visited a sales branch, he would make it a point to discuss with each representative the related position of each account in terms of what competition was doing. On one occasion he was being taken to the airport by a company representative. On the way to the terminal the manager asked the representative what a competitive station was selling at the pumps (monthly gallonage). The company representative indicated that he did not know what the gallonage was. The manager asked the sales representative to stop the car and go over to the dealer *now* and find out what his gallonage was. It is debatable whether or not the sales representative obtained accurate information when forced into a situation like that, but the sales manager did impress upon him the importance of knowing all that is possible about competitive accounts.

DEVELOPING SELLING EFFECTIVENESS

One manner in which the sales representative can increase sales is to develop in the dealer's sales organization a greater skill in selling the product. This is accomplished in two ways. One is the use of sales seminars, which are usually held in the evening. This approach is particularly helpful when a new product is being presented to the market. Car manufacturers typically hold meetings in July and August across the country, where the company representatives and car dealers gather to examine the new models. If there are important engineering changes appearing on a model, an engineering specialist may be available to help the dealers and their staff, both sales and service, understand the functional significance of the product. The second approach is one in which the company representative spends time with the dealer selling the product to the buyer. There is a distinct possibility of using these two procedures together: first present a sales clinic, and then bring the practical use of the product knowledge or sales techniques directly to the selling activity. Here the sales representative is in a position to use the material presented in the sales clinic as supportive knowledge, related directly to selling techniques.

LEGAL CONSTRAINTS

The manner in which the sales representative develops his relationships with his accounts is influenced by contractual agreements between the parties. In the petroleum industry there are two legal contracts which affect this relationship.

One is the *lessee-lessor agreement*, whereby an individual dealer (lessee) has the privilege of using the service station facilities owned by the petroleum firm (lessor) for a period of time, usually 1 to 3 years. The other contract is a *product agreement*, in which the lessee, or dealer, indicates he will buy certain products from the lessor, or petroleum firm.

Another type of agreement is *exclusive agency*, where a firm allows a retailer or wholesaler the privilege of selling its products within an expressed geographical area. Exclusive agencies are frequently given to expensive clothiers, such as Hart, Schaffner, and Marx, Kuppenheimer, and Society Brand. The primary distinction between the lessee-lessor agreement and exclusive agency agreement is that there is apt to be a closer working relationship between the lessee and lessor, primarily because the petroleum firm has considerable investment in the physical plant.

Another category would be the situation where *no* agreement is involved, but a relationship evolves based upon the company representative being able to fulfill the needs of the retailer. This situation could apply to the pharmaceutical sales representative calling upon drugstores.

DEVELOPING A WORKING RELATIONSHIP

It usually takes a period of time before the sales representative acquires the confidence of his accounts. Therefore, the first goal of a company representative should be to establish a good relationship. The welding together of the wholesalers, retailers, and sales organization of the manufacturer into a smoothly working organization becomes the company representative's responsibility. Although this effort is not directly related to selling activities, it is so intertwined with the selling aspect that mention here is essential.

There are certain factors that will influence this harmonious relationship. One is the determination of a geographical area. This involves an area of market potential which allows the dealer a reasonable opportunity to develop his sales potential. A clothing firm may allot the downtown area of a metropolitan city to one dealer; if he becomes successful, the question might arise as to whether to divide the territory or anticipate that the present outlet can adapt to the larger market segment. Either decision will affect the relationship between the company representative and his account. Another example would be a petroleum firm's decision to build new service stations which could infringe upon the market of existing locations.

Another factor that will affect the relationship involves specific services offered by the firm to the dealer. For example, is a beer distributor responsible for placement of holiday promotional signs in retail establishments, or will the company representative also participate in the activity? When a car manufacturer introduces a new model, new service equipment may be required for proper maintenance standards. If so, must the dealers bear the brunt of the entire cost of this new equipment? Shaeffer pens are sold on the basis that the "little white dot" assures the owner that he may return the pen to Shaeffer for necessary repair at a nominal charge. The service must be accomplished through retail outlets, and therefore the attitude of the retailer toward accomplishing this function becomes a part of the service factor.

Another factor that affects the relationship between the sales representative and the account involves the credit terms upon which sales are made. In the petroleum industry, the product is usually sold on a "load to load" basis; that is, before another "drop" is made, the present amount must be paid in full. Before the transportation department places the account on its delivery schedule, it first checks with the credit department to determine the account's status. In the day-to-day operations, problems can occur. Suppose you are a company representative and you receive a phone call from a fuel oil distributor in Kellogg, Idaho. It is 5 below zero and the distributor has been denied the privilege of a dump of furnace oil because he has not yet paid for his last drop. He informs you that either you make arrangements to have furnace oil shipped to his bulk plant or he will call a firm in Missoula, Montana, that will ship the product to him. You have two alternatives: stand by the decision of the credit department not to ship product until full payment is received, or recommend to the sales manager that he override the credit department and ship the product, probably on the promise of acquiring payment at a specific date in the near future.

The operational problem of welding together into a working organization the various retail and wholesale outlets that take part in the selling activities is a real challenge for the sales representative. In order to develop a working relationship with his accounts, he must be able to speak their language, which involves precision in communications. A distributor in the hinterlands of Idaho does not express himself in the same manner as a distributor in Denver, Colorado, would. There must be a sharing of confidence in accepting each party's integrity and intentions. Each must have an intimate understanding of the other's background in the trade, so as to interpret his point of view objectively. Each party must be able to make an intelligent evaluation of the entire situation, to see the consequences of his action. The development of the positive attitude of mutual interdependence requires that the sales representative assume the leadership in the cooperative effort.

DEVELOPING THE SELLING SYSTEM

In fulfilling the role of sales representative, you will focus your efforts upon the intangible, or selling ideas. These ideas become the fertile garden from which the sales of products will emerge. Where the direct salesman, such as a business forms salesman, measures his success in direct reference to specific sales, the sales representative measures his success in terms of how effective the dealer is in selling to the consumer.

The need for planning becomes extremely important in this sales activity, because the selling of an idea frequently involves changing patterns of behavior or attitudes. This can be done only when the idea is presented in a manner which clearly specifies a *need/benefit* relationship to the dealer or his sales organization. Planning here involves clearly considering the relationships of the functions of the sales representative—sales performance, promotional activity, service given to the customer, and balanced sales effort.

An example may help express how these categories are used. The sales representative for the ABC TV Corporation is evaluating his sales figures on a large department store account (see Table 17-1).

From a percentage viewpoint, the account is down slightly over 2 percent, which is no real cause for worry. Evaluating the sales figures, he can see that there is considerable strength in the fact that the sales group has gone considerably over the objective with models ADZ and ATM, indicating a serious sales effort is being made by this firm. Since this is the first quarter of sales, it is quite possible that the salesmen are not familiar with the sales features of the more expensive models or with how to demonstrate these features. With these facts to use for action planning, the company representative finds *needs/benefits* (increased sales of models ADL, AKM, and AJI) as the basis for the following plan.

1. Company representative plans to work a full week with the retail sales organization, using this time to help each salesman increase his sales efficiency.

2. Use $1,000 on cooperative advertising to promote the more expensive models during the week the company representative plans to work.

TABLE 17-1   FIRST-QUARTER SALES: ACCOUNT 107

Item (retail price)	Objective	Sold	Over/under objective
Model ADZ $350	$10,000	$15,000	Over $5,000
Model ATM $425	12,000	20,000	Over 8,000
Model ADL $550	20,000	18,000	Under 2,000
Model AKM $650	25,000	20,000	Under 5,000
Model AJI $795	20,000	12,000	Under 8,000
Total	87,000	85,000	Under 2,000 (−2.3%)

3. Dealer offers a special $100 bonus to the salesman who sells the largest volume of models ADL, AKM, and AJI.

This plan of action, or idea, fills the role of the *product* in the selling system. The importance of selling becomes more obvious when we realize that the plan involves a monitary outlay by the dealer. In determining whether or not the dealer would agree to this idea, the company representative now uses the *preapproach* mentally to relate this sales strategy to the dealer's needs. An important factor in this planning state is an appraisal of the dealer's attitudes and motives toward such a promotional plan. The company representative may develop a variety of sales activities, but they become reality only when the dealer commits himself and his sales organization to the proposed plan.

Based upon the above discussion, the following conclusion can be stated: When planning the sale of an idea, the company representative takes into account all factors that relate to the account. This includes company sales reports, activities of competition, and particular status of the dealer directly involved with the proposed plan.

Using his three points as the base, the company representative now uses the other steps of salesmanship in the same manner as presented in Part One of this book, always keeping in mind that his selling activity involves the selling of a concept or a commitment rather than a specific product. When the dealer becomes committed to the idea, the results directly affect the responsibilities of the sales representative, as previously stated. In the *interest step*, the company representative asks exploratory questions that focus upon developing the dealer's awareness of the need for increased selling effectiveness. For example, the company representative might ask these questions:

"Bill, have you had a chance to get an idea how those new models are selling?"

"Would you like to see a comparison of last year's sales to what you are selling this year?"

"Have you seriously considered the market potential you might be losing in the middle- and upper-priced market?"

"Bill, I know you are an outstanding salesman yourself. Ever wonder what could be done to instill your personal drive into your sales organization? We know a professional sales organization is the key to any successful operation."

Based upon the above discussion, the following generalization can now be made: The company representative utilizes his human evaluation of each account to plan the kinds of questions that will most effectively bring need awareness to the account. This is similar to any other professional "probing" to develop rational needs. The doctor also probes the patient with questions to determine the particular cause of his illness. It is the principal of the matter. The company representative who takes the time to develop these kinds of questions will discover that he is continually thinking in terms of the account, and therefore he increases substantially his opportunity positively to influence the account.

The *conviction step* utilizes all the inputs of the selling system, again emphasizing the sale of ideas rather than products. The idea here is a promotional program involving the use of advertising, a special bonus for the salesmen, and the company representative working with the salesmen on the floor. Using the is-do-means concept, *is* would be the promotional program involving the entire plan; *does* would be the increase in sales ratio of the higher-priced models and increased strength within a competitive market; *means* would refer to the benefits that the program would develop in terms of personal values to the dealer. It could include greater profits; a stronger sales organization, resulting in gaining a higher share of the market; the recognition by the other dealers within the company framework that you have the market perceptiveness to implement such a program. Whatever selling needs the company representative develops, this is the area where he presents the plan he developed in the preapproach. However, when he presents it he does so in terms of *benefits to fulfill needs*, not as merely a plan. The impact of this approach cannot be overemphasized. When the company representative bases his plan upon needs/benefits, it becomes a positive factor in developing the strength of the dealer. On the other hand, if he were to use the same plan to overcome the *lack* of sales in the middle and upper price range, the plan would become a negative force in overcoming a weakness on the part of the dealer, and the dealer might fail to recognize its positive impact because he felt it to be a form of criticism.

The *desire step* becomes a matter of following the techniques expressed in the selling system. *Benefits lost* would be the lost sales in the middle and upper price ranges. *Benefits offered* would be a revitalization of sales efforts toward this market by the sales organization. *Benefits used*, using the present tense, could be visualization of the impact of newly found sales effectiveness. The *close step* would be a determination of when the promotional plan could be initiated. The choice close could be used: "Should we use this promotional approach the week before Thanksgiving or right after?"

CONCLUSION

This chapter raises the question of the primary function of a company representative—salesman or business consultant. Using the selling system as the basis of our rationale, we must conclude that the function of a company representative is that of a *professional* salesman who concerns himself with not only the direct selling of his firm's products, but also the selling of *ideas* by which the dealers and wholesalers who sell to the consumer become more successful. In order to do this successfully, the sales representative must be a sales consultant, particularly in his ability to evaluate the flow of sales activity involving sales results, new products offered by competition, pricing and promotional activities, and selling environment of each dealer. Yet, in the final analysis, the success of the company representative will depend upon his ability to use the selling system in making the dealer aware of how the company representative's sales-consultant ideas can fulfill the dealer's needs.

PROBLEMS

1. Discuss the role of a company representative for the Chevrolet Sales Division from the aspects of (a) sales performance, (b) promotional activity, (c) service given to customers, (d) balanced sales effort, and (e) awareness of competitors' activities.

2. Discuss two ways a company representative for Whirlpool washers and dryers can increase retail effectiveness.

3. What are the differences between a lessee-lessor agreement and an exclusive agency agreement? Why would these differences be important to a company representative calling on both types of accounts?

4. Discuss three factors that could affect the working relationship of a company representative and a petroleum distributor.

5. Why do we say that a company representative is primarily concerned with selling ideas? What factors affect the planning preapproach activity in developing an approach to selling an idea?

6. You are being interviewed by Parke, Davis & Company as a possible sales representative for their pharmaceutical firm. Your principle function will be to call upon doctors and hospitals to explain the benefits of your product line in the medical field. Your beginning salary will be $750 per month. (a) What educational requirements should you possess? (b) What areas of study would be of particular value? (c) What personal characteristics would be significant? (d) Should you be flexible as to where in the country you want to live?

7. Interview a local firm which uses sales representatives and present a report of your impressions.

8. As a sales representative, would your relationship with a dealer who has a lessee-lessor agreement with your firm be the same as that with a dealer who owns his own building and equipment?

9. As a distributor representative calling upon hardware wholesalers, would you find it helpful to develop skill in utilizing the I-M-P approach to solving problems? In making decisions? Why do you suppose that decision making is such an important function of a company representative?

10. Do you sell an idea any differently than you sell a product? Explain.

See pages 283–291 for an additional case study.

Chapter Eighteen
Applied Salesmanship

In discussing the functional role of the salesman within the system, particular reference was made to techniques that could be applied to accomplish a particular step in salesmanship. In Part One we discussed the salesman in relation to the customer, particularly stressing the impact of motives, attitudes, and knowledge on the development of need awareness. In this chapter we will focus upon specific actions the salesman can take to improve his sales results. Although these techniques are not directly related to a specific sales step, they relate most closely to the planning discussion in Chapters Eleven and Twelve.

ADVERTISING AND SALES LETTERS

The classic definition of advertising is "salesmanship in print." If more advertising was prepared with this definition in mind, people would find ads even more interesting and rewarding to read, view, and hear, and merchants would find advertising more profitable to run. The same principles, and many of the same techniques, that mean successful selling to individuals also mean successful selling to many people at once, in mass selling through advertising. One of the most important things to remember in preparing or planning any advertising, sales letter, or other promotional material is this: you are always communicating with only one person at a time. A printed ad or a TV commercial may be seen by millions of people, but each person sees it as an individual. Selling through advertising is still one salesman talking to one prospect. For effective advertising, you "talk" to people; you talk simply and directly. You talk to them sincerely, and you talk to them about needs and benefits.

There are two formulas that are extremely helpful in preparing advertising. The first is the standard formula. This is its most used version:

Attention

Interest

Desire

Conviction

Action

It is very similar to five of the steps of selling, but the words have slightly different meanings. This may help show the similarity, the difference, and how the formula can be applied in planning an advertisement:

Get the reader's attention. Gimmicks, illustrations, and other devices are often used, but needs and benefits are especially powerful.

Build his interest in your message or product. Needs and benefits are the best way to do it.

Build the desire to buy. Make the reader see what you are selling. This actually corresponds to the conviction step of selling, and the key technique is to talk about benefits.

Build conviction of value. Give evidence to substantiate your claims. Give the reader excuses and reasons to buy. This corresponds partly to the conviction step and partly to the desire step of personal selling.

Ask for action. Let the reader know what you want him to do. Give him the information he needs so he can do it.

The second formula that you may find useful, especially for sales letters, is the formula for selling an idea:

Need: The need for your idea or product, the problem it will solve

Idea: The idea, product, or proposal to fulfill the need

Gain: The benefits to be derived

Proof: Evidence to support the benefits and to disprove possible objections

Action: The action wanted or recommended

This has been called the all-purpose formula. It can be used to tell your children why something must be done, to prepare an advertisement or sales letter, to prepare reports, for office or plant suggestions, or for a talk in favor of any particular course of action. Once you learn this simple formula, you will find yourself using it almost every day in your speaking and writing. The basis of this formula is one of the keys to all effective speaking, communicating, persuasion, supervision, and teaching: you start with your listener or reader where he is, with his needs or problems, and lead him step by step to where you build upon them toward the known and familiar, and build upon that toward the new and unfamiliar.

TELEPHONE SELLING

THE SALESMAN'S ASSISTANT

The telephone can be your assistant, a handy and efficient time saver. It enables you to multiply your time and effectiveness many times over. Often, you can accomplish as much in a few minutes on the telephone as you could in a personal visit taking an hour or more. One of the strongest advantages of the telephone is the fact that it can be used when it might be inconvenient or impossible to make a personal call, in the odd moments between other calls or customers or when the weather or other circumstances interfere with making calls. The telephone also has the advantage of being immediate and direct. It is often the most effective way to make contact with people who are difficult to see. Here are a few of the many ways the telephone can be of use to you:

Setting up sales appointments: Calling ahead is often good manners and a good way to organize your day's schedule for efficient use of your time. A brief call helps make sure the prospect will be there and ready to see you when you arrive.

Following up sales calls: Sales calls sometimes need a follow-up: to make another attempt to complete the sale, to confirm details, to pass on additional information, and so on. This can be done by phone instead of in person.

Following up orders: When the sale has been made, it is a good idea to check up to make sure the customer has been satisfied. The customer may have questions you can answer or possibly complaints or misunderstandings you can clear up. Whatever the situation, the buyer appreciates and values your interest in his satisfaction.

Keeping in contact with customers: In general selling, particularly for the salesman covering a wide area or many customers, it becomes difficult to visit every customer regularly and frequently. In many cases, it is possible to alternate telephone calls and personal calls. The customer is contacted twice as often, and you know immediately if a special personal visit is necessary.

Goodwill calls: Part of the snowplow system is to keep in touch with your potential customers. The telephone is a quick, friendly, informal way to do this, by calling prospects to congratulate them on something they have done or to pass on some information they may find interesting or valuable.

Handling complaints: When complaints and misunderstandings arise, customers want and appreciate prompt attention. You can give immediate attention by telephone, and often save yourself a personal call.

Hunting for additional prospects: In both retail and general selling, you can use the telephone to search for additional prospects. You can use selected lists, such as the birth announcement list for a baby shop or a neighborhood list for a service such as appliance repair. Also, you can use the telephone to check or "qualify" a list of possible prospects. As in regular selling, it is best to start with a general, interest-provoking question rather than a specific one. For example: "Does your television set bring in a perfect picture for all three TV stations?" rather than, "Do you want to buy a new TV aerial?"

Encouraging customers to order by phone: It is quick, easy, and convenient to order or to buy by phone. Many customers who will hesitate or delay going out to buy something will gladly pick up the phone and order it. Encourage your customers to do this; it saves your time and theirs. Many firms offer to pay charges on out-of-town calls. One reminder: Anything delivered in response to a phone order should be sent "on approval," with the customer allowed to return or exchange it if it is not what he had in mind.

SELLING BY TELEPHONE

Nearly everything, from shoes to subscriptions to structural steel, can be sold by telephone. Telephone selling is used more and more in both general and retail selling. In retail selling, particularly, the snowplow system is valuable. It can be used to advantage whenever business is slack, even before the store is open or after it closes. The telephone is also a quick and profitable way to tell customers that new merchandise has arrived. Using the telephone to sell on the snowplow basis is the difference between going out after business and sitting waiting for it to come in. It is a service to your customers and profitable for you.

Selling by telephone is little different from any other kind of selling. The same steps are followed; the same principles apply. The main difference is that the customer cannot see you or what you are talking about. Your voice and your words must work harder to help the customer *visualize*. The things you say and the way you say them must carry the full burden of the sales effort.

Speak clearly and distinctly, and with a smile. Try to keep your voice pleasant and friendly, and be sure to keep the tone of your voice low; speak from your chest rather than your nasal passages.

Listen carefully. Try to visualize the customer as a person rather than a body-less voice. This will help you talk *with* the customer instead of at the telephone.

Be sure you are understood. Since you cannot see the customer's expressions, you will have to ask more questions than in face-to-face selling. Keep checking to be sure you are being understood.

Use visual words. Use words that describe things vividly, that help bring a picture to the customer's mind. Specific words help: "It's the same golden honey brown as a cocker spaniel," instead of, "It's a beautiful shade of brown."

Watch your manner. Use good manners, just as you would with your friends and your guests. The best manner is one that combines directness with courtesy. For example, in talking to a secretary, you might say, "Mr. Brown, please," rather than, "I want to talk to Mr. Brown," or "Could you tell me if I might talk to Mr. Brown?"

Keep your call brief, concise, and direct. Because people cannot see you, long pauses or rambling conversation can become very annoying to some customers. Know what you are going to say, and say it.

Have your objective in mind. As in all selling, keep working toward your goal. If your goal is to make an appointment, keep working in that direction. Know where you are going.

Be sure you get the customer's name and address, particularly when someone calls you. Ask for them, and be sure you get them right. A direct question, particularly if it offers a benefit, is much better than a trick. "I'd like to send you some literature so you can see if this product will fulfill your needs. What is your name and address, please?" is far better than, "How do you spell your name?"

When Customers or Prospects Call In

A customer calling in to inquire about something you sell is the same as a customer walking into your place of business. He should be treated with courtesy and respect and made to feel welcome. The customer who calls in is almost always in the interest step of the selling, or buying, process. You should proceed with him on the same basis as you would with a face-to-face customer in the interest step. Ask questions to determine his interest, needs, wants, and desires. Ask questions to help him develop his interest and understand his needs. Lead him toward a linking of his needs with the abilities and strengths of what you sell.

TELEPHONE TECHNIQUE

The Appointment

The call to make a sales appointment is one of the most frequent calls you will make. Let us consider the appointment. When you call most business offices, you first encounter the telephone receptionist or the businessman's secretary. She will have questions to ask you, usually the same questions you have been asked a thousand times before. By expecting these questions, you can be prepared and able to answer them easily. When the phone is answered, say: "Mr. Prospect, please. This is John Carter calling." Do not bother to say, "May I please," or "I would like to speak to Mr. Prospect." There is no reason to "beat around the bush." Be courteous and direct.

She may ask, "What did you wish to speak to him about?" Answer confidently: this is another information question, not an objection. State your business, justifying your call. For example: "Mr. Jones, of the ABC Company, asked that I get in touch with Mr. Prospect. Is he in now?" "It is in regard to a letter I sent him. Will you please put me through to him?" "I'm interested in making an appointment to tell him about a new office machine he will probably find valuable. Is he in his office?" Note that each statement is followed by a question, a direct or implied request for action. This is a particularly effective technique to use with the occasional secretary who seems to feel it is her duty to shield her boss from the outside world. You can match the firmness of your answer to the behavior of the secretary. If the man you are calling is out, or if he is in conference, ask: "When will he be available?" or, "Will he be in his office tomorrow morning?"

When you are talking with the prospect and seeking an interview, keep your purpose in mind. There are only two things you need to tell him: who you are and that you would like an appointment. "Mr. Prospect, this is Frank James, of the ABC Company. I would like to see you tomorrow for a few minutes, about 10 A.M. or 10:30 A.M. Will you be in your office then?" How many things can he say to you? Here are a few:

"Yes." Thank him for the appointment and hang up.

"No."

"What did you want to see me about?"

"I'm too busy to see you."

"Tell me about it in a letter."

"I have no money to spend now."

"I'm not interested in your product."

"I buy all my products from XYZ Company."

For anything that he can say, there is an answer which will help you get an appointment. Clues to the type of answer to use are found in

The approach or interest step of selling, particularly in the principle of offering a benefit.

The close techniques, for you are attempting to close on the arrangement of the appointment.

The reason given in the resistance the prospect presents. This is the same as the principle that the objection contains the reason to buy. For example, if the customer says, "I cannot see you tomorrow. I'll be out of town," the logical and natural answer is, "Will you be back in your office the following day so we may get together then?"

Selling over the Phone

Many salesmen sell over the phone. They call up their old customers for orders, and many sell new customers over the phone. When talking to customers, a salesman must be sure to identify himself. The customer must understand clearly who is calling. The sales conversation over the telephone is most often a shorter sales presentation. It must be organized for clarity and speed. The salesman asks the same questions over the telephone when attempting to get an order as he would in person. Answer these questions before calling. Tell the answers to the customer when calling.

You follow the same six steps of selling, from the preapproach through the close. You are helping the buyer with the same five buying decisions. To help guide your planning before making telephone sales calls, think about these questions and answer them for yourself:

What is the purpose of my call?

How will my products help the customer? (What are his needs?)

What benefits will he receive?

What will the customer get out of it by purchasing now?

Be ready to answer any questions the customer may raise; always have your order blank ready on your desk and a pencil in your hand.

How to Answer the Phone

1. Answer promptly. No one likes to be kept waiting, particularly when he cannot see the reason for the delay.

2. Give a friendly greeting. Let the warmth of your personality shine through.

3. Identify your company and yourself clearly. Concentrate on this; take enough time to do it properly. We get so accustomed to identifying ourselves that there is a tendency to bark or condense the words, or to use phrases that may mean nothing to the customer.

4. Remember that one of the first things in the customer's mind is whether he got the right number. If you bark "Acme!" the confusion still may exist. If you say, "Good morning, this is Acme Appliance Company, Mr. Brown speaking," there is no confusion.

5. Resist the temptation to answer by giving your telephone number. This usually only creates confusion.

6. Identify the caller. There are any number of direct, polite questions you can ask. One way is to say, "My name is Dick Markson. What's your name, please?"

7. A secretary or receptionist handling a call can say, "May I tell him who's calling?" or, "What's your name, please?" when referring a call. The tone of voice is all-important; this is not a cross-examination or an obstacle, but a polite request for information to pass on to the person being called. The world would be a more pleasant place if secretaries were trained not to say, "Who's calling?" This gives the impression of abruptness and suspicion, as if the call will not be put through unless the caller is of sufficient importance.

8. If the caller must wait, or the person being called cannot answer at the moment, explain the situation in a friendly way: "I'm sorry, he's on another line right now (or tied up for a few minutes). Would you like to wait, or shall I ask him to call you?" or "I'm sorry, he's out right now. We expect him back about 3 o'clock. May I have him call you then, or would you like to leave a message?" or "I'm sorry, he's in a meeting right now and asked me to hold all his calls. Would you like me to take a message in to him, or could I have him call you as soon as the meeting is over?"

Note: In the last answer, it is recognized that only the caller knows how important his call may be. It puts the burden of deciding whether to interrupt the meeting on his shoulders, where it belongs. The secretary is being helpful rather than an obstacle.

When a caller must wait, make progress on his waiting time. Keep in contact with him, and keep him informed. If you are still trying to locate the person he is trying to reach, let him know. If the other party is still busy, let the caller know, and ask again if you can take a message or if he will wait for a few minutes longer. The same principle applies when you have to look up information for a caller. If you find out it will take a few minutes, let him know how long the wait will be, and ask if you can call back with it. The principle is this: Do not let the person feel forgotten or neglected. Keep the caller informed of the progress being made in serving him, or of your attention and interest in serving him.

There are several cautions on handling telephone calls, several things that sometimes happen, but never should. We discussed one of these—the use of "Who's calling?" Another is, "He's in conference." To many people this sounds pompous and self-important. It is just as easy and natural to say, "He's in a meeting," or, "He's talking with another customer." Another thing to guard against is phrases that reflect upon your own organization or company, such as, "He's out to coffee," or, "I can't seem to find him; I don't know where he went." It is just as easy, and makes a better impression, to say, "He has stepped out of the office for a few minutes. May I have him call you when he gets back?"

Do these things: Be courteous. Be sincerely helpful, and tell the truth in a friendly manner.

BID SELLING

In selling in bid and price situations when yours is not the lowest price, look carefully at the needs—the specifications. As we often discover, buyers do not always have a clear idea of their needs. This is as true of people who buy by bids and specifications as it is of the average buyer. If you can discover needs that only your product can adequately fulfill, or if you can discover needs that are not adequately covered by the specifications, you have strengthened your chance for the sale. You have gained a slight edge on your competition by rendering a real service to the buyer. Sell the benefits, and particularly your exclusive benefits—your strengths, your slight edge. Work to sell the difference in quality and benefits that make the difference in price. For a slight edge, look particularly to your *source* if the competing products are standardized. Sell such factors as guarantee, reputation, delivery, service, and availability.

Prove the price. Give a breakdown of the factors that went into figuring it, so the buyer can see how it was determined. You may be able to show that it is fully justified and that a lower price would seriously damage any firm's ability to deliver at the quoted price. Remember that if you can sell each item that goes into a price, the total makes logical sense. Give the buyer a choice of benefits and prices, especially if you feel the original specifications are not correct. Let him see and compare several bids from your company—the product exactly as specified and a number of other possibilities from a minimum proposal to an ideal one. Continually translate sales points into benefits into visualization. Tell and show not only what your product *is*, but also what it will *do* and *mean*.

ESTIMATING

Define your terms. Be sure you and the buyer both understand what you are talking about. An estimate is a guess as to the probable price of merchandise or service. It can be a rough guess or a detailed, carefully figured guess. In normal usage, since it is a guess, it is not a firm or binding figure. A *bid* or *quotation* is a firm price, an offer to do a service or supply merchandise for a specific amount of money.

When you are estimating, overestimate slightly. There is important psychology behind this. It is the idea of helping the buyer feel he is getting the best of the bargain, that he is getting a little extra instead of a squeeze. People always like to pay a little less than they expected to pay, but it disturbs them to pay even a little more than expected. Prepare your estimate item by item, explaining each one fully, then hide or code the total. The item-by-item estimate enables you to sell each item individually, with its benefits, cost, and value. It allows the buyer flexibility and choice, since he can make some selection from the items proposed. He can see how reducing the benefits will cut the cost, and also how cutting the cost will cut specific benefits. The reason for coding the total is to get the buyer to look at each item rather than the final figure, to let him get into the act by figuring the total for himself, and to allow you to change the total as the items are changed.

Be sure you know your own costs. Do not be too eager to make the sale. You cannot lose money on every job and hope to make it up in volume. Work on average. You can afford to lose on one job if you know you will recover it on others. Give the buyer as firm a figure as you can, based on averages, so that there will not be any "possible extra problem" for him to pay for, as having a sword over his head. Emphasize what will remain to be lived with after the job is done and paid for.

THE PHILOSOPHY OF PROFESSIONAL SELLING

Whenever you sell, you buy something in return. You must buy part of people's dreams and ideas—part of their loneliness, hope, or vision. You must buy part of the fisherman's thrill of landing a big one, and part of the businessman's pride in doing his job well. You buy part of the customer's joy of accomplishment—or part of his hope of accomplishment.

Selling is a profession to be proud of. As a salesman, you help people fulfill their needs. You help them realize more benefits from life. It is a worthwhile service, a fair exchange of merchandise and money. It is one of the most satisfying and personally rewarding occupations.

This is what distinguishes the professional salesman from the average salesman: He feels he is helping people rather than conquering them; serving them rather than tricking them; bringing them advantages rather than taking advantage of them. He does not need to apologize for being a salesman, for he has made salesmanship noble.

The professional salesman sells to earn money, of course. We all have the necessity of earning a living. But he gives full value and more, in service and benefits, for the money he receives. He sells, not for the love of money, but for the love of people.

PROBLEMS

1. List three questions that secretaries may ask you when you call for an appointment with a prospect, and give your answers.

2. List four resistance or lack-of-interest statements that a prospect might make when you are seeking an appointment, and give possible answers you might make. Remember the principle of offering benefits.

3. In preparing a sales letter, what point must always be kept in mind?

4. Prepare two advertisements for a 14-inch portable color TV set, using both formulas discussed in the chapter in preparing your advertising message.

5. Discuss five ways a telephone can be helpful in selling life insurance. In selling real estate.

6. List eight factors to consider when using the telephone as a sales tool.

7. Distinguish between a bid and an estimate.

8. Discuss four techniques in proper bid preparation.

9. As a retail saleswoman for high fashions, how would you use the telephone to increase your selling effectiveness?

10. If you are unable to reach a person through personal contact to his office, is it proper to call his office on the telephone in order to make an appointment? Can you think of any situation when you would not do this?

See pages 292–293 for a case study.

PART FOUR
SALES MANAGEMENT

Where Part Two focused upon development of the salesman's capabilities with the selling function and his relationship to the sales manager, Part Four deals with the other side of the coin — the relationship of the sales manager to the salesman and the sales manager's responsibility to the organization. Chapter Nineteen discusses the importance of managing the selling system within the formal organizational structure, particularly recognizing the importance of objectives, policy, and planning. The constant theme of this chapter is the responsibility of the sales manager to utilize his authority so as to hold the salesmen accountable for their actions and at the same time foster an environment wherein the salesmen's reactivity will grow. Chapter Twenty deals with those statistical factors a sales manager must utilize in realistically appraising sales objectives, developing sales strategies, and guiding the salesmen in their striving to achieve these objectives.

Chapter Nineteen
Managing the Selling Organization

The power and impact of organization is found in every segment of human life. An organization can exist only in a living or organic environment. The term itself is defined as *any vitally or systematically organic whole; an association or society*. Within this definition we find elements which utilize energy to bring action to some conclusion. "Vital" informs us that the component parts of the organization are of significant value; thus each part has an important role to play in an organization. "Systematically" indicates that there is a particular relatedness among the various components of the organization. "Organic" suggests that an organization must have growth of some kind, since the word "organic" applies to a *living* organism. "Whole" suggests that somehow parts become united in order to comprise a *new* body, or whole. Thus in a selling organization the achievement of particular sales results implies organizational growth and has the effect of changing the organizational body in direct relationship to the impact of the sales upon the firm. The organization is *not* the same organization after the sales are concluded, just as every living body is constantly changing in terms of activity and results.

SALES MANAGER: THE ROLE OF THE SALES ORGANIZATION

Accepting the definition that an organization is a vitally organic whole, implying *future* fulfillment and future growth, we can also accept the supposition that the term "organization" implies *potential* energy that can attain results when the elements of the organization are linked in a significant manner. The relationship, or linking of components, is of critical importance, for it is through this linking process that something new evolves from the individual parts of the organization mix. Perhaps comparative examples can best illustrate the importance of this point. The component parts which form an organization called a "tornado" (an organized body) include air pressure, a wind funnel, and land. Separately each of these parts has a particular identity but would not be called that organized force, a tornado. The wind funnel may be seen over land and is quite harmless unless the air pressure reaches the critical point where the wind funnel touches land or water. Once these three component parts are interrelated, we have a powerful organized force, a tornado. Notice that at no time does the land, the wind funnel, or the air pressure lose any of its basic characteristics; it is because of the peculiar relationship of these three components that a new force takes place.

Another example would be a particular organization classified as a "brick wall." The components necessary to bring this organized force into being consist of the bricks themselves, mortar, and the skilled labor (activity) of the bricklayer. The bricks, mortar, and bricklaying skill do not lose their individual identity;

rather, their identity is strengthened through identification with the organized force, the completed wall.

A sales organization comprises economic resources, skilled personnel, and potential customers; it becomes an effective organization when all these elements are united systematically as an organic whole. Unification takes place through the meaningful relatedness of the individual activities of the sales organization. How effectively these parts are brought together will determine organizational success. Consequently, sales manager effectiveness is judged in terms of organizational sales results, making it essential that the manager understand the functional activities required of a progressive sales organization and the relationship of these activities to the previously discussed selling system. The sales manager is given sufficient authority to effect the results for which he is held accountable. This authority takes form within the constructs of a sales organization; so it is that the principal activities of the sales manager are accomplished through the organization. For this reason the professional future of the manager depends on how well he is able to bring the organization to its true potential. The sales manager will display his effectiveness by developing objectives, wisely interpreting policy in maintaining operational balance, and implementing a plan of action.

SALES OBJECTIVES

Objectives are the ultimate results desired through performing particular selling tasks. Objectives and a clear understanding of consumer needs are two sides of the same coin, for a well-defined sales goal can be achieved only in terms of need satisfaction. Although many sales organizations fail to develop stated objectives thoughtfully, in reality objectives of some type are inherently present within any selling organization. The mere activity of opening the doors for business implies unspoken objectives of attaining sales that business day. However, the development of formal objectives becomes the basis upon which the sales manager utilizes organizational energy in developing a sales strategy.

Objectives can be long term or short term. Long-term objectives are desired results which are to be attained over a time span greater than one year; it is possible that no specific time span is set. Usually they are broad in scope, affecting the entire selling organization. The long-term objective of the sales organization of Del Monte Corporation might be to achieve a leading position in the sale of high-quality canned fruits and vegetables, with emphasis upon (1) quality product, (2) strong sales penetration in the grocery store level, and (3) strong distributor relationships. Short-term objectives are concerned with accomplishments which can be finalized within one year, are concrete in nature, and have application to a definitive segment of the marketing organization. The sales objective for the Los Angeles division of the RCA Corporation to sell 500,000 TV sets in 1973 would be a short-term objective.

Through the development of a selling strategy, objectives make possible "management by objectives" rather than management in response to crash programs and special drives. When objectives are not formally stated and clearly understood by all personnel, the solutions of immediate emergencies are dignified as objectives, and as such they become a series of short-term projects lacking cohesiveness and frequently contradictory in fact.

The sales division of Shasta Beverages, a subsidiary of the Consolidated Foods Corporation, illustrates the role of objectives. The long-term sales objective is "to create consumer demand through brand awareness by developing a strong product line, with a wide range of product flavors, thereby making it possible to exploit competitive weakness." Notice that this long-term objective meets all the requirements previously stated. It has a duration of time greater than one year. It is abstract, and universal, in its commitment to action. For example, the term "brand awareness" is an abstract concept and conceivably could apply to any brand which would create consumer demand. "Developing a strong product line" does not limit or extend the variety of product flavors available to the market, but simply states a sales philosophy. Short-term objectives would be the specific accomplishments which are supportive to fulfilling these long-range objectives; for example, the Phoenix district sales manager may have an annual sales objective of 1.5 million cases as a 1973 short-term objective.

A sales manager for Shasta Beverages used objectives as the basic framework in developing his sales organization to function most effectively. In practice, clearly defined long- and short-term objectives functionally interact in three ways. First, they allow the sales manager a well-defined frame of reference in developing a positive interaction with the sales organization, the large food chains, and the grocery wholesalers. All decisions and other managerial activities are evaluated in terms of their supportiveness to *both* long- and short-term objectives. This is an important concept, particularly in evaluating the impact of short-term objectives upon long-term objectives. For instance, if a salesman were to offer an especially low price on root beer in 12-ounce cans to compete against another soft drink firm, the action might result in a significant increase in sales and possibly gross profit also. The effect of this course of action might lead to the attainment of a short-term objective, that of selling a specified amount of soft drinks. However, it could have a negative impact upon long-term objectives, in that with the store managers favoring the selling of root beer the other flavors might not be ordered. The net effect would be that the "strong product line" concept would be weakened. As a consequence this short-term goal achievement could have far greater long-term negative implications.

A sales manager's position is one requiring clear decision-making ability. In addition, the typical on going decision making takes place with little time for reflection, let alone the opportunity to gather all the information one would like to have. Successful sales managers maintain their true perspective to the selling environment by evaluating their actions in terms of supporting long- *and* short-term goal achievements.

The second way that clearly defined long- and short-term objectives functionally interact is by giving the salesmen in the territories a clear understanding of how the sales organization views its reason for existence. Consequently the salesmen are in a better position to identify their selling role. With Shasta Beverages, this might be related to the manner in which the salesmen function.

Third, objectives mirror the needs of customers and in the process give the sales manager a clearer understanding of how his product relates to customers. Again, this knowledge is important to guide the organization in an efficient manner. The objectives of Shasta Beverages mirror the needs of customers in the three- to twelve-year-old-age group. The rationale which led to this particular objective-customer relationship was based upon these important factors:

1. Shasta wished to identify itself with children of ages three through twelve, who represent the third largest market potential age group.

2. A full flavor line is well suited to children's tastes.

3. Children are influential in family brand selection.

4. Brand loyalty could be created at an early age.

5. Shasta could be exposed to the entire family through the child.

6. Competition was concentrating on teen-agers and young adults.

7. Objectives had been successfully met in the past.

Once there exists a clearly defined, broad objective which validly displays a relatedness to a particular group of potential buyers, more specific objectives are formulated. When the functional merits of objectives are viewed within the sales organization, the concern is not with *who* develops the objectives, but rather with how they relate to the total effectiveness of the organization. They may be the result of decisions made at an upper management level. Another possibility is that the sales manager himself developed the objectives for his particular sales organization. Wherever their initial start, the sales manager would do well to evaluate their importance to the total organization and how his particular sales group can best relate itself to goal achievement. One final thought: objectives imply results. They are most effective when offering a realistic challenge.

SALES POLICY

In its broadest context, policy is a well-conceived statement or managerial decision which guides the sales organization in accomplishing its objectives. Policies become standing guideposts which are used as the basis for evaluating important recurring decisions. The quality of decision making within the sales organization is proportional to the quality of decision making at all levels of the system, particularly at the sales level. This relatedness of policy to decision making is so important because the operational environment of the sales organization is that of an open system, where the impact of the inputs into the organization, as well as the intended results, may vary.

For example, decisions faced by the Los Angeles district division of United

Petroleum Corporation differ from those of the Spokane district division of United Petroleum. In the Los Angeles district, which covers Orange County, are found 25 percent of all the automobiles in California. By contrast, the Spokane district, comprising Spokane County, eastern Washington State, and northern Idaho, has a significantly smaller number of automobiles requiring petroleum products. Because of this contrast in market potential, the sales environment of these two areas is not the same, and consequently each district sales manager faces a different set of challenges. However, in both cases the basis of their decisions will be the same sales policies, those of United Petroleum. Since each geographical area of United Petroleum will have characteristics unique to that area, the sales manager's success will be judged by how well he applies sales policies to achieving sales objectives. Probably the interpretation of policy is one of the keys to a successfully functioning sales organization; properly developed policies should allow a degree of flexibility in interpretation so that they may become adaptable to divergent sales environments. One sales executive expressed the importance of proper interpretation of sales policy this way:

> I find that one of the main reasons sales managers fail to actualize true potential is that when they are placed into positions of management responsibility they begin to interpret policy as they think I want them to interpret it, rather than using their experience and good judgment to use policy as a guide in meeting particular selling challenges.

Selling policy might be compared to a two-sided mirror. On one side it reflects the objectives of the firm, and on the other side it reflects how a specific plan of action will be implemented.

Since selling policies act as guidelines in the realization of sales objectives, the sales organization is usually supported by specific policies which have relative application to that specific segment of the organization. An overall set of corporation policies would be too broad in scope to be of real value. For example, Shasta Beverages has a specific marketing policy relating to how the product will be sold. It reads as follows: "Shasta will sell to food wholesalers or food chains under the stipulation that the wholesaler accept the responsibility of transferring the stock from Shasta's warehouse." This policy is contrasted with that of the Coca-Cola Company, which has a sales organization selling directly to the customer, or retailer. Here are contrasting policies which have far-reaching effects upon the method by which each of these two beverage firms will utilize the elements of the sales organization to accomplish their particular objectives. The success of each will be evaluated in terms of how each develops its policies to meet objectives.

SALES PLANNING

Planning refers to the sequential action taken to accomplish long- and short-term objectives, using policy as a guideline. For the sales manager it involves an evaluation of his organization in terms of present performance, measured against past accomplishment, in order to more accurately predict its future effectiveness. From a functional reference point, the terms "planning" and "plan" should be defined separately. "Planning" refers to the activity of utilizing present and historical facts in developing sequential steps of activity through which the goals of the firm are translated into specific accomplishments. From an activity standpoint, the "planning function" is the key which brings about the intended organizational results. As previously stated, policy acts as a guideline which charts the course that planning takes. The "plan" becomes the finished product of the planning phase, specifying in concrete terms the steps which members of the sales organization will take. Figure 19-1 depicts the relationship of objectives, policy, planning, and the plan. Planning does not eliminate the element of risk, but it does provide the basis for stating in precise terms the degree of risk involved.

DEVELOPING A SELLING STRATEGY

Since planning is an activity, it forms the basis of all sales strategy and in the process makes specific use of the sales organization. To illustrate how objectives, policy, and planning can be applied to a selling situation, here is how the Seattle district manager of Shasta Beverages applied these managerial ingredients to a sales promotion. Beginning with the long-term objective of creating consumer demand through consumer acceptance of a quality product line, the Seattle district manager had the 1972 short-term objective of selling 1.5 million cases in the Seattle district. This area included the entire northwestern section of Washington State. Using these long- and short-term objectives, the manager evaluated the district's 1969, 1970, and projected 1971 sales performance. These sales figures indicated that the district had made increases of 6.54 percent, 8.29 percent, and 9.75 percent. The manager was quite pleased with these results, but he also realized that a significantly greater increase had to be forthcoming to meet the 1972 objective — a 13.5 percent increase over 1971. The manager felt that he would have to reevaluate the company's policy of "allowing the district

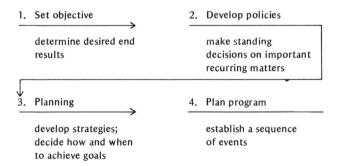

1. Set objective
→
   determine desired end
   results

2. Develop policies
   make standing
   decisions on important
   recurring matters

3. Planning
→
   develop strategies;
   decide how and when
   to achieve goals

4. Plan program
   establish a sequence
   of events

Fig. 19-1 Relationship of objectives, policy, planning, and the plan within the sales organization.

managers of Shasta beverages to attain the highest level of profit without jeopardizing Shasta's competitive position in the market." In evaluating the application of this policy (guideline) to the Seattle territory, the district manager noted these factors: (1) Shasta was a growth company and does not hold a dominant position in the soft drink industry. (2) The firm had in mind a sizable increase in the 1972 market position. (3) If his district was going to achieve this objective, he had to apply the above policy in a different manner. Whereas in the past he had encouraged his sales organization to achieve their sales growth solely on the basis of competitive pricing and superior service by the entire sales organization, including everyone from the secretarial staff to the salesman, now he would have to consider a greater price break in order to overcome the strong sales position of Coca-Cola. (4) He was convinced that the 1972 interpretation of Shasta's sales policy, although a new approach for the Seattle district, was the proper one and therefore supported the accomplishment of the firm's objectives.

The sales manager called for an evening sales meeting the last week in November. The timing afforded an opportunity to review the 10 month's sales figures of 1971 and provided ample time for the entire sales organization thoroughly to develop with him their individual approaches toward meeting the 1972 objective. The meeting was devoted to three related subject areas: (1) The sales manager reviewed the excellent 1971 sales effort, complimenting publicly those who were significantly instrumental in attaining those sales results. (2) He clearly presented the objectives for 1972 and gave an area-by-area breakdown of specific quotas. These were distributed to each member of the organization for their permanent file. (3) The sales manager presented two important tools which the Seattle district division would use to meet this sales goal. One tool was to reduce the cost by 30 cents per case. This was possible because Shasta had a much lower delivery cost figure. Shasta's delivery policy was to have the purchaser accept the responsibility of the product at the plant location. The price reduction would offer an extremely competitive position in the Seattle area and better utilization of organizational resources. Also, sales research done by the district manager indicated that the most popular flavor in his territory was wild raspberry. His advertising budget allowed $100,000 for the promotion of his 1972 sales. He contacted a local television station to determine the cost of developing a 60-second commercial to sell Shasta's wild raspberry, Seattle's "hot" product. The station not only gave him some accurate cost figures (between $40,000 and $50,000 to develop a 60-second color commercial) but also recommended an advertising agency which was capable of handling this assignment. At the sales meeting the manager showed a filmstrip of the commercial and gave a complete breakdown of when the commercial would be played to reach all markets over a 15-week period (Table 19-1). Note the district manager's exclusive use of children's shows, thereby appealing directly to the primary sales objective.

In conclusion, this particular strategy was developed by a sales manager who clearly understood the objectives of his firm and the policies which evolved

TABLE 19-1   TV SCHEDULE FOR SPOT COMMERCIALS OF SHASTA
BEVERAGES

Network	Day	Program	Number of commercials per week
ABC	Sat.	*Lancelot Link, Secret Chimp*	15
	Sat.	*Will The Real Jerry Lewis Please Sit Down?*	15
	Sat.	*Hot Wheels*	15
	Sat.	*Sky Hawks*	7
	Sat.	*Motor Mouse*	14
	Sat.	*Hardy Boys*	3
	Sun.	*Here Come The Doubledeckers*	15
	Sun.	*Smokey Bear*	3
	Sun.	*Jonny Quest*	15
	Sun.	*Cattanooga Cats*	15
	Sun.	*The Bullwinkle Show*	14
	Mon.–Fri.	*That Girl*	10
	Mon.–Fri.	*Bewitched*	8
CBS	Sat.	*The Bugs Bunny Show* and *Roadrunner*	6
	Sat.	*Sabrina* and *Groovie Ghoulies*	12
	Sat.	*Josie and the Pussycats*	10
	Sat.	*The Harlem Globetrotters*	7
	Sat.	*Archie's TV Funnies*	10
	Sat.	*Scooby Doo, Where Are You?*	6
	Sat.	*The Monkees*	5
	Sat.	*Dastardly and Muttley*	9
	Sat.	*The Jetsons*	9
	Sun.	*Tom and Jerry*	4
	Sun.	*Perils of Penelope Pitstop*	5
	Mon.–Fri.	*Captain Kangaroo*	12
	Mon.–Fri.	*The Lucy Show*	4
	Mon.–Fri.	*The Beverly Hillbillies*	5
	Mon.–Fri.	*Family Affair*	6

Average weekly impressions: Homes — 44,103,000; Children — 44,337,000

Total   256

from these objectives. He wisely chose to be flexible in his interpretation of policy guidelines in his planning. In the area of planning, he displayed a keen interest in the historical efforts of his sales organization, enabling him more accurately to develop a specific plan of action which would meet the objectives bestowed upon his organization. Finally, the sales manager realized that the interaction of objectives, policies, and planning could take place only through the efforts of the people in his selling organization, and he used the sales meeting as a tool for bringing together the human resources of the organization. This sales meeting is not to be construed as the final reel of a Western movie, where the hero rides his white stallion into the sunset and we somehow get the feeling that all is well with the world. There are certain challenges to be overcome before the objectives are met. What is implied is that the sales manager will best succeed with an effective organization which draws upon its total potential in reaching goal achievement.

THE MANAGER: ROLE OF PERSONAL COMMITMENT WITHIN THE SALES ORGANIZATION

The sales manager's success in maintaining an efficient sales organization rests with his ability to gain the salesmen's personal commitment to utilize their sales ability in such a manner that personal goals harmonize with those of the organization. "Commitment" in this sense refers to that mental decision by which the salesman judges his sales achievements in terms of personal values and consequently freely wills his personal efforts to the accomplishment of sales results. The critical point here is that he performs the action specifically to satisfy *personal objectives*, but because this personal objective achievement also fulfills a formal organizational goal, the salesman's commitment to action is viewed as supportive to the effective organizational results desired by the sales manager. Once this commitment is achieved, the individual elements of the organization blend together into a cohesive force called an organization. When this total commitment is given, and when the individual component parts of the sales organization are blended into a purposeful whole, there exists a positive acceptance of the sales manager's leadership role.

A comparative study of a symphony orchestra would be helpful in illustrating this point. Each member of the orchestra is a skilled professional in his own right (as each salesman is skilled in his own right). Each musician sacrifices a degree of his or her individuality in order to reach a greater achievement level than could be attained as an individual — that of playing a symphonic masterpiece. In fulfilling this objective, each member of the orchestra gains a high degree of personal satisfaction by following the demanding instruction of the leader (conductor) freely and willingly. The accomplishments of the symphony orchestra or the sales organization are in direct proportion to the personal commitment given to the objectives of each organization by its participating members. In the sales structure a degree of organizational success will be reached if the sales management is committed to the goals of that organization, however, it will reach a higher degree of success if the other members of the sales organization also find a direct relationship between their personal goals and those of the organization.

To return to the concept of the organization within the symphony orchestra, the individual commitment of each member of that symphony means that individually the members will practice long hours in order to contribute more fully when playing together as an organized whole. The musician's personal identity or nature is not lost because of his high involvement with the orchestra, but rather he emerges as a greater person for having the opportunity to become involved in greater musical accomplishments vis-à-vis the formal organization of the symphony orchestra. Similarly, the salesman's identity truly becomes involved in selling activity, and personal commitment occurs when the salesman's desire to use his personal skill and ability becomes interrelated with achieving sales goals by satisfying legitimate consumer needs.

Figure 19-2 illustrates how the goals of the symphony orchestra, as an organization, parallel those personal goals of the individual members. The objectives of the organization are so closely interwoven with the personal objectives of the musicians that they emerge as one. This occurs within this organizational arrangement because the accomplishments, or objectives, which the organization seeks demand professional skilled people who are already individually committed to the creation of fine music.

Figure 19-3 illustrates the parallel relationship between the personal goals of sales management and the formal objectives of the organization. Here we see that the personal objectives of sales management are in direct harmony with the goals of the business organization. Sales management requires this high degree of commitment, and the professional activity of leading the sales organization lends itself naturally to such a complete congruency of goals.

As can be seen in Figure 19-4, the personal objectives of individual salesmen are not in complete harmony with the organizational objectives. There is, however, some congruency of goals, and it is within this area of congruency between the salesman's personal objectives and formal organizational objectives that commitment occurs. Since so much of the potential organized power of a sales

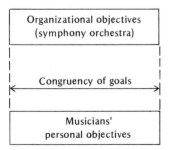

Fig. 19-2 The close relationship between personal and organizational objectives.

Fig. 19-3   With high personal commitment, personal goals can match organizational goals.

Fig 19-4   The relationship between the salesman's personal objectives and organizational objectives.

force depends upon the salesman's creative ability to develop customer need awareness, individual commitment by each salesman to develop his selling ability so as to enable personal goal attainment, and in the process also achieve organizational objectives, is of vital concern to the sales manager.

The particular methodology employed by the sales manager to involve the salesman within the organization-salesman relationship will depend upon: (1) the degree of harmony between the salesman's personal goals and the organizational goals; (2) the skills, abilities, and experiences of the sales organization; and (3) the emerging role of personal involvement within the sales organization. The personal goals and the organizational goals are very much intertwined with the skill level of the members of the organization and thereby affect the manager's leadership approach, which may be authoritarian, democratic, or laissez faire.

In order to obtain a strong commitment level, the sales manager should keep in mind the fact that he cannot expect his salesmen to have the same degree of congruency between personal goals and formal organizational goals as he has. How can the sales manager expect the salesmen to have his degree of personal commitment to the firm? They have not experienced the thrill of managerial involvement in major organizational decisions, nor the privilege of dining in the executive dining room when at the home office, nor the large expense account — all supportive experiences which draw the sales manager into the bosom of the organizational structure. It is of little practical value to place the carrot in front of the salesman by suggesting that, if he develops the intensity of commitment given by the sales manager, someday he will be as successful as that manager — and share in his privileges. Rather than attempting to obtain this level of commitment, and thereby risk a negative reaction by the sales organization, the sales manager should be realistic in accepting the area of goal congruency that exists and deepen the commitment within this area.

Members of an organization at different structural levels may view that organization from various perspectives. Peter Drucker expressed these variances in perspective in this manner:

> Each of the groups sees the same thing, the enterprise, from a different viewpoint and within a different angle of vision. What one group sees as obvious and plain fact, the other simply cannot see at all. Each group, though seeing only a part of the picture, fancies that it sees the whole. And each group, convinced that it sees the whole, is convinced that its viewpoint is fair and logical. Present management efforts [to communicate] are, by and large, like the attempt to establish communication between a Chinese and a Spaniard by putting them both on the telephone; unless one of them knows the language of the other, the most perfect telephone system will not enable them to talk to each other.[1]

Thus is it that difference of experiences or perspective may deprive the sales manager of the common language he requires to develop within the salesman this personal commitment.

An example of personal commitment might involve the telephone sales personnel for the *Yellow Pages*. Basically their function is to sell *Yellow Pages* advertising within a defined geographical market. Specific objectives are clearly defined by the sales manager; these include the number of sales calls made during a day's activity, the percentage of repeat sales, and a monthly sales objective. Every member of the sales team will probably make the required number of calls, but the effectiveness of each salesgirl will vary in direct proportion to her personal commitment as judged by the percentage of customer reorders and new-account acquisition. This is where commitment to personal objectives becomes important. When the salesgirl relates her work activity to personal growth or achievement, the motivational forces which play an important role in attaining successful sales results are more readily applied by the sales personnel. An effective sales manager for the *Yellow Pages* would do well to become familiar with the personal objectives of every member of the organization, for like customer needs, the personal values of the salesgirls, which trigger commitment to objectives, will also vary. Consideration should be given to understanding the impact of sincere recognition, constructive performance evaluation, specially designed training programs, extra bonuses, and sales contests, to name but a few

---

[1] Peter Drucker, *The New Society*, Harper & Row, Publishers, Incorporated, New York, 1950.

areas of concern. The important point always behind the managerial function is that the intensity of personal commitment is related to its impact upon *personal* goal achievement, not organizational goal achievement.

In his effort to develop this commitment, the sales manager should evaluate himself in three categories. First, has he taken the necessary steps to become aware of the economic status and sales potential of the area? Second, he should reflect upon his capability to evaluate accurately the potential of each salesperson and to further the capability of each salesman by suggesting activities which would sharpen the salesman's performance. This requires an atmosphere of mutual respect: the salesman respects the manager's perspective and judgment in presenting him with specific suggestions for self-improvement; the manager respects the salesman's ability and desire to implement these suggestions. Such a working relationship encourages the important, but fragile, element of trust between parties. This element of trust may itself become an important commitment factor by adding to the personal goals of the salesman that particular goal of proving to someone of responsibility and authority that he is worthy of the trust and confidence bestowed. Finally, in utilizing personal commitment to develop the true potential of the sales organization, the manager himself must be a proficient salesman. He must maintain his ability to communicate customer needs to the customer. This allows the sales manager a clearer understanding of the inputs he must bring to the salesman in order to gain greater results from his personal commitment.

THE MANAGER: ROLE OF THE SELLING SYSTEM WITHIN THE SALES ORGANIZATION

A sales organization is unique in several ways. First, the sales organization is "people oriented" to the extent that every important area of achievement takes place in terms of human values — the relationships of salesmen to customers, customers to peer groups, sales managers to salesmen, and sales managers to sales organizations. Second, the sales manager must rely completely upon the salesman's ability to make the sale. A production manager may closely supervise the manufacture of a technical item and actually become involved in the production process. A sales manager, however, other than making a "swing through the territory," must accept the salesman's capacity to develop the salesman-customer relationship. Third, the salesmen who constitute the major segment of the organization require an organizational environment which develops in them a feeling of trust toward their capability and their efforts to attain sales results. When we refer to this trust, we are assuming an *effective* sales organization, one in which personnel are well qualified and sincere in their desire to achieve significant sales results.

Fourth, the sales manager continually seeks improvement of his organization by helping his salesmen become more proficient, adjusting individual behavior patterns where necessary and thereby achieving a more productive sales organization. In order not to upset the delicate balance of mutual trust between the salesmen and the manager, it is important that this behavior readjustment occur in a positive manner. The value of the behavior principle "Build upon your strengths" becomes of vital importance in positive performance evaluation and consequent increase in sales results. There is no faster way for a sales manager to assure his professional decay than to build his managerial philosophy on fear and transfer this philosophy to the salesman in the form of threats. An effective sales organization cannot function in an environment of fear and distrust.

Within this context the selling system plays a significant role in effective utilization of human resources. The selling system gains particular strength in its ability to function as an organized *human* activity within the boundaries of the *formal* organizational structure. Human nature, which forms the basis of human resources, functions best in a social environment where a natural sharing of experiences, challenges, and aspirations leads to shared achievements within the selling system.

Since the selling system is primarily people oriented, the functional value of the system is dependent upon how well the human decision-making process provides attractive goods and services to the consumer. It is by allowing salesmen to develop their potential by individually reaching selling decisions that the system really develops its organizational impact. The selling system is recognized as an open system in that there are certain inputs which cannot be directly controlled and thus results that cannot be predicted. These include competitive activities, customer reaction to the product, and the changing needs of the customer. Because these factors cannot be regulated, organizational impact results from proper application of the selling system by the salesmen. There is no one way to relate the component parts of the system, and the sales manager should encourage each member of his sales team to apply the system relative to his particular personality mix. The result is that the selling system becomes supportive to stimulating personal creativity, which in turn strengthens the commitment to attain personal goals congruent with formal organizational goals.

A STUDY IN EFFECTIVE UTILIZATION OF OBJECTIVES, POLICY, AND PLANNING

Moore Business Forms, Inc., is by far the world's major producer of business forms. With its forty-one plants in operation, Moore's 1970 sales were $388 million, with its nearest rival grossing $102 million and number three, UARCO Inc., grossing $98.6 million. The sales leadership of Moore Business Forms becomes even clearer when we realize that the total purchases of business forms in the United States during 1970 were $1.2 billion, and there were 500 printers who produced business forms for their local markets.[2] This gave Moore 32 percent of total sales in 1970.

[2] Forbes, *Moore Corp.,* Oct. 15, 1971, p. 39.

Moore's long-range objective is to design the most effective form possible to meet the changing customer needs. Through the years, dating back to 1899, when Moore purchased Boston's Kidder press, this sales-oriented firm has seen this objective met and surpassed many times over. In the early 1900s this firm produced the first Whiz hand register, making it possible to write sales receipts in three copies without inserting carbon between each sheet. After World War II there was the Speediset snapout form which had throwaway carbons in each form set. With the advent of computers, Moore realized this long-range objective in another manner. It developed a specialized technique of crimping the edges of multicopy computer forms (Speedi-flex), making it possible for the forms to withstand the pressure of the computer's printer tension and thereby use the computer printout in two, three, or more copies per set. This locking process allowed forms to be used in computer preparation of large payrolls, by printing the amount payable on each check and also printing the informational second copy. It immediately fulfilled major customer needs for firms which began running accounts received in the computer.

Moore also made special application of its long-range objective in meeting the particular needs of hospitals. Accurate records of patients' medical progress is a vital part of a hospital's function. In performing this activity, there was a constant problem of maintaining high sanitary conditions, since carbon from the forms was smearing fingers, uniforms, and hospital items. To meet a particular customer need, Moore went to "ncr" (no carbon required) paper, a specially treated paper which transfers a carbon copy to all subsequent sheets when pressure is applied to the original sheet.

Moore's sales policy, used as a guideline in successfully meeting the firm's objective, is to rely heavily upon management to provide a master system of controlling customer reordering and maintaining a record of competitive accounts, complete with potential reorder dates by the user and the price paid for the form. Because of the Moore's high volume and efficiency, each sales manager is permitted to cut prices in order to maintain a high volume. As 1970 indicates, competition cannot meet Moore head on. In that year Standard Register Co. made no sales gains and had a 12 percent drop in profits, while Moore raised sales 8.3 percent to $431.8 million (this figure includes the sale of forms in the United States as well as in other parts of the world), a profit increase of 5.1 percent. Even with price cutting, Moore netted better than 11 percent on stockholders' equity. Moore's management denies that this sales policy crushes the competition through sheer size. David Barr, executive officer, expresses the competition relationship in terms of organizational effectiveness with these words: "We simply control costs better."

Typically sales managers must clear capital expenditures above $5,000 through Barr. While Moore's policy is to control cost expenditures at the top management level, Moore also allows its operational sales organization complete autonomy in planning sales strategy and evaluating results. This is particularly evident in the highly trained sales force. A new employee spends the first months in his district's home office learning the functional value of every form classification that Moore prints and how to price the form in terms of size, quality and weight of paper, various ink colors, and particular use of shading and partial form blackout, to name a few of the variables. Assignments are also given by the trainee's manager. For example, the trainee is requested to design a purchase order to be used by a hardware retail chain. The problem might include specific decisions as to where the control numbers should be placed and how to indicate that the second and third copy go to the accounting and receiving departments respectively. Throughout this training period there is a strong working relationship developed between the area sales manager and the budding salesman. While explaining the intricate use of forms in all phases of business, the manager has an opportunity to relate them to the sales area the salesman will soon encounter.

Once in the territory, the salesman's customer "call plan" for the month is given to the sales manager the first calendar day of every month. This is possible because Moore breaks down each salesman's territory by a series of "blocks." Each block represents a geographical area including (1) all accounts now buying from Moore and (2) potential accounts the salesman feels have sales possibilities. To fully develop sales penetration of the block concept, each account is recorded on a specially printed fold-over 3- by 5-inch card. This record is maintained on potential customers as well as active accounts. The information placed on the card includes the specific form used by the customer, date of sale, cost per 1,000, and rate of usage. Rate of usage is determined by consistently checking the control numbers remaining in inventory. This system allows for a close supervisory control by the sales manager. For example, sales manager Ted Wilson plans to work with salesman Frank Holmes on December 4. Wilson looks at the territorial planning sheet for December 4 and finds that Holmes will be working Block 417. Before going into Block 417 the sales manager may take time to review the individual card file on each account, in order to assist Holmes in further developing his territory. An account may have purchased payroll checks but may buy his voucher checks elsewhere. The sales manager might suggest sales planning (preapproach) in selecting samples of voucher checks used by other firms and developing a sales analysis around the example. This preparation might also include a discussion of the kinds of interest questions which might be asked to develop customer need awareness.

Another control device which requires planning appears on the salesman's sales order blank. The information requested by Moore includes a section directing the salesman to specify a reorder date for this form. If the salesman were to state January 1974, then a "status request" from the sales manager's office would be automatically sent to the salesman 6 months prior to this date, in this instance in July 1973. The salesman, on his next block call to that area, would determine the present status of the supply and then reply to the request by verifying that a reorder will in fact occur within that time period, or by providing a more accurate reorder date. Perhaps it should be moved back 4 months, to April 1974. If this were the status report submitted by the salesman, he would receive another status request in November 1973.

Every movement of a Moore salesman is dictated by computer, even down to which side of a street he will work on a particular afternoon. One might question the degree of commitment the sales manager might anticipate from such a high degree of regimentation. Yet effectiveness of this sales structure cannot be ignored. A strong commitment *must* take place within a Moore salesman, because creativity plays a dominant role in developing forms that fulfill complicated business functions. This creativity, the function of designing and engineering forms, offers a high degree of personal involvement leading to fulfillment of personal goals. This opportunity for personal creativity allows the salesman to use his expertise in satisfying his customers' complete needs and is actually supported by the strictly regulated sales organizational structure because it affords the salesman the best opportunity to understand the total forms needs of his customers.

CONCLUSION

From the sales manager's perspective, the sales organization is a potential force which materializes under his direction. Since the sales organization is a living organism, in the sense that it is capable of growth, the manager's activity focuses upon realizing positive results and in the process gives a stronger identity to the organization's character. The essential ingredient of the selling organization is that activity of bringing together the component parts in such a manner that they acquire a new state of being but do not lose their specific identity. There are three managerial devices the sales manager uses in achieving organizational results. The first is clearly stated long- and short-term objectives. Objectives are important for two reasons: (1) they identify in selling terms the firm's functional relationship to the customer and (2) they give a specific sense of direction to the sales personnel. The second managerial device is sales policy. Policy acts as a guideline, developing clear boundaries within which the salesman is free to operate. Policies are most effective when they afford the greatest degree of freedom relative to the salesman's capacity. Because no two salesmen have the same degree of ability or experience, organizational policy increases in effectiveness when there is flexibility of application. The third tool is planning, that sequential activity which utilizes sales policies as a guideline in accomplishing sales objectives.

This becomes the basis of specific sales results which ultimately turn *potential* energy of the sales organization into goal accomplishments. The sales manager can best achieve sales planning and its implementation when the salesman's personal goals are in a reasonable harmony with the formal goals of the organization. The sales manager will realize a high degree of commitment on the part of the sales organization when its members function in an environment of trust and confidence. This positive organizational atmosphere evolves when the sales manager has the ability to evaluate objectively the economic potential of each territory, can evaluate the true potential of each salesman, and has the sales proficiency needed to develop the sales potential of each member of the organization.

PROBLEMS

1. Define the term "organization." Compare the components of a sales organization with those of a production organization, indicating their differences and similarities.

2. Why do we say that when the sales organization attains certain positive achievements, a new organization evolves because of these efforts?

3. Discuss three important elements of the sales organization.

4. Explain the role of objectives, policy, and planning in developing an effective sales organization.

5. How does "management by objectives" differ from crash programs?

6. Evaluate the objectives of Shasta Beverages and the policy developed by this organization in formulating a plan of action. Do you feel Shasta's 1972 sales strategy had merit? Why?

7. Using the United Petroleum example as your basis, explain why a sound sales policy must have a degree of flexibility in its interpretation.

8. Discuss the difference between planning and the plan.

9. How does the sales manager achieve personal commitment of the sales organization?

10. Discuss why the sales manager's personal goals parallel more closely the formal goals of the sales organization than do the personal goals of the salesmen.

11. Discuss the role of congruency of goals in attaining commitment of the sales organization.

12. How does a personal objective vary from a formal organizational objective?

13. Why is Moore Business Forms, Inc., classified as an effective sales organization?

14. How does creativity play an important role in developing personal commitment within Moore's rigid organizational structure?

See pages 294–296 for an additional case study.

Chapter Twenty
Understanding Sales Potential:
A Managerial Function

The preceding chapter dealt with the sales manager and his role in developing the sales organization. A major portion of that chapter dealt with relating objectives, policy, and planning to organizational effectiveness. This chapter focuses upon those broad statistical characteristics which the sales manager can use in accurately appraising the sales potential of the organization and also in developing meaningful objectives. Market information in terms of customer trends is important, for it forms the manager's basis in training sales personnel to meet changing trends. A regional manager of the Ford Motor Corporation expressed it in these words: "In today's competitive market selling skills come about through more effective education — education of the salesmen, education of the dealers, and education of the changing market."

This chapter provides the basis for sales territorial evaluation by presenting those statistical trends which will have the greatest influence upon the selling activities of the 1970s.

STATISTICAL DISTRIBUTION BY AGE

Grouping the population by age is of value in determining the sales potential of products. For example, a firm selling mobile homes ranging in price from $8,000 to $25,000 can look to elderly people who find the mobile home an inexpensive way to maintain a comfortable home, particularly after retirement. The increasing percentage of people over fifty-five years of age is significant to our sales potential. In 1966, according to Table 20-1, there were 35 million people in this category, whereas in 1975, 42 million are projected. This is an increase of 7 million in sales potential, or an 18 percent potential increase by 1975.

TABLE 20-1 NUMERICAL DISTRIBUTION BY AGE

Age	1966 (in millions)	1975 (in millions)
0-14	60	70
15-24	32	40
25-34	24	31
35-44	25	22
45-54	22	23
55-64	17	18
Over 64	18	24

SOURCE: U.S. Bureau of the Census, *Statistical Abstract*, 1967, pp. 8–9.

This trend in population categories is further substantiated by a study conducted by *U.S. News and World Report.* Table 20-2 represents the population trends from 1970 to 1980. The figures presented in these two tables substantiate the conclusion that important shifts are taking place during this decade which will have profound influences upon the market potential into the 1980s. The increase in population of persons over sixty years of age suggests a rapid climb in store for this market segment. The surge in marketing prospects promises greater demand for apartments, medical care, nursing homes and hospitals, and a corresponding rise in the need for large quantities of pharmaceutical products. Because of rising government benefits and the growth of private pension plans, there is a greater degree of financial independence by older people. Already marketers are showing increasing interest in the market for luxuries such as travel, books, recreation, fashionable clothing, and cosmetics.

In Chapter Nineteen the objective of Shasta Beverages was discussed in connection with that company's appeal to the youth market, the three- to twelve-year-olds. Looking ahead, it becomes apparent that the growth potential is there: 79.3 million in 1975 and 82.2 million in 1980.

The trend of the future appears to be toward a nation of young adults. By 1980 the total United States population will be about 232 million, and nearly one in every three Americans will be in his or her twenties or thirties. From a numerical viewpoint, it appears as though the young adults (ages twenty to thirty-nine) will have a dominant influence in shaping the markets of the 1970s and 1980s. Between 1971 and 1980 the number of young adults will grow by 18 million, up 34 percent. People in all other age groups will increase by 9 million, or a mere 6 percent. In other words, two of every three Americans added to the population in the coming decade will be young adults. This stems from the "baby boom" in the years just after World War II; these Americans

TABLE 20-2 POPULATION GROWTH, 1970–1980

Age group	1970 (in millions)	1975 (in millions)	1980 (in millions)
Children and teen-agers	78.1	79.3	82.2
Young adults, 20–39	53.6	62.1	71.7
Middle-aged, 40-59	45.4	45.3	45.2
Over 59	28.3	30.8	33.3

SOURCE: "What the U.S. Will Be Like By 1980," *U.S. News and World Report,* Jan. 11, 1971, pp. 38–40.

now are coming of age, moving through the colleges, marrying, and starting and raising families. Young adults spend and borrow freely for cars, clothing, recreation, housing, and the multitude of products that go into new homes and apartments. Styles and fashions, increasingly, will bear the stamp of young people.

The Ford Motor Corporation has had considerable success in its marketing of the Pinto, a low-priced car appealing to the young adult market. Persons who would most readily purchase this car are in the twenty-five to thirty-four-year-old age group. Table 20-2 indicates that there will be an increase of 8.5 million people in this group by 1975. With this market potential available, all the manufacturers will be competing and developing a portion of their marketing strategy to capture this share of the market. Ford is well aware of the fact that once the buyer in this age group purchases a Pinto, he gains through experience knowledge about Ford products and in the process forms a buying pattern. If this pattern is favorable, there is a potential market in the higher-priced models, particularly in the future, higher-income years. Looking ahead to the 1980–1985 period, the age group consisting of persons thirty-five to forty-four years of age will reach significant size. The members of this group will have a number of years of work experience behind them and should have an influence upon placing this group into a higher income classification. They will have a different variety of consumer needs closely related to their work environment. The marketing impact will be upon more luxurious homes, possibly fashionable apartments, expansive travel plans, more high-fashion clothing, selective meal preparation, greater reliance upon all kinds of services, *and* more expensive automobiles.

GEOGRAPHIC DISTRIBUTION

In the development of a marketing strategy from a geographical viewpoint, four factors play a role. The first is the climatic peculiarities of the particular section of the country. Automobile firms find a greater potential for convertibles in Southern California, the Southwest, and the South than in the Northern states, while snow tires have their sales potential in the Northern states and the high mountain country. Another factor is the ethnic population in the particular segment of the country. The San Francisco area is highly populated with Italian and Spanish ethnic groups. This has a profound influence upon the sale of food and drink items; the Italians, in particular, enjoy wine with their social activities. The Germans in Wisconsin have followed their family heritage in drinking beer, making this geographical area a good potential for that product. The color preference in automobiles is also related to geographical areas. In Seattle, where the rainy season lasts from October until April, bright-colored cars are most popular, while in Spokane, a more conservative city with a great deal more sunshine, the subdued shades are more popular.

The third factor to be considered is the population trend in the particular part of the country. There is a constant shifting of people from one section of the country to another, which is caused by three basic factors: (1) The young working force finds initial employment in that section of the country which offers the greatest promise; (2) people are transferred by major companies to different sections of the country; (3) the economic conditions of particular sections of the country influence population size. Table 20-3, showing population trends by geographic areas, indicates that the South and the West will have the fastest growth in the coming decade. According to census experts, the urge to move toward warmer climates and the ocean shores is a strong one. Population in the Northeast and the central part of the country will show the smallest gains, yet these areas will still contain the majority of Americans and therefore still provide an important market potential.

TABLE 20-3 POPULATION GROWTH BY GEOGRAPHIC REGION

Region	1971	1980	Percent gain
New England: Maine, New Hampshire, Vermont, Massachusetts, Rhode Island, Connecticut	11,848,000	13,000,000	10
Middle Atlantic: New York, New Jersey, Pennsylvania	37,153,000	40,600,000	9
East North Central: Ohio, Indiana, Illinois, Michigan, Wisconsin	16,324,000	17,400,000	7
East South Central: Kentucky, Tennessee, Alabama, Mississippi	12,804,000	13,800,000	8
West South Central: Arkansas, Louisiana, Oklahoma, Texas	19,322,000	22,000,000	14
Mountain: Montana, Idaho, Wyoming, Colorado, New Mexico, Arizona, Utah, Nevada	8,282,000	10,000,000	21
Pacific: Washington, Oregon, California, Alaska, Hawaii	26,525,000	33,100,000	25

SOURCE: U.S. Bureau of the Census; 1980 estimates by *U.S. News and World Report*'s Economic Unit, Jan. 11, 1971, p. 39.

The fourth factor to consider in developing a marketing strategy from a geographical viewpoint is the continued shift from rural to metropolitan areas. This shift to a metropolitan living environment will have a tremendous impact upon the social environment and consequently upon marketing strategies. There will be a diminishing influence of such reference groups as the family and community, resulting in attachments to different reference groups. The implications of this geographical shift might be better understood by considering the situation of a young man who has just arrived at a military basic training camp. This new recruit knows no one other than those who came to camp with him, and his surroundings are totally new. Immediately he begins to develop new living patterns, with particular emphasis upon the basic elements of living: where he sleeps and where and when meals are served. In the process of developing these patterns, he makes friends with those adjacent to his bunk or living area or ahead of him in the chow line. Soon a social relationship is formed, one which is totally different from anything he has ever known. Within the framework of this friendship the new recruit finds interest in other patterns of living — visiting the P.X., perhaps having a beer or two at the club, or attending the post theater.

When those who live in rural areas move to the city, the tendency is to locate in the outskirts, or suburbs, rather than in the central area of the city, for the suburbs most closely resemble their home environment. The suburban area forms the basis for one important marketing segment, recognized by retail stores which make up shopping centers. Although the shopping center is a far cry from the downtown section of Small Town, U.S.A., it has certain characteristics which attract those oriented toward the rural life. For example, the informality of the center allows the entire family to shop in their casual clothes; the carnival atmosphere complete with balloons, popcorn, and frequently carnival rides is an attraction; the large number of small shops allows a great deal of browsing. One of the reasons for the outstanding success of shopping centers has been the recognition of this market potential and the close affiliation with this social group. On the other hand, this geographical trend has had a negative impact upon the downtown retail areas. The J. C. Penney Company thought long and hard before it renewed its downtown lease in Seattle, while in San Francisco this company no longer has a downtown store. By 1980 it is estimated that 60 percent of the metropolitan population will live in suburbia; this should give continued impetus to the growth of shopping centers.

OCCUPATIONAL CHARACTERISTICS

Since men and women spend the major share of their lives working, there is a significant relationship between work activity and fulfilling human needs. The concern here rests with the direct behavioral impact upon the market. In order to develop an in-depth understanding of what constitutes this sales potential, we will study occupational characteristics from as many viewpoints as possible.

Working Women

More than 50 years have passed since the 1920 enactment of the Nineteenth Amendment granting women suffrage. Since that time there has been considerable progress made by women in attaining an influential position in the employment market. In this 50-year span important progress has been made in changing attitudes and dispelling myths about women's capabilities, motivations, and potentialities. The relative contribution a wife makes to a family income has remained constant through the 1960s. In 1968 the median proportion of the family income contributed by the wife's earnings was 27 percent, reaching as high as 37 percent for wives who worked full time the entire year and as low as 13 percent for those who worked less than a full year or all year at part-time jobs.[1] About 50 percent of all working wives supplied between 20 and 50 percent of their family's income, while only 2 percent supplied 75 percent or more. The contribution to family income made by Negro wives with some work experience in 1968 was not significantly different from that of white wives. The more education women have, the more likely they are to be in the labor force; the more education they bring to their jobs, the higher their earnings. Figure 20-1 presents further characteristics of women in the work force.

[1] Elizabeth Waldman, "Women in the Labor Force," *Monthly Labor Review,* June 1970, p. 12. Elizabeth Waldman is an economist in the Division of Labor Force Studies, Bureau of Labor Statistics.

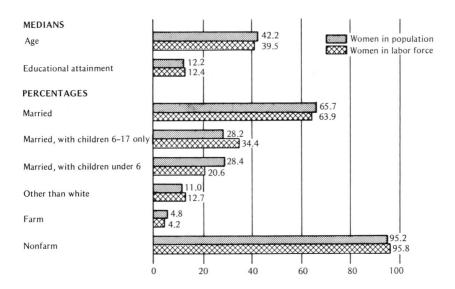

Fig. 20-1 Characteristics of women in the population and the civilian labor force, 1969. *(From Janice Hedges, "Women Workers in the 1970's" Monthly Labor Review, June 1970, p. 21.)*

Women's attachment to the labor force seems strong for the 1970s. The lengthening work life of women, the increasing percentage of women working full time and year round, and the significant contribution working women are making to family income testify to the strength of that attachment. Work in the labor force is becoming an ongoing way of life for a growing proportion of women in the United States. This segment of the population, working women who are married or maintain a private household, will have an influence upon the food market, particularly in the purchase of finished products such as frozen dinners, desserts, and vegetables. The service industries, such as dry cleaning and transportation, will be used more extensively by working women.

Figure 20-2 illustrates the difference between the traditional organizational structure and the possible organizational shape of the future. In the past the pyramid structure has proved effective, particularly at the lower end of the organization, where the structure broadens to compensate for the fewer skills required to perform the job, since larger numbers of people are substituted for skill levels. The 1960s saw the growth of technology, automation, and particularly computer control systems which were highly instrumented, using automatic control techniques (cybernetics). In mid-1968 a total of about 1,700 process computers were installed or on order in the United States. This number is only a fraction of the total potential, with an estimated 5,900 to be in use by 1975.[2] Where computer processes have been utilized, there has been an upgrading of the occupational structure. This has increased the need for supervisors, usually experienced engineers, to be in charge of a specific process group. College graduates now staff about 65 percent of new computer jobs, while high school graduates and employees with some college education fill a significant number of new key positions.

[2] "Manpower Implications of Computer Control in Manufacturing," *Monthly Labor Review*, October 1970, p. 3. For a specific example of how technological changes are affecting the employment structure, read Robert V. Critchlow, "Technological Changes in the Printing Industry," *Monthly Labor Review*, Aug. 1970, pp. 3–9.

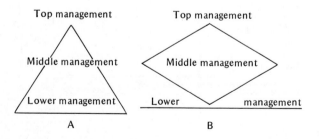

Fig. 20-2 Traditional organizational structure (A) compared with possible future organizational structure (B).

This sophisticated equipment appears to affect the structure of the work force. Control systems and automation will continue to take the place of the unskilled or semiskilled employee at the bottom of the traditional organizational structure. Fewer employees will be needed at the lower level, but there will be a larger demand for employees with the necessary skills to plan, develop, maintain, and interpret data emanating from these computer-oriented systems. This will result in a new, diamond-shaped organizational structure, as shown in Figure 20-2 (B). Changes in process computer technology in the 1970s and 1980s are expected to lead to continued growth in installations and an expansion in the type and scope of applications. Two trends in the manufacture of process computers are under way. One trend is toward small, low-cost computers which are economically feasible for control of a single small process. The other trend is toward large-scale computers capable of controlling many different units in a plant, thereby lowering the cost of control over individual processes.

Here the influence upon the market will be a trend toward a larger segment of the work force possessing either a higher level of occupational skills or a college degree. These members of the work force will form new kinds of reference groups which will have a direct bearing upon the kinds of products they buy, where they shop, and where they live. A large segment of this work force will be in the middle-to-upper area of the organizational structure, with higher incomes, while a substantial number are likely to be transferred from one geographical area to another.

Leisure Time

Leisure is intrinsically bound to the quality of life. Its distribution among the population over a lifetime and the uses to which it is put are indicative of the well-being of a society. Yet in the United States the increase in time free of work and available for leisure activities has been far less widely noticed than the increasing output of goods and services. The relative neglect of leisure as a measure of the nation's advance in living standards is related to its elusive quality. Work time, and its reduction over a period of years, can be measured statistically; it is more difficult to tell whether leisure time has actually grown. Even to define leisure is difficult. Perhaps the most comprehensive definition of leisure is that of Sebastian de Grazia, who states that it is "a state of being in which activity is performed for its own sake."[3]

Significantly, most current definitions of leisure use work as the reference point. That is, leisure time or leisure activities are contrasted, implicitly or explicitly, with work time or productive activities. In some other societies, leisure has been the reference point. In Greece, in the fifth century B.C., for example, "business" was the negative form of the word *schole*, which we

[3]Sebastian de Grazia, *Of Time, Work and Leisure*, The Twentieth Century Fund, New York, 1962.

translate as "leisure." And the Latin word for "business," *negotium*, is the antonym of *otium*, which is "leisure." In Athens or Rome, the Bureau of Labor would have been the Bureau of Leisure! But times have changed. The definition given by de Grazia serves as a proper background in discussing leisure as time free of the necessity to earn a living. This free time can be viewed from three perspectives, each with a significant influence upon a market potential.

1. *Extended leisure time.* The 5-day workweek is now a reality for the majority of workers, while the 4-day week is gaining greater momentum. In 1970 about 7,000 workers in a small number of firms distributed throughout the United States were on a 4-day week, although many companies that have gone to the 4-day week require their workers to put in 9 or 10 hours a day.[4] The adjustment of national holidays to fall on Mondays has a considered impact upon leisure time. In 1971 federal law shifted five midweek holidays to Monday. Earned vacations are steadily increasing from the standard 2-week vacation.

2. *Lumps of leisure.* Lumps of leisure, in contrast to small bits of leisure added each day, have been gaining favor.[5] Retirement years represent one such lump of leisure that is growing. By 1980, the labor force participation rate for men age sixty-five and over is expected to *decline* to 22 percent, down 4 percentage points from 1968. Improvements in social security benefits and private pension plans are enabling increasing numbers of older workers to choose retirement over work. The sabbatical leave is another form of lumps of leisure that may become more extensive in the future. The sabbatical, first established for college teachers in the 1880s, was adopted in the steel industry in 1963, at which time the union contract provided 3 months of paid vacation every 5 years for workers in the top half of the seniority roster. Those with lesser service became eligible under the 1968 negotiations for 3 weeks of paid vacation every 5 years in addition to their regular paid vacation time.

3. *Leisure time for additional work income.* Among those who work long hours are the "moonlighters," those who hold two or more jobs.[6] In May 1969, about 4 million persons, more than 5 percent of the work force, held two or more jobs at the same time.[7] About half of them worked 55 or more hours

---

[4] For a comprehensive discussion and evaluation of the 4-day workweek and projections of its acceptance into the future, refer to Riva Poor, ed., *Four Days, Forty Hours,* Bursk and Poor, Cambridge, Mass., 1970.

[5] Juanita Kreps, "Lifetime Tradeoffs between Work and Play," *Proceedings of the Twenty-first Annual Winter Meeting, Industrial Research Association,* 1968, pp. 307–316.

[6] For a more comprehensive understanding of moonlighters, read Vera C. Perrella, "Moonlighters: Their Motivations and Characteristics," *Monthly Labor Review,* Aug. 1970, pp. 57–64.

[7] Geoffrey H. Moore and Janice Neipert Hedges, "Trends in Labor and Leisure," *Monthly Labor Review,* Feb. 1971, p. 7.

during the survey week. Most moonlighters work at two or more jobs because they value additional income over leisure. In 1969, two out of five moonlighters cited the need for additional income for regular household expenses. One out of five said he worked at two or more jobs either to pay debts or to save for the future. The importance of economic reasons for multiple job holding is supported by data on marital and family status. The moonlighting rate was less than 4 percent for single men. Among married men, rates were about 6 percent for those with no children under age eighteen and rose as the number of children in the family increased. The rate for men with five or more children under eighteen was 11 percent.

The increase in leisure time has a significant influence upon the market potential. With an increasing amount of time away from the work environment (other than the moonlighters), the consumer inevitably turns to goods and services to secure higher personal fulfillment. Maslow's hierarchy of needs finds particular value as a standard for evaluating the consumer's motivation to achieve particular plateaus of satisfaction. For example, long weekends, extended vacations, and more 3-day holidays make expenditures for boats, motors, and hunting equipment more plausible. The motivation factor could be a social need — the consumer's need to enjoy the companionship of members of his reference group or his immediate family.[8]

Airlines are purchasing large fleets of 747 jumbo commercial jets with the anticipation of more travel by those who will be enjoying longer vacations, sabbaticals, and earlier retirement. Needs which serve as motivators to seek air travel are varied: (1) the need for social relationships, where reference groups take vacations together; (2) self-esteem, in being in a financial position to be categorized as a person who travels throughout the world; and (3) self-actualization, whereby in experiencing the cultural and historical heritage of particular geographic areas, the consumer more fully develops his personal growth as an individual and his potential for further achievements. Greater leisure time also develops the popularity of do-it-yourself activity, which to some extent represents a substitution of unpaid labor for the earning of an income. As leisure-time activity, it could also fulfill the need for personal accomplishment.

In addition, economic growth and higher living standards cause an increasing variety of demands upon time. As Linder observes, "the material richness of advanced societies are apparently incompatible with the superfluity of time that is characteristic of materially poor cultures."[9] An example is the economic commitment to maintain and service durable goods, such as automobiles and washing machines, that goes with their ownership.

[8]For further study of this subject, see "The Pattern of Leisure in Contemporary American Culture," *Annals of the American Academy of Political and Social Science*, 1967, vol. 313, p. 14.

[9]Staffan Burenstam Linder, *The Harried Leisure Class*, Columbia University Press, New York, 1970.

Finally, leisure offers time to acquire further education, which has the effect of developing new work skills, greater understanding of our culture, or motivational needs to find new participative avenues within the social structure. Whatever the rationale in seeking more educational knowledge, the use of leisure time in acquiring this knowledge is important to understanding market potentials, for often the learning process creates new needs to be satisfied, as well as establishing new reference groups and new motivations requiring achievement.

POPULATION MOBILITY

The significance of the mobile family is important in market determination. This group constitutes a significant quantitative market segment, for over 35 million American consumers change addresses each year. In twenty surveys dating back to 1948, movers have made up approximately 20 percent of the nation's population.[10] According to Dr. James E. Bell, Jr.,[11] each year nearly two-thirds of the movers make local and intracounty moves, one-sixth go to different counties in the same states, and one-sixth move to other states. The geographically mobile market segment is now nearly twice the size of the nation's black population. Furthermore, projections anticipate that by 1975 some 47 million people will be changing their residences each year. This estimate is based upon a projected population of 226 million for the nation and a yearly mobility rate of 20.8 percent by 1975.[12] Based upon the classification of movers from March 1966 to March 1967, by 1975 some 15.6 million persons are expected to make moves taking them outside the counties in which they resided at the beginning of the year.

After we accept the fact that this is a significant market segment, we must understand some of its behavior characteristics. Because each move involves rebuilding shopping patterns, recognizable marketing outlets and brand names form the basis for developing new buying habits. Mobiles who have strong product brand loyalties are able to choose suppliers based upon the distribution of such brand items. However, when these products have widespread distribution, retail selection decisions must be based upon such traditional factors as convenience, price, service, or credit. Dr. Bell's research in this area was performed in a detailed study of 147 families moving into a metropolitan area with a population of 200,000. The information was secured from a local welcoming organization. Sixty percent of the households contacted had moved to the study area from out-of-state locations more than 80 miles away. Women interviewers held comprehensive in-home interviews with housewives in each family after the

[10] U.S. Bureau of the Census, *Current Population Reports, Population Characteristics*, ser. P.-20, no. 171, Apr. 30, 1968, p. 1.

[11] "Mobiles: A Neglected Market Segment," *Journal of Marketing*, Apr. 1969, vol. 33, pp. 37-44.

[12] "Consumer Dynamics — Part 2: The Movers," *Progressive Grocery*, Nov. 1965, p. 138.

mobiles had been in the community for a mean time of 23 weeks. A 20 percent callback was made to verify data collected. The following purchase categories were studied: food, beauty parlors, dry cleaning, financial institutions, insurance, furniture, appliances, women's clothing, men's suits, and medical service.

Significant Conclusions in Developing Mobile Shopping Patterns

In normal traffic, the mobiles in Bell's study could reach by automobile virtually all parts of the study community within a half hour. As a result, new families could regard most outlets in the area as sources of supply. Convenience played a major role in the supplier selection process, and initially suppliers were most frequently selected on this basis. After families became familiar with the community, subsequent patronage decisions rested heavily upon: (1) prior experience with the firm, (2) quality, (3) price, and (4) service. Mobiles used personal information more than any other source in rebuilding shopping patterns. Searching was the second most vital means of gaining potential supplier information. In no purchase category did newcomers place primary reliance on impersonal information sources. For example, almost no use was made of *Yellow Pages* advertisements. Furniture and appliances were the only categories where newspapers played a vital role in shopping selections. In the beauty-parlor and dry-cleaner categories, personal information was generally secured from representatives of local welcoming organizations; co-workers, employers, and real estate representatives provided the majority of personal information on financial institutions. In the insurance area, company sales personnel typically provided the "personal" contact. Medical services were selected by sixty-eight families based on personal information from nonprofessional sources — people who were in the same age category, always married, and generally of the same sex, and who had incomes similar to families studied.

Real estate personnel, new neighbors, and co-workers were all used to gain information about furniture and appliance outlets. Searching was instrumental in choosing supermarkets and played a secondary role in the choices of dry cleaners, banks, furniture stores, appliance outlets, and clothing stores. However, as length of time in the community increased, searching declined in importance and mobiles relied increasingly upon personal conversations for the necessary answers. As expected, wives selected beauty parlors and virtually all dress shops. In addition, wives made two-thirds of the supermarket and dry-cleaning choices. Sole responsibility for selecting physicians and dentists rested upon wives twice as often as husbands. Decisions of husbands were primarily confined to choosing the family bank, insurance firms, and men's clothing stores. However, supermarket, physician, dentist, furniture store, and bank selections were also frequently made after mutual discussion.

It is important to view the background characteristics of the mobile group in terms of income, education, and occupational levels. Table 20-4 shows the percentage income relationship of mobiles to the general population. Families

TABLE 20-4 FAMILY INCOME, 1966

Income range	Intercounty mobiles		Total nation
	Number	Percent	Percent
Under $5,000	2	1.4	28.2
$5,000–6,000	11	7.5	17.8
7,000–9,000	39	26.5	24.4
10,000–14,000	57	38.7	20.4
15,000–24,000	35	23.8	9.2
Over $25,000	1	0.7	....
No answer	2	1.4	....
Total	147	100.0	100.0

SOURCE: U.S. Bureau of the Census, *Current Population Reports, Consumer Income*, ser. P-60, no. 53, Dec. 28, 1967, pp. 1–8.

interviewed showed a mean pretax income of $12,600 for 1966. This figure, less estimated tax expenditures, closely paralleled the area's 1966 *buying* income of $9,729 per household.[13] Income levels of this magnitude placed mobiles in the upper 30 percent of the nation's families. Nearly 90 percent of the mobile household heads were white-collar workers. Regarding *geographic* characteristics, mobile families had a history of past geographic mobility. On the average, each family in the nation makes one long-distance move every 16 years; mobile families average one long-distance move every 3 years, a mobility rate nearly five times the national average.

Regarding the *household* characteristics of mobiles, mobile couples were found to have been married an average of 11 years, and two-thirds of them had children under five years of age. Slightly more than 19 percent of the housewives worked outside the home, generally on a part-time basis. In 95 percent of the families, wives drove automobiles, while nearly half the mobiles were two-car families. When they moved into the study community, over 80 percent occupied one-family dwellings. Ownership of the place of residence was assumed by 55 percent of the families.

A 1966 study of 148 long-distance geographically mobile families in Philadelphia by Alan R. Andreasen[14] has particular relevance to this study. The Philadelphia study revealed that mobiles possess higher levels of education, occupation, and income than the rest of the population. Willingness to be mobile, ambition, and relative youth were also found to be distinguishing

[13] "Annual Survey of Buying Power," *Sales Management*, June 10, 1967, pp. 8–44.

[14] Alan R. Andreasen, "Geographic Mobility and Market Segmentation," *Journal of Marketing Research*, Nov. 1966, pp. 341–345.

characteristics of this market. Almost identical income levels, educational achievement, and mobility histories were found in Bell's and Andreasen's studies, which were conducted several hundred miles apart. Based on the two investigations, it appears that long-distance mobiles moving into metropolitan areas exhibit homogeneous socioeconomic and life-cycle profiles independent of the destination involved. In both studies families contacted had generally been geographically mobile in the past.

The relatively high proportion of white persons with some college training and working in upper-level white-collar occupations suggests a positive relationship between socioeconomic status and migration. At the same time, the relatively high proportion of unemployed and unskilled suggests a negative relationship. Thus migrants appear to be of two types: (1) unemployed people moving to search for job opportunities and (2) people holding professional or managerial positions moving in response to a greater demand for services.

In the area of *occupational* characteristics, nearly 90 percent of the mobile household heads were white-collar workers. Of the mobile males, 80 percent worked in professional or managerial occupations; in contrast, only 25.1 percent of all males in the nation held occupations in these two categories. A more complete comparison of the nation and mobiles regarding occupations is presented in Table 20-5.

TABLE 20-5 OCCUPATION OF HOUSEHOLD HEADS

Occupational category	Intercounty mobiles		Total nation, 1965
	Number	Percent	Percent
Professional, technical, or kindred	66	44.9	11.9
Managers, officials, and proprietors	48	32.7	13.2
Clerical workers	0	0.0	7.0
Salesworkers	14	9.5	6.0
Craftsmen and foremen	7	4.8	19.0
Operatives	3	2.0	20.8
Nonfarm laborers	0	0.0	7.9
Service workers	6	4.1	6.9
Farm workers and others	3	2.0	7.3
Total	147	100.0	100.0

SOURCE: U.S. Bureau of the Census, *Statistical Abstract*, 1968, p. 225.

HOUSEHOLD CHARACTERISTICS

Demographically, the structure of households can be viewed in terms of age groups, previously discussed under the broad category of population. For example, Table 20-1 indicates that those in the age group of twenty-five to thirty-four will number 31 million by 1975, while those between thirty-five and forty-four years old will number 22 million. What is of particular importance here is translating these numbers within particular age groups into consumer needs of families. This can best be accomplished by relating this numerical age grouping to the family's life cycle; while families vary in their life cycles, much can be learned for use in market strategy from consideration of average patterns.[15]

The Beginning Family

The beginning family is usually composed of the young couple alone. This stage continues a year or two, on the average, until the birth of the first child. In this category the needs for food and clothing are low. The beginning family needs small and inexpensive private quarters. Its medical needs are probably low, and recreation needs are moderate. During this period some couples seek to complete their education or repay premarriage debts.

The Expanding Family

The expanding stage includes the childbearing, preschool, and grade school years, and lasts about 13 years, until the oldest child reaches adolescence. Food and clothing needs of the family are increasing throughout this period as the children progress from the preschool through the grade school years. There are likely to be high medical expenditures for the birth of the children, preventive care for them, and treatment of childhood diseases as the first child starts to school. The family's shelter needs are increasing, as it requires more space in a place where children are permitted and a place close to schools and other community facilities. Recreation outside the home is probably negligible, although some should be provided, especially for the mother. Since the mother's duties are heavy at this stage, provision needs to be made for the purchase of labor-saving equipment (washer, dryer, etc.), extra household help, or the use of outside services.

The Launching Family

In this stage the family is concerned with completing the formal education of its children and launching them on their careers. The stage begins when the first child reaches adolescence and presumably ends with the marriage of the last, a

[15] Virginia Britton, *Personal Finance*, American Book Company, New York, 1968, pp. 6-12.

period averaging about 17 years. During this stage of the life cycle, food, clothing, recreation, and shelter needs are high and increasing. Education expenses increase as the children progress through high school, especially if they continue into college or graduate work. The family may help the children start in a business or profession and start their homes, including the provision of weddings.

The Middle-age Family

The middle-age family is again composed of the husband and wife after the marriage of their children and before retirement or widowhood. While the children are now generally self-supporting, the parents may have some children living with them, particularly early in this period. On the average, the period lasts about 11 years, beginning when the husband is fifty-four years old and the wife fifty-two, at the marriage of their last child, and ending when the husband is about sixty-five. During this period, the parents' needs are low for food, clothing, and shelter. Entertainment, particularly of their children, may add to their food and housing costs. During these years, their medical needs are likely to be rising. Recreation expenses rise as they engage in more social activities, travel, and develop wider interests for the retirement years. In addition, they may need to help their elderly parents. They will work to replace worn-out durable goods, repay debts, complete payment of insurance premiums, and increase savings for old age, when income will decrease and medical costs will rise.

The Old-age Family

The period of old age might be considered to begin with the retirement of the husband or the death at about that time of one of the spouses. For half of the couples, marriage is broken by death of one of the spouses by the time the husband is sixty-six years old. Since the wife is more likely to be the survivor because of her younger age at marriage and the greater longevity of women, she will probably be a widow for a number of years. Needs are low for food, clothing, and shelter. Recreation needs are moderate, including social activities, hobbies, and perhaps travel. But medical needs may be high and growing as chronic illness develops, and there may be increasing need for household help.

RELATEDNESS OF SALES POTENTIAL TO NEED SATISFACTION

Based upon well-defined objectives discussed in the previous chapter, the marketing potential becomes the foundation for long-range sales strategy. The use of analysis is of value in evaluating the market. This is best understood when we view the customer within the boundaries of his personality, as shown in Figure 20-3. This conceptual arrangement shows the interaction of four variables: (1) need satisfaction, (2) long-range sales potential, (3) personality, in terms of motives, attitudes, knowledge, social environment, and reference groups, and

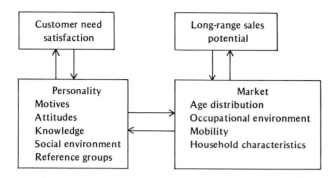

Fig. 20-3   A system's relationship between need satisfaction and long-range sales potential.

(4) market, in terms of age distribution, occupational environment, mobility, and household characteristics.

By properly relating all the factors, this systems application allows for a more accurate appraisal of the buyer potential. When the factors are viewed as an entity, there is a significant degree of credibility in the appraisal. For example, a life insurance company could develop a future market potential by considering the number of new families which will evolve from the age group comprising persons twenty-five to thirty-four years old (see Table 20-1). These young families would be concerned with providing safety needs (motives) for their growing families. Continuing with this example, the insurance company would gather more in-depth knowledge concerning the characteristics of this age group. This would include whether or not the wife works, where men in this age group are employed; whether they move frequently from one city to another; the average size of their family; the educational background of this age group. Gathering and analyzing demographic information would permit the insurance company to develop sales programs which more closely satisfy the specific needs of various segments of this market. For the rising young executive thirty-three years of age with three children, ages seven, ten, and fourteen, the emphasis of his insurance plan would be to provide not only financial protection, but also funds for the children's college education and possibly his retirement. Since his firm moves their executives frequently, he will be interested in gaining access to the services provided by a national firm with offices throughout major cities. Professional men in this age group, such as doctors, dentists, and lawyers, are seeking insurance programs which will protect their income level as well as the other needs mentioned for the young executive. Through proper market evaluation the sales manager can determine which of these statistical areas are of significant value; their importance will vary with the product or service offered and the consumer needs to be satisfied.

Successful sales management relies upon the manager's gathering market information *and* using it. There is also, however, a creative aspect involved in the process of understanding markets. Data on population, ages, incomes, and household characteristics can be very useful. The sales manager needs to know about these things, but this knowledge alone is not enough. Since sales potential begins with "people needs," it is vital for the manager to develop a real sensitivity toward people. It is also vital to project this sensitivity into the future and to act even when there are risks. In the 1920s Henry Ford rightly sensed the public's willingness to buy cars on a low-price appeal. He was slow, however, in changing his product and adding such options as new colors. Sears, Roebuck & Company prospered as its sales management responded to urbanization by adding retail stores to the mail order operation and in 1931 by adding insurance to the mail order catalog. Steam locomotive manufacturers lost markets by concentrating solely on their traditional product while the market moved into other forms of transportation equipment.

Perhaps the only certain feature of sales markets is that they will change. It is easy to look into the past for examples of such change; the real challenge is to be able to recognize the sales strategy required to meet future needs. This is the responsibility of the sales manager.

CONCLUSION

In order to utilize fully the resources of the sales organization, the sales manager must be able to relate objectives, policy, and planning to the changing needs of customers. Selling is always concerned with the future, since its primary objective is to fulfill presently unsatisfied needs. This can take place only in the future. The sales strategy of relating objectives, policy, and planning to the future needs of customers is best accomplished when the sales manager has a comprehensive understanding of the marketing potential. This chapter has discussed in depth four important statistical areas in terms of customer characteristics: (1) age distribution, (2) occupational environment, (3) mobility, and (4) household characteristics.

PROBLEMS

1. Discuss the importance of market information to the sales manager. Do you feel that this information will assist the manager in utilizing his sales organization to reach objectives? In setting realistic objectives?

2. Discuss two important population trends occurring within our country. How would they affect the sale of condominiums? The sale of campers? The sale of Ford Pintos?

3. Do you feel that selling activities of the 1970s will be influenced by the following age groups? Give them a numerical order of importance, along with an explanation of your choice.

0–19
20–39
40–59
Over 59

4. In the discussion of work characteristics, the chapter suggested a trend toward more leisure time. What kinds of products would a family of five (children range in age from seven to sixteen; parents are forty-one and thirty-nine; income level is at $13,500) purchase with the advent of greater leisure time?

5. Relate the product or service people fifty-five to sixty years of age would buy with more leisure time. Be sure to consider the *family life cycle* in your choice.

6. Which geographic section of the United States appears to offer the greatest population potential in the 1970s and 1980s?

7. Which statistical trends would support the building of more shopping centers by retail stores?

8. List five products whose sales should increase with retirement age dropped to sixty.

See pages 297–298 for an additional case study.

Additional Case Studies for
Chapters One to Twenty

SALESMANSHIP: AN ANALYSIS
Chapter One

The following remarks were made by William A. Reasoner, president of Waddell and Reed, Inc., a Kansas City-based financial-service complex which manages and sponsors United Funds, Inc., and United Continental group of mutual funds, whose assets approximate $2.5 billion.[1]

> Unfortunately when today's college student hears the word "salesman" he often thinks of poor old Willy Loman in *Death of a Salesman*; he doesn't realize that Willy is a figure of the past. Some of the best paid people in our economy, and among the most challenged and useful, are those who sell products, services, or ideas. Today's students should consider that whether a person's "status title" is marketing expert, account executive, registered representative or other variation, this person is basically a specialist in a very important field, selling. He makes good money and is held in high esteem, but regardless of the carpeting on the floor, he is a salesman. Many people forget that a large percentage of our corporate leaders come from the ranks of selling, or, if you will, marketing.
>
> High schools, colleges, or even schools of business administration, ignore a truth of economic life when they fail to provide courses on the technology of selling or avoid the word as if it had unpleasant connotations. It could be, in fact, that salesmen haven't done enough selling of their own profession. They never truly have taken up the cudgel to defend their way of life. Sure, we talk with each other at meetings, but they already are sold on what they are doing. This is not unlike ministers conversing with each other about faith. They must help erase that Willy Loman image and impart to young people how much salesmen contribute to the nation's economy. Young people should be made aware that there is a new breed of salesman increasing in evidence today. He is not the man of the old traveling-salesman jokes, an itinerant, crass pedler with glib tongue and a penchant for farmers' daughters. Today's salesman is most likely to be an articulate, well educated, solid-citizen type. He's often a former athlete or war hero. Of course he's still glib, but what successful attorney or advertising man isn't too, for that matter?
>
> The American economic and political systems are based essentially on persuasion. Neither customer nor decree can determine what people will

[1] Excerpt from *The Seattle Times*, Aug. 10, 1971, p. 6, from an article written by the *Times* business columnist, Boyd Burchard.

buy or for whom they will vote. Education is the key. Today's salesman has to be educated and efficient if he is to inform and persuade the increasingly sophisticated clients with whom he must deal. He no longer can rely on the goods and gossip he used to bring to the frontier. He must bring facts and know-how. In the financial-service field the salesman, to be properly effective, must have the training to consider all aspects of a client's financial problems, not solely insurance or investments or banking. He must be able to look them all over and come up with a financial prescription, much as does a physician in considering the needs of a patient. This applies even if he is specializing in one aspect of the field. More and more women are finding the field of selling a winning way of life, and not just at the store-clerk level. From running a household, they often have a grasp of the basic economic facts of life. Maybe their entry into the field will put a stop, once and for all, to the old traveling-salesman stories.

PROBLEMS

1. Does Reasoner's evaluation of a salesman match your understanding of the selling function? Discuss your answer in terms of the article and the chapter.

2. Does your personal experience suggest that Reasoner is correct in stating that some educational systems are remiss in not teaching the *technology* of selling?

3. Relating selling to the 1970s, discuss the correlation between marketing and selling. Give an example of a specific selling activity where the functions of marketing and selling are mutually supportive.

4. Why does Reasoner state that today education is the key to developing salesmen?

5. Give a one-page evaluation of Reasoner's analysis of selling in the 1970s. Note particularly how Reasoner has influenced your attitude toward salesmanship.

Professor Ainsley poses the following question to his class in salesmanship. "Suppose," he begins, "I made this statement about the purchase of an electric organ by a father for his daughter: 'This organ will make your daughter happy.' Does this statement by the salesman turn you on?"

There is no response from the class. Professor Ainsley then reads the example from the text of Mr. Swanson buying an organ for his daughter's enjoyment. Ainsley then asks the class members what their reaction is to the statements made by the salesman.

"It's a bit sticky," one student replies.

"Aren't they putting it on a little thick?" another asks.

"I would be embarrassed to say that to a customer," a student states.

"If that's selling, count me out," retorts another.

Professor Ainsley smiles and goes on to say, "You students have just proved to yourself the communication power of relating motives to human values. In the first instance, I merely referred to the motive of desiring "happiness." In itself it is a vague term, requiring personal interpretation by the customer. In the second case I developed the motive in specific human values, and most of you immediately reacted to these values, just as the customer would. I am not concerned with the fact that many of you have a negative response to the value expressed; in fact I encourage you to develop the values as you feel they apply. The selling system is designed to be flexible in applying the techniques by which you relate the component parts of the system. What is important is that you recognize the impact of effective development through communication of motives by translating these motives into human values."

PROBLEMS

1. Read the example in the text again. Do you agree with the students in this case study?

2. Develop a one-paragraph narrative expressing how you would envision the purchase of an electric organ in terms of human values. How about a sports car?

3. Has Ainsley proved his point? Discuss.

Fred S. Thompson, representing the Acme Control Records Corporation, has prepared the following product analysis, which he plans to utilize in selling his product to the personnel department of Lockheed Shipbuilding and Construction Company. Acme provides a service to accompany the product, which is their *Personnel Management Policies and Practices Manual*. Once a firm buys the manual, it will receive a biweekly supplement of the current developments in personnel management and labor negotiations, plus NLRB decisions which relate to the firm's industrial classification.

Name: Fred S. Thompson   Date June 18, 19

PRODUCT: PERSONNEL MANAGEMENT POLICIES AND PRACTICES MANUAL

1. Selling point	2. What it is	3. What it will do for the buyer; why or how it will do it	4. What it means to the buyer	5. Buying motives
Unique binder	Exclusive patented binder that lies flat for easy use	Book and pages lie flat for easy turning and reading.	No eyestrain trying to read curved or bent pages. No difficulty in turning 1 or 100 pages. Easy to use.	Ease
Overlapping rings	Exclusive patented overlapping rings (5) that expand to release pages	Gives stability to the pages, yet allows them to be turned or removed or inserted with amazing speed and ease.	Simplifies updating and makes it a pleasure for your secretary to file.	Ease
Biweekly supplements	Biweekly newsletter of all the latest developments, plus new pages to replace old or obsolete information	Keeps you abreast of the news on personnel management with what, where, and how to do things.	Saves you time, effort, embarrassment, and money by giving you the latest developments in good personnel management. Also keeps you up on the changes in laws that you should know about.	Money Security
Recognized authority	Recommended by ASPA, and in use by thousands of businesses in the United States, also government agencies at all levels	Gives you authoritative current answers to all problems or questions on personnel management.	Gives you the tools to run an efficient, happy, and productive work force with the least effort. Gives you the best return on your payroll dollar, and ease of mind.	Money Time, security
Indexed and cross-referenced	Over 150 pages of alphabetical index noted in the field for its completeness	Has you reading the complete answer to your problem in seconds.	Saves you time in locating the exact information you need.	Money, time

PROBLEMS

1. Has Fred done an adequate job of listing the important selling points? Do the benefits he expresses relate to customer values? How?

2. Judging from the depth of analysis, would you classify Fred as a professional salesman? Discuss.

3. How does this analysis illustrate the point that the differences make the sale?

4. What specific product characteristics is Fred emphasizing in his sales analysis?

5. In relating this case to the ABC Fertilizer Company case, do you feel that Fred is selling "elephants" or "ponies"? Discuss.

The children had all gone to school and Mary Kerns was enjoying her second cup of coffee while watching her favorite morning quiz show. The commercial flashed onto the screen, showing a silver United Airlines jet gracefully streaking across the blue skies of Hawaii. Mary was reminded of the beautiful color slides Beth O'Riley had shown at their bridge club just last week. Beth had said that it was amazing how interesting the culture of the island was, and that she had enjoyed visiting with the small villagers more than being on the sandy beaches of the large resorts.

Mary thought to herself, "Beth knows how to really live. You can sense from her conversations, and the places she has visited, that her background is excellent. Our bridge group is lucky to have a lady like Beth. The fact that John O'Riley is a successful surgeon and that she has been educated at one of the better Eastern finishing schools hasn't affected her outlook on life one bit! . . . It seems to me that Spence [her husband] is due for his annual bonus soon. Wouldn't it be nice if just the two of us could spend three weeks in Hawaii!"

That evening Spencer drove their 1964 Buick Special into the driveway. Beth noticed that he seemed to be in a particularly good mood. "Something must have happened," she thought. "He hasn't had time to stop at the club!"

Spencer did have a special bounce to his walk that evening. He could hardly wait to tell Mary: "Guess what," he began. "I received my bonus check today, and it was $1,200 more than I expected! The total came to $3,500. What color car do you want, Mary, because we're going to trade in that clunker soon!"

Mary countered, "You know, Spence, we aren't getting any younger, and the children are able to take care of themselves. Why don't we put off the purchase of the car until next year and take that trip to Hawaii we've always talked about? Beth says that it's really great in the fall."

"From what you've mentioned about Beth's trip," Spencer said, "I know how much you would like to see the islands. The Buick needs tires, a battery, and a tuneup, but we can make do. Why don't you call the travel agency in the morning and make arrangements for the first week in October?"

"That's really nice of you, Spence!" Mary exclaimed. "I know we'll have as much fun as the O'Riley's did! Which reminds me, we'd better clear the dishes in a hurry; we have a bridge game with the O'Riley's, Swensons, and Coles."

After the party, Mary and Spencer reached their car in a rainstorm. As Spencer turned the key, he heard nothing but the click-click of the starter motor.

"Battery's dead, Mary," Spencer said. "I'm going to call the service station."

"Oh Spence," Mary moaned. "Why did it have to happen right in front of our best friends? There go the O'Rileys in their new sportscar; I wonder what that smile means? I'll bet her car starts when she turns the key!"

After the garage man had come and the Kerns were on their way home, there was not much conversation until Mary said, "Why don't we put that trip off until next year, Spence? It's more important that you have a safe car in driving to work. I'd never forgive myself if you had an accident because I wanted to take a trip to Hawaii. Your well-being is far more important to me than all the trips to Hawaii."

Spencer smiled and thought to himself, "Thanks, old dead battery, you couldn't have gone bad at a better time. Mr. Jacobs [his company's production vice-president] just bought a new Cadillac; it's sure a beauty. I think it's about time Mary and I stepped up to a Cadillac. We deserve it *and* they're safe cars!"

PROBLEMS

1. Which of the following played predominant roles in affecting the decision to purchase a car: attitudes, motives, knowledge, reference groups, social class? Discuss your answer. Which played the least important role?

2. Describe the reference group to which Mary found a close relationship.

3. Give three consumer needs a trip to Hawaii represented to Mary.

4. Does the case give evidence of a reference group that influenced Spencer? If so, discuss.

5. Which of the following influenced Mary to change her mind about a trip to Hawaii in favor of buying a new car: reference groups, social class, psychological needs? Discuss your choice.

6. Which of the following influenced Spencer to decide on a Cadillac: safety needs, reference group, self-esteem?

7. Using the information in this case, utilize the selling system to develop one selling point of a Cadillac that would be important to Spencer.

TONY THE BARBER GETS A NEW CUSTOMER
Chapter Five

Bert Owens, sales representative with Foremost Barber Supplies, Inc., had attempted for more than a year to sell Tony Coniglero his complete line of shaving cream, shampoo, hair lotion, clippers, razors, and strops. Tony's shop (a ten-chair affair in a large Hilton Hotel) was the biggest account in town. In researching Tony, Bert reached two conclusions: One, since Bert had a ten-chair account like Tony's in Philadelphia, he knew from experience that the account was worth about $50 per month in sales commission. Two, Bert was certain that his product line was superior to that presently used by Tony and also that he could give Tony better service. In spite of this knowledge, Bert was unable to find the right time to discuss his product in the correct selling environment. If he came to the shop in the morning, Tony was busy with his special customers, for Tony gave the best and closest shave in town. In the afternoon he was either cutting hair or reading the paper. Bert knew from experience not to interrupt Tony while he was reading, and he also knew that it was no good to talk to an inattentive person.

Bert flew into Chicago Sunday evening, planning to spend the week in the Chicago area. One particular objective was uppermost in his mind — sell Tony! While driving in from the air terminal, he mentally began retracing the constant factors of this situation and how those factors could best be related to the selling system. His mind always seemed to return to one overriding characteristic of Tony: *Tony gave the best shave in town.*

"That's it," Bert muttered excitedly. "Approach the sale from Tony's strength."

The following morning about 8:30, Bert was in the shop. Tony looked at him quizzically, but said nothing. Tony was more surprised when Bert took his turn in the chair and asked for a close shave with lots of hot towels. Tony, caught off guard, did not talk much; maybe he was concentrating on proving to Bert why he had the reputation of top shaver in town. Bert made no mention of his product. When he left, he complemented Tony on the fine job he did, giving Tony a 25-cent tip.

"Have a cup of coffee on me, Tony," Bert said. He knew the money meant nothing to him, but he also knew that a good barber like Tony expected a tip as recognition of his performance.

Tuesday morning Bert was waiting at 8:30, first in line for his shave. "You know, Tony, that shave you gave me yesterday felt so good I thought I'd try another one," Bert said as he climbed into the chair.

Tony was pleased that a tonsorial salesman would show such interest in his abilities. He began telling Bert about his earlier days in the business, particularly the first shave he had given in this same hotel 30 years ago.

"When that guy left here," Tony said, "I wasn't sure whether I should call the hospital for an ambulance or see my attorney." They both chuckled over that experience.

By Wednesday Tony was half expecting Bert to drop in again; Bert had mentioned earlier that he would be in town most of the week. Tony was not disappointed, for at 8:40 Bert was in the chair, looking forward to that shave. He realized now why Tony's reputation had grown through the years.

"Tony," Bert began with enthusiasm, "I'm going to miss your shave next week. You actually spoil a guy's beard! I'm not sure if you are aware of it, but we have a new shaving cream compound that I'd like you to try. Would you mind if I left you a jar now and dropped by tomorrow to see how you like it?"

"No problem," replied Tony. "I'm always glad to try something that will improve my touch. What's in this new compound?"

"Well, Tony," Bert began, "it's a patented cream blended into the soap, which penetrates under the whiskers to give immediate skin protection."

"Sounds pretty good, Bert," Tony replied. "You come by for a shave in the morning, and we'll talk about it then."

PROBLEMS

1. Does Bert's tipping tell us something about his understanding of Tony's personality? Was he appealing to Tony's attitudes or motives or knowledge gained through experience?

2. Do you feel that Bert was sincere when, in returning for his second shave, he complimented Tony on his professional skill? Does it really matter? Discuss your answer in terms of *principles of behavior* presented in Chapter Five.

3. Did Bert make a wise choice in waiting until Wednesday to talk to Tony, or could he have saved time by attempting to gain his attention on Monday? Discuss your reasoning.

4. Did Bert achieve the primary purpose of the attention step, that of gaining favorable attention? Discuss.

5. Which principles of behavior discussed in Chapter Five are apparent in this case?

6. Which techniques did Bert apply to gain favorable attention?

John was about to call on Fred Winston, the owner of an interstate trucking line. After getting Winston's attention, John prepared to develop need awareness through the interest step. As preparation for this portion of the selling system, John first made a product analysis of his product's strength as shown on the *product analysis sheet* below.

Name: John Hanks   Date Oct. 11, 19--

PRODUCT: MOBIL DELVAC 1130 MOTOR OIL

1. Selling point	2. What it is	3. What it will do for the buyer; why or how it will do it	4. What it means to the buyer (benefits)	5. Buying motives
Universal oil	The use of one oil	Will allow you to stock only one oil for your fleet of trucks.	Last year you lost two engines because your vacation-relief mechanic used the wrong oil (cost of overhaul, $6400 each). You are presently using 30-weight oil in the GMC trucks and one 30-weight oil in the Detroit Diesel trucks. This oil will work in both engines. The chance of error is eliminated.	Money
2104C oil	Oil meets U.S. Specification Mil-L-2104C	An oil that meets this specification will maintain warranty standards as specified by GMC and Detroit Diesel.	This specification is harsher than any standards in your fleet. It is doubtful that you would ever exceed the government standards. Since this oil meets the U.S. specification and the manufacturer's, the use of it will allow you to operate under guaranteed conditions, without the worry of engine failure.	Guarantee of performance
30-weight oil	Single-viscosity oil	Allows you to use one weight of oil all year long and will perform all duties demanded by your trucks. It will protect all engine parts by effectively applying the right amount of oil at the correct time on the proper part. It will help eliminate the common problem of sticky valves, broken seals, and varnished cylinders.	90 percent of all fleet owners use a 30-weight motor oil; it costs approximately one-half as much as multiviscosity oils. It has the ability to correctly prevent metal-to-metal contact; there is less downtime due to engine failure. Purchasing expensive engine parts and major overhauls can be eliminated.	Conformity Money
Detergent/ dispersent additives	Cleansing power	Will actually clean the engine by picking up dirty particles or metals and floating them in the oil until they are forced through the filter and caught.	A clean engine means cleaner air. A clean engine will last longer because harmful deposits have been dispersed. These harmful deposits cause faulty ignition, dirty oil, and unneeded repairs. A clean engine runs longer and better, thus eliminating downtime. Downtime last year cost your company $6,000.	Ecology Health Money

1. Selling point	2. What it is	3. What it will do for the buyer; why or how it will do it	4. What it means to the buyer (benefits)	5. Buying motives
Extended drain interval	Longer period between oil changes	The oil molecules will not break down after prolonged stress and use, allowing engines to perform longer without having to change oil.	A $7,564 savings as follows: *Present practice:* 80 trucks x 2 changes/month x 12 months/yr = 1920 changes/yr Oil 2.5 gallons x $.80 = $2.00 labor 1 hr/change x $5.00/hr = 5.00 Filter = 2.30 $9.30 1920 changes/yr x $9.30 = $17,856/yr for oil changes *Proposed practice:* Using Mobil Delvac 1130 you can safely extend the change interval to once per month on most vehicles. 80 trucks x 1 change/month x 12 months/yr = 960 changes/yr oil 2.5 gallons x $.95 = $2.38 labor (see above) = 5.00 Filter = 2.30 $9.68 960 changes/yr x $9.68 = $9,292 $17,856/yr - $9,292/yr = yearly savings $7,564	Money

On the basis of this product strength reflected in the selling point, he presented the following interest questions to Fred Winston:

1. "Fred, judging from the size of your operation, you must have about the same amount of trucks as ABC Trucking. Is that the case?

2. "As you probably know, we service that account. It's been our experience that over 90 percent of their trucks use a single viscosity oil. Is that about the same ratio for your outfit?"

3. "Fred, we know that one of the really big expense items for a trucker is his percentage of downtime due primarily to air pollution in faulty exhaust systems. How much of your truck downtime is caused by this situation?"

4. "If you could use those trucks just 25 percent of that downtime, what do you figure it would be in increased earnings?"

5. "When I came into the yard, Fred, I noticed a considerable number of drums sitting in your yard. Do you use two types of oil? Any problems?"

6. "How often do you figure your maintenance man spends changing oil, Fred? Have you ever computed the costs of oil changes over a period of one year?"

PROBLEMS

1. Relate each of the questions to one of the selling points on the *product analysis sheet* and specify a customer need you feel could be developed from this relationship.

2. Why does the selling system become an effective instrument in developing customer need awareness toward John's product and services?

3. Did John apply the technique of leading with his strengths by basing his questions upon specific selling points of his product? Discuss.

4. What specific kinds of questions was John using? Are they phrased properly to develop an expanded customer response?

The following advertisement appeared nationally, discussing the particular merits of buying a Mercedes-Benz:[1]

OUR NEW 280SE 4.5 COSTS ALMOST THREE TIMES AS MUCH AS THE "AVERAGE" CAR. BUT WE THINK THERE ARE 10,000 AMERICANS WHO CAN APPRECIATE THE DIFFERENCE.

The average car buyer can be taken aback at the price of our new Mercedes-Benz 280SE 4.5. At nearly $10,000 it is not only well above average, it is some $2,000 more expensive than the highest priced domestic luxury sedan. And new import taxes will only serve to increase this disparity in the future. Whether it's worth that difference to you may be answered only by what you expect of a motor car. The 280SE 4.5 is a touring sedan in the best European tradition. Designed to provide every motoring comfort for a party of five. And engineered to cope with driving situations that vary from the descending switchbacks of an Alpine pass to the 100 mph cruising speed of an Autobahn. A concept so fundamentally different from that guiding the design of a domestic "luxury" car that Mercedes-Benz engineers used the punishing Nürburgring racing circuit as its final testing ground.

The difference begins with an engine unlike any built in America. An overhead-camshaft, electronically fuel-injected V-8 displacing 4.5 liters. It has no carburetor. Instead, a computer monitors engine speed and load, temperature and altitude, then electronically meters fuel to each cylinder. This more precise method of fuel delivery provides high-speed touring capability with the greatest possible efficiency.

A three-speed automatic transmission makes gear changes almost imperceptible to passengers. Yet it can be shifted manually by the driver who prefers to control gear selection. The fully independent suspension was designed for ruts and bends, not just boulevards and turnpikes. It's so roadworthy, *Road and Truck* contends that "no domestic luxury sedan is even in the same ballpark." The recirculating-ball steering is so accurate, it seeks a straight path on its own. Its power assist is so responsive *Car and Driver* calls it "unquestionably the most precise unit of its kind ever developed." And to match its performance abilities, Mercedes-Benz engineers have equipped it with four power-assisted disc brakes, ventilated in front to resist fading. The result is an automobile that performs with equal aplomb on the 174 curves of Nürburgring, or the unwavering concrete ribbon of an interstate highway.

[1] Reprinted by permission of Mercedez-Benz of North America.

And the new 4.5 is further endowed with almost every comfort. Power brakes and steering. Electric windows. Air conditioning and tinted glass. Electricity heated rear window. An AM-FM receiver. Even a central locking system that secures all four doors, the trunk and even the gas port at the touch of a button. Because we think such "options" should be standard on any car of this magnitude.

In addition to the 280SE 4.5, Mercedes-Benz builds two other V-8 touring sedans in similarly miniscule quantities. The 280SEL 4.5 is identical to the SE except that it is longer. Longer in the Mercedes-Benz sense — an increase of four inches that is translated directly into rear-seat leg room.

The 300 SEL 4.5 adds air suspension to the list of performance features unavailable on any domestic automobile. Instead of metal springs, cushions of air soak up shock and vibration. Under varying passenger and trunk loads this unique suspension instantly returns the 300 SEL to its normal level with a barely audible hiss. Pull a lever and the entire car raises two inches for additional road clearance.

In total, these three high-performance touring sedans will account for less than one of every 400 cars sold in the United States this year. If you can accept a car that is "different," we invite you to take a thorough test drive. Discover the real differences in a car built to be the best — not the best seller.

PROBLEMS

1. List five selling points of the Mercedes-Benz, what the selling points do functionally, and what they mean to the buyer in terms of personal values (benefits).

2. If you were a salesman for Mercedes-Benz, would this advertisement be of assistance in product analysis? How?

3. How might you relate this product to the principle of the slight edge?

4. Give an *example* used in the advertisement to develop a particular selling point.

5. Do you think the demonstration would support particular selling points? Discuss.

6. Give three illustrations showing the use of *descriptive language*.

7. How does this advertisement illustrate why the conviction step is also called the knowledge step?

8. Does this product message support the function of the conviction step? How?

9. Develop five interest exploratory questions you would use in determining whether or not a prospective customer has needs which the Mercedes-Benz might fulfill.

10. Is the emphasis in the advertisement upon the price of the item or the customer values it represents? From a sales strategy viewpoint, is it an effective "want creator"?

"Now that you have read the case in the text of the salesman using visualization to develop mental ownership within Mr. Benson, the customer, what is your impression of how the salesman handles the future benefits being enjoyed?" asked Professor Ainsley.

One member of the class raised his hand and offered this observation: "I feel that he did a great job of using creative words to develop a word picture, making it possible for Mr. Benson to place himself into this situation and thereby gain mental ownership. At the same time, I feel that the salesman really 'overkilled' the point, especially the part about the customer coming in and finally being sold because for the first time that summer the office was comfortable. To me, a little of that visualization goes a long way."

"You have an excellent point, Martin," replied the professor. "What you are saying is that in order for the visualization to become effective in attaining mental ownership, not only must the salesman have the ability to use creative words, but the thought content must also relate to that customer in terms of believability. You will find when you become involved in a real selling situation that if you properly understand the relationship of this selling step to the total selling system, and if you have made an effort to develop a good flow of descriptive communication, the process of bringing the customer into the future, using the present tense, of course, will come quite easily and naturally to that particular buying relationship. Remember, in the one-to-one relationship of salesman to customer, you are able through selflessness to become directly involved in the selling environment, so that you actually can mentally visualize with the customer the mental need satisfaction."

"For the sake of discussion," Professor Ainsley continued, "let me present some other thoughts on developing this mental image and see what your reaction is. In Winston-Salem, North Carolina, a traveling sales representative for the Winston-Salem *Journal-Sentinel* found that by painting word pictures he had greater success in selling paper boys upon entering a prize contest. He would paint a word picture of the boys enjoying the prize — which was a trip to the shore. He pictured the bus ride to the resort, the meals in the hotel, the games on the beach, the dip in the Atlantic. He made them feel the rush of the bus, the taste of the meals, the smell of salt air, the feel of salt water. Before he finished, the boys eyes were shining. Apparently it was quite successful; on one occasion the boys sold forty subscriptions in 2 days. Now, Marty, if you were going to present this word picture to the boys, how would you do it?"

PROBLEMS

1. As Professor Ainsley requested of Martin, prepare a word picture which would assist the paper boys in visualizing their trip to the beach.

2. Do you agree with Professor Ainsley that selflessness on the part of the salesman plays a role in properly developing the mental picture?

3. Give your evaluation of Martin's summation of the salesman's use (in Chapter Eight) of the desire step.

Discuss the closing technique used in each of the following situations.

Phil Kilmer was trying on a particularly stylish suit at the Olympia Men's Shop. He had shopped here exclusively for several years, principally because he liked the people who ran the store as well the quality suits they sold.

"Yes, Phil," John Roark, salesman for Olympia, went on as he adjusted the shoulders, "that's about as perfect a fit as you'll ever get. I'll ring for the tailor."

Mary Shelton was looking into the mirror, trying to make a decision about the camel's-hair coat. She liked it very much but just could not make up her mind. At this point the saleswoman asked: "Would you like to wear it home, or shall we sent it?"

Jake Cramston gingerly rang Mrs. Johnson's doorbell. As Mrs. Johnson opened the door, Jake said: "I've been out here four or five times to see you about buying that new sewing machine, and I've told you about the proposition, so I've come out this morning to ask you for the order."

"I know," Mrs. Johnson replied. "I've been trying to give you the order, but you wanted to have a demonstration. My sister has one of your sewing machines and I know all about it. I'll take that model we discussed."

Calvin Johns, salesman for Consolidated Plymouth, was ready to use the closing technique he felt best fit this customer. "Bill, if you buy your new station wagon this month, we can give you ten free chassis lubrications and oil changes. That's about a $60 value."

Fred Aspley was ready to close a sale of 50,000 purchase orders. The prospect appeared to be interested and agreed with Fred that the form design was more than adequate to meet his needs, but. . . . At this point Fred asked: "How soon will you need the forms?"

Beth and Ken Hollingworth sip their hot coffee as they thoughtfully talk with Tom Haywood of Westward Realtors. All three have just returned from inspecting a house which Tom feels just suits the Hollingworths' needs. It is within three blocks of a grade school, easy walking distance for their two youngsters in the third and fifth grades, while their boy in high school catches the bus directly across the street. The house itself is a two-story affair: upstairs, a master bedroom with a full bath, downstairs, two bedrooms, a large living room, rec room, and a New England brick kitchen with sliding glass doors opening onto a beautiful backyard. Not only is there much room and privacy, but the natural background of woods and trees even attracts wildlife! The present owner said that he always kept a box of dry cat food on hand to feed a family of raccoons that came by every evening.

"Yet," Tom thought to himself, "there's something that's bothering those two. No, that's not right. Ken is actually sold on the house; he likes the idea of that large garage with space for tools as well as both cars. If my selling instinct is correct, the problem here is with Beth. I'm going to try pinning down the *real* problem."

"Beth," Tom began, "do you think the children will enjoy having bedrooms of their own? I know ours seem to enjoy the privacy of their room as they grow older."

Beth sets her coffee cup down as she says, "Yes, Tom, the children will love the house. In fact, they already have selected names for those raccoons we told them about last evening. I guess that I'm the one who is dragging her feet. Frankly, I'm a little embarrassed to tell you why."

"Now, Beth, you can't feel that way. When you and Tom invest $55,000 and years of dreaming, you want to be right. Maybe if you let me know, I can suggest a way out. You know, being your agent means more to me than just finding a house. The important thing to me is that you and your family find the happiness a good home can bring," Tom replied.

"Well," Beth began again, "I have been rather proud of my activities in charitable and political organizations within our neighborhood. In fact, this year I'm the UGN chairman for our area, and am committee woman for the Young Republicans. If we move out to the suburbs, I'll have to start all over again, probably taking the pledge cards around the neighborhood. It's not that I don't mind starting from the bottom, but it's tougher after you have been near the top."

"I can understand how you feel, Beth," Tom said. "My wife spent many years with the Red Cross, and she had to make a similar move in positions when we selected our present home. Making this kind of a change isn't easy, but it probably eases the pain when you realize that you and your family will have a much more enjoyable family life. Didn't you mention that one of the reasons you wanted to move was to give the children an opportunity to live the relaxed life you and Ken enjoyed when you were children?"

"That's right, I did," Beth replied. "You know, Ken and I grew up in a small town and always felt that if we had the opportunity, we would give the kids a chance to discover the joys of living in a smaller community. Times have changed since our youth, but I do feel that this area comes closest to a small-town environment. When did you say they wanted to move out, Tom?"

PROBLEMS

1. When Tom asked Beth Hollingworth how the children would enjoy their bedrooms, was he attempting a close? What kind?

2. Judging from her response, was Tom utilizing the selling system effectively? Discuss.

3. What technique did Tom employ to bring Beth's objection into the open?

4. Evaluate Tom's response to Beth's reluctance to tell him why she was reticent to commit herself to the purchase. Discuss your answer in terms of needs/benefits.

5. Of the five customer buying decisions, which would you determine to be the cause of Beth's objection?

6. To which selling step did Tom return in order to respond to this cause?

7. Summarize in a one-page paper how this case illustrates the effectiveness of the selling system in determining the cause of an objective and then taking the correct action to turn the objection into a reason to buy.

8. In place of Tom's response to Beth's reasoning for not wanting to move, assume he says the following: "Beth, you know as well as I that you have to pay a price for anything you do. Is your leaving the prestige you enjoy in your club activity too much to ask for a family residence of this caliber?" Do you feel that this response would be more/less effective than the original? Discuss your answer in terms of need/benefit, buyer decisions, and their relationship to overcoming objections.

It was 7:15 A.M. when Ted threaded his way down the narrow canyon road of Walnut Creek. He reached the Bay Freeway at 7:35. "I'm 5 minutes late," Ted muttered to himself. "This means I'll probably spend about 20 minutes getting across the Bay Bridge. Oh well, I shouldn't complain. If it weren't for people like myself there wouldn't be a need for all these freeways, and I wouldn't have the opportunity to sell heavy equipment in the San Francisco area." Ted had been with Consolidated Manufacturers, Inc., for 5 years and was far more successful than he had felt would be possible. Last year his W-2 form showed an income of $31,000, and this year should be even better.

"Better move it," Ted thought. "I've an appointment at 10:30 this morning with Bill Jefferson. Bill's done one heck of a job with ABC Construction this year. Which reminds me, I'm glad I made that trip to the county highway office last week. It gave me an opportunity to learn that Bill had been awarded that 50-mile freeway stretch to San Jose. I know it's been at least 2 years since he's purchased *any* heavy equipment. With the type of earth removal that job will require, he should be in the market for at least ten of our heavy-duty carriers, to say nothing of the 'cats' he'll be needing. This could be a $500,000 order for the firm – and a fat commission for me."

Ted was ushered into Bill's office promptly at 10:30. "Bill, your secretary informed me on the way in that you have an important meeting with your construction crew at 11 and probably won't have a great deal of time to spend with me. Rather than discuss your equipment needs now, may I just leave a couple of brochures which illustrate the main features of our latest earth removers?"

"Thanks, Ted, for being understanding," Bill replied. "This meeting came up quite suddenly and just couldn't be postponed. As you probably know, our outfit was awarded that San Jose job. We aren't going to start on it until 4 or 5 months from now, but in order to get started then, we'll have to wrap up work we are presently on so that I can utilize all my crews on that project. So, I'm meeting with my key men to find out exactly where we are on those other jobs. Could we get together sometime next week? I at least owe you the opportunity to show me what you have."

"You bet, Bill. Could we get together a week from today about the same time?" Ted responded.

On his return to the office, Ted began laying the foundations for his sales presentation the following week. He mentally reviewed the kinds of equipment Bill would require on the project and paralleled these needs with the equipment Consolidated manufactured. He felt confident that his firm had the best equipment to fulfill the needs, but he also knew that the sales representative for Diamond Trucking was a personal friend of Bill's and thus far had gotten most of Bill's business. "I'm going to have to do something I'm not doing now to get

267

that business. Maybe Tom Olsen [division manager] will have some ideas to help."

Ted, while having lunch with Tom Olsen, explained the terrific potential this sale had. He also told Tom that he had not been very successful in selling Bill on Consolidated's products.

"Ted," Tom replied, "I know from what you've told me and my experience with your ability that you've done everything possible to sell Bill on a logical, rational basis. Sometimes this isn't enough; sometimes the emotions play an important role in a sale. They may be *more* important in this case. Because of the importance of this sale, I feel it calls for some creative selling. In the past I've called upon a private investigation agency to give us the kind of information we would need to make a sale. These guys are real sharp in digging up facts that are of real value."

"My gosh, Tom!" Ted exclaimed. "Do you think it's right to go that far?"

"I don't feel there's anything wrong in it, Ted," Tom replied. "Any professional salesman makes a concerted effort to find out as much about his customers as he possibly can. In this case we simply hire another professional to do the job for us. It isn't as though we were trying to find out anything derogatory about Bill; we simply want to gain a better insight into his personality. Besides, it's very personal, and will never go past my office."

Friday of that week Tom Olsen called Ted into the office. With a big smile on his face Tom said to Ted, "Ted, old buddy, I think we've found the key that will turn Mr. Bill on. The agency I used came up with only one really important characteristic, but it's a dandy! He found out that Bill was originally from Los Angeles and after leaving The University of Southern California tried out for the Los Angeles Rams. He didn't make the team, but made some lasting friends with the Rams' organization. Shortly thereafter he accepted his father's offer to run the San Francisco end of his construction business. That was 7 years ago, and Bill still talks about the day he can move his operation down to Los Angeles again."

Ted looked a little puzzled as he said, "What's that got to do with the sale of earth movers, Tom?"

"Only this," Tom continued enthusiastically. "Here are two tickets for next week's home game in Los Angeles against the Packers. Give Bill a call and invite him to fly down to the game in the company plane. I've alerted the company pilot to stand by."

Sunday evening Bill and Ted were flying comfortably back toward San Francisco replaying the game. It was particularly satisfying since the Rams had won a big one.

As they disembarked at the airport, Bill turned to Ted and said, "You know, Ted, we're going to start on that San Jose job in about 3 months, and we'll be needing some newer equipment. Our present stuff just can't handle a job like this. I've been looking through those brochures you left the other day, and I like what I saw. Could you drop by the office tomorrow to talk about it some more?"

PROBLEMS

1. Which was more important in this case, product analysis or customer analysis? Discuss.

2. Which specific techniques were employed by Ted and Tom?

3. Do you feel Ted should have at least begun a sales discussion while in Bill's office the first time? Why?

4. How did Bill tip off the size of the San Jose job?

5. On his return drive to the office, was Ted properly evaluating his pre-approach? Discuss.

6. Do you agree with Tom's evaluation of the role of logic and emotion in a sale? Can one be more important than the other in completing a sale?

7. What do you think of Tom's decision to use a private investigator? Does this involve a matter of ethics? Discuss your answer.

Professor Ainsley was enjoying a small group discussion after class. One of the students made the statement that the successful salesmen he had known had two characteristics: they were optimists and they were lucky.

Ainsley nodded, interested, as he lit his pipe, and asked the student, "What do *you* mean by luck, Bob?"

To which Bob replied, "Luck, Professor, is that characteristic of being at the right place at the right time, through no fault of the salesman."

"Ah," the professor mused, "the old flip-of-the-coin story, Bob. I suppose there are situations where events uncontrolled by the salesman can have a positive influence upon the sale. I feel, though, that these do not occur as often as one thinks. You see, Bob, every action is related to a cause and effect, even though uncontrolled. In most selling situations the salesman refers to being lucky or unlucky only when he is *not* fully aware of this relationship of cause and effect. In other words, he has not developed an in-depth understanding of how the selling system works. As we discussed earlier in the course, the buying decision on the part of the customer is a *conscious* act of relating a need to a benefit. Therefore, what the salesman often refers to as luck is really unawareness of those related factors which resulted in a completed sale."

The professor continued, "It has been my experience that a professional salesman makes his own luck in the sense that he knows where he is going and has considered all the steps necessary to get there. Another way of putting it is that he realizes the importance of planning and takes the necessary time to understand all the factors which will be of value in making the sale. I do agree with you, Bob, that the successful salesman is an optimist, which leads me to ask another question: What is an optimist? Or, to put it another way, what are those characteristics which give some people the ability to see the success side of life?

"From what I have seen of salesmen, the term 'optimist' is just another way of describing a salesman who has confidence in his selling ability, awareness of the many strengths of his product line, a deep understanding of the customer needs these products will fulfill, a personal desire to bring his products' benefits to the customer in terms of an objective, coupled with a realistic plan which tells him how to do this. That says a great deal, Bob, but gives you some understanding of how the professional salesman is able to turn *all* his activities into positive acts. Even if he may fail in a well-planned sales effort, he will see the positive side. The dedicated salesman will not fear that failure; rather, he will evaluate it very carefully to see what he can learn from experience to be a greater success in the future.

"I am constantly impressed with your interest in life, Bob, your desire to want to succeed in what you do. With this attitude you should succeed. Your future is in a sense success unfulfilled. It's a bright selling future, and with a goal in mind, guided by proper planning, you will have a lifetime to enjoy this future."

PROBLEMS

1. Discuss a salesman whom you consider to be the "lucky" one Bob described.

2. Do you really believe that optimism is important to success? Why?

3. Evaluate Professor Ainsley's position on luck.

4. Do you feel that objective and planning are important?

5. What do we mean when we talk about the person who turns failure into success?

Phil Carter, sales representative for the Mutual Petroleum Corporation, was reviewing the quarterly sales figures of the twenty-three service stations assigned his territory. One station particularly caught his attention, S.S. 113-094 leased by Gene Adams. Gene had been in that location for 13 months, and the sales figures indicated that he was having a problem. His gasoline sales had decreased by 22 percent, his oil sales were behind the previous year by 17 percent, while his tire sales were behind by 45 percent. In fact, there was not one item that indicated a positive sales trend. This concerned Phil for two reasons. First, Gene had spent 6 weeks going through the training program. During this time he learned all segments of managing a service station. Second, there was only one other station in Phil's entire area that showed negative sales results, and that was because the freeway had bypassed the station.

Phil did not have an opportunity to discuss the matter with Gene during the day, but he decided to drop by in the evening with the thought that Gene might still be there. He was not, but what Phil saw was quite revealing. A young lad, around seventeen, was exhibiting a charitable trait toward his personal friends, allowing them to make use of the lube bays for their own cars, while two other buddies were burning rubber on the inner lot. It reminded Phil of a mini-300 race. One other point caught Phil's attention: there were no cars coming into the station for purchases or service work.

The following morning, Phil did make Gene's station the first stop of the day. Upon entering the station lot Phil saw that Gene was busy in the lube bay with a lubrication. That offered Phil an opportunity to make a little survey of Gene's operation. First, he entered the men's restroom, where found that it badly needed a general cleanup and a new supply of soap powder and hand towels, and three tiles were missing. Going on to the office, he found that the shelves were dusty, still displaying the summer waxes (in October). Gene was wearing a greasy overcoat and hat; Phil winced as Gene ran out to the pump island to wait on a customer, greasy cape flowing in the wind. As Gene reached for the front hood latch to check the oil, greasy thumb prints appeared on the hood of the new Cadillac.

As he walked back into the office thinking about what was the best way to discuss this problem, Phil noticed that Gene had recently installed an old leather chair in the office.

PROBLEMS

1. Using the I-M-P approach, evaluate this problem in terms of identifying its cause, deciding on what method to use in rectifying the situation, and proceeding with the necessary course of action.

2. If you were Phil, would you seek other than your personal observations?

3. Do you feel that Gene realizes that a problem exists? If so, would the thinking of Gene and Phil be along similar channels?

Wayne Harlan, department manager for men's sportswear at the Vogue Department Store, slowly worked his way out of his car, leaving his Pontiac safely tucked away in the parking lot while he inched toward the doorway and the light drizzle outside. It was still dark; Wayne checked his watch for the time.

"Seven fifteen," he muttered to himself. "What an unholy hour of the morning to be going to work. Well, I guess it's really a small price to pay for being a member of management with the opportunity to share in major store decisions. There really isn't much time to prepare for our 8 A.M. department meeting. I want to check this week's sales figures."

Wayne quickly crossed the intersection, nodded to the doorman as he unlocked the south entrance, and went directly to his office. The total sales for the month indicated that the department was ahead of objectives for the month as well as for the year. He then looked at the item breakdowns to see how individual items were selling. Two interesting totals deserved further investigation. He noted that the sale of sweaters was over the objective by 18 percent, while dress shirts were down by 12 percent. The remaining items were plus or minus 5 percent. Wayne wondered if his sales organization was really making a sales effort with dress shirts. With total sales doing so well, Wayne felt justified in assuming that the total sales effort was an effective one. He decided to give an extra 50-cent bonus on each shirt sold during the month and to run a feature article in the store magazine. He reasoned that this stimulus would develop a positive selling attitude, resulting in better selling efforts with other product lines.

"Seven fifty-five," Wayne thought. "Guess it's time to put the parts together for the meeting."

Wayne began the meeting by congratulating the entire sales organization for their successful efforts in placing the department's sales above its objectives. He singled out special honors for Kathy Smith, a twenty-three-year-old with 2 years of college, for her outstanding sales record last week. Her sales showed the greatest increase over sales for a similar period the previous year. Wayne went to considerable effort to obtain this kind of information from the accounting records, feeling that when members of his sales staff performed in an outstanding manner, they were due proper recognition. Then he announced that a bonus of 50 cents per shirt would be paid this month. Also, the individual who sold the largest volume of shirts during this period would receive a $25 bonus. From the expression on their faces, he could tell there was a high degree of enthusiasm.

Frank Bunker, twenty-five, who held a degree in business administration from New York University and had been a managerial trainee for the past 9 months, asked Wayne if he would give him a few extra selling points on the $17.95 Irish linen line which was placed into stock last month. "Customers look at the shirt," Frank said, "and ask why this *cloth shirt* sells for nearly $18 when they can buy a wool plaid for $20. Frankly, I don't really know why, and what usually happens is that the customer doesn't buy *any* shirt!"

"That's a really good question, Frank," Wayne replied. "Any of the rest of you have a similar problem?" The vigorous nods indicated that the question applied to others in the department. "Pass one of those shirts up here, Kathy," Wayne continued. "I'll see if I can give you some of the better sales features of this shirt. First, take the cloth itself. If you hold it up to the light you'll notice the close weave of the fiber. This not only gives the cloth twice the durability of a normal weave pattern, but also gives the wearer a *crisp* shirt which will not wilt under normal wearing conditions. This means, for example, that a salesman wearing this shirt will have as professional an appearance at four in the afternoon as at nine in the morning. You'll notice that the buttons are *molded* from synthetic pearl. It gives the shirt a unique look, while the buttons will not crack when placed in the washer. Notice the *tapering* from the shoulders to the bottom of the shirt. It gives the wearer a molded appearance, much as a tailored shirt does. Look carefully at the pockets. Notice that the design of the shirt is carefully aligned with pocket material so that the pattern is in complete harmony. The stitching on the collar is accomplished by hand and done in two separate operations. One, on the outside of the collar, and two, on the inside. This makes it practically impossible for the collar to wear out, particularly when you further examine the material placed into the collar itself; it has two layers of cloth, giving added wear to that area of the neck where most of the friction occurs."

Marilyn Neering, forty-three, asked about an interpretation of Vogue Department Store's current policy of stating that the store would gladly give full credit or proper exchange for any item with which the customer was not happy. She asked Wayne if he would give a clearer interpretation of that policy, because she felt that customers were taking unfair advantage of the store. Marilyn had been with the store 15 years. Although she lacked in post-high school education, she knew the department inside out; for this reason Wayne had made her assistant manager.

"Last Tuesday," she went on, "a woman brought a sweater back, asking for a new one; she said that the sweater had shrunk two sizes. I asked her if she had read the instructions, which specified that Woolite soap be used in washing. She replied that the instruction card was not in the box when she took the sweater out of it, and since she was not able to read the instructions, she could not be held accountable. I gave her a new sweater, but felt that she didn't deserve it. Could you give us a clear guideline by which to judge our decisions?"

Wayne replied that he was encouraged to have such concern from his sales organization regarding a just relationship between the store and its customers. It made him realize that they were sincerely interested in their selling activities.

"As you know," Wayne pointed out, "the primary objective of Vogue Department Store is to build a strong loyalty between the store and its customers so that a family tradition develops to shop our store. In order to bring this objective into the environment of the 1970s it was felt that Vogue should develop a policy of giving the salesman complete discretion in determining the necessary store action to maintain this respect and loyalty for Vogue Department Store. The plan of action for return items is to give the sales personnel complete authority to sign the credit memos and make whatever adjustment they feel is necessary. Using your sweater return as an example, Marilyn, it is understandable that from your perspective it would appear that a customer may be giving us an excuse. However, remember that when the store developed this long-range objective, it was well aware that there would be occasions where customers would take advantage of the store. It also realized that the majority of the customers who frequent the store and in time develop a relationship of trust and loyalty would not take that kind of advantage. The opportunity to further a relationship with this kind of customer warranted giving the other customers 'a free ride'."

The 9:20 bell rang, leaving 10 minutes until the store's opening. Wayne thanked his sales organization for their participation in the sales meeting, and suggested that they use the next 10 minutes to prepare for the day.

PROBLEMS

1. Discuss the backgrounds of Kathy Smith, Marilyn Neering, and Frank Bunker. From Wayne Harlan's reactions to their questions, would you conclude that Wayne varies his leadership technique when dealing with them? Discuss.

2. Does Wayne Harlan fit the definition of a leader found in the text? If so, how?

3. Are there any indications in this case that Wayne employs the I-M-P approach to solving problems?

4. Do you feel that Frank Bunker will succeed with the firm, and possibly become a successful sales manager? Why?

5. In this selling activity would Wayne Harlan be wise to employ the open-door policy?

6. Would you define Wayne's style of leadership as autocratic, democratic, or laissez faire? Give your rationale.

7. How would you evaluate Wayne's investigation of the department's sales results? Did he try to relate cause and effect? How?

8. Does Wayne understand the true potential of his sales organization?

9. Do you feel that the bonus for shirt sales during the month will be a good motivator?

10. Was Wayne's time well spent in gathering information on sales performance by his staff? What connection might group recognition have to personal achievement by the sales organization?

11. Does Frank Bunker's question on pricing offer some insight into why shirts have not been selling?

12. From Wayne's explanation of the sales features relating to the $17.95 Irish linen shirt, do you get the feeling he knows something about his product lines *and* how to sell them? Is this important for a sales manager? Discuss.

It was 4:40 P.M. when Hank Sandstrom parked his car in the company lot. He had just about enough time to complete his paper work and sales orders for the day, such as it was. Hank was somewhat droopy as he walked toward the sales office; he had spent the better part of the afternoon attempting to find out why his company's shortening was not giving the proper results for the ABC Baking Company. "The production manager had a pretty good point," he thought, "particularly when he gave me one of the doughnuts to sample. There was a definite taste of stale grease."

"I wish I had a little more background," Hank thought, "in being able to trace all the critical activities in these industrial accounts. I still feel certain that it is not the fault of the shortening, but the way they are applying it. I've got a hunch that they're getting the temperature up too rapidly and it's breaking down the chemical composition of the shortening, but I can't really prove it. On the other hand, I don't have the confidence in my technical background to cast any reflection upon their operational standards."

While sorting his incoming correspondence, Hank noticed that Dick Wohlard, the district sales manager, had dropped him a note reminding him that they were to meet at 9 A.M. to discuss Hank's performance for the year. "It's amazing how fast the years go by," Hank mused to himself. "Hard to believe this will be my fifth annual interview."

Driving to work the next morning, Hank for the first time in those 5 years did not really want to discuss his progress and performance with the firm during the past year. It was not that he did not like his job, or the firm, or that he felt on shaky ground. "I guess I'm still thinking about that ABC problem yesterday," Hank thought. "It bugs me when I can't get to the bottom of that kind of a problem."

Dick Wohlard had arrived at the office a little earlier that morning. He wanted to review Hank's record and personnel background before their 9 A.M. meeting.

"Let me just summarize Hank's personal background," Dick reflected. "To me that is always the key to increasing ability and performance. Now, Hank came to us directly from the University of California at Santa Barbara, where he earned a degree in business administration, majoring in marketing and minoring in sociology and political science. He spent his first 2 years working retail stores in the San Diego area and then was transferred to Denver, where he continued calling exclusively upon grocery stores. Two years ago he was transferred here [Portland, Oregon]."

Dick had felt Hank should acquire some exposure with commercial accounts, so he had assigned him ABC Bakery, a large restaurant chain, and five hospitals in the Portland area. "Hank's developing a good background with our firm," Dick thought. "He has the mental capacity to make good decisions and the personal discipline to see them through. He's a real asset to the firm."

With that background clearly before him, Dick reflected, "I've got to find the right opening to make Hank aware that we've got to develop his ability to sell industrial accounts. From his educational and work background, it appears as though he could get more depth in this area. I think I'll make this the high watermark of our discussion."

As Hank entered the office, Dick grabbed him by the arm and said, "That phone's been ringing off the hook all morning, Hank. Let's jump in my car and go down to the club for a quiet cup of coffee — and a chance to talk in real comfort."

When they were comfortably seated before the fireplace in overstuffed morris chairs, watching the fire send sparks up the chimney, Dick broke the silence: "Hank, as you probably know, we are extremely pleased with your contributions to the firm. I want you to know that I personally will give you my support the next time a request for area manager nominees passes my desk. You are too valuable a man to leave out in the field more than 1 or 2 more years. There really isn't much I have to say, Hank. Are there any particular points you would like to discuss with me?"

"First off, Dick," Hank replied, "I sincerely appreciate your trust in my ability and want to thank you for your personal interest in my promotion. It's guys like you that make this the fine firm it is. Really, though, there is one area of activity that concerns me. A good example is yesterday. The production manager for ABC Bakery gave me a call in the morning, asking me to come over as soon as possible. They were baking doughnuts, and the reaction of the shortening within the dough was causing a foreign flavor, not complimentary to the doughnut. He was right; the first thing I did was taste the doughnuts, and they had a lousy flavor. Although he may have been right in blaming this flavor contamination upon our shortening, Dick, I honestly didn't know the proper steps that would give us a conclusive answer. The situation made me aware of the fact that I do not have as sound an understanding of industrial applications of our products as I should have."

"Hank," Dick replied, "what you just said took me back 15 years when I made just about the same statement to my boss. I have always said that our sales organization would do well to spend about 4 weeks developing industrial procedures before sending a man into the field. I think I'll send off another memo stating my position once more when we get back to the office. The answer, of course, is in education. You simply don't understand the inputs into this element of the selling system. Tell you what. This summer we are going to select five trainees for the firm. As soon as they are trained, I'm going to request that we get one of them up here on a training status. We have a really sharp industrial salesman in our Oakland office. As soon as we can get this trainee up here, I'm going to send you down to work with this fella for a month. How does that sound to you, Hank?"

"All I can say, Dick, is thanks!" Hank replied. "I can't tell you how relieved I am to know that this experience gap will be rectified. You know, I was a little worried when I was driving in this morning, but I understand now why the company requires that my background be evaluated every year. It brings things out in the open — the right way."

PROBLEMS

1. Do you feel that effective communication was achieved in this discussion?

2. Were the three elements necessary for proper performance evaluation utilized by Dick Wohlard? In what way?

3. Was Dick wise in bringing the discussion into the informal club atmosphere? Is this important?

4. Should Dick have made a point of confronting Hank with his lack of industrial expertise?

5. Do you think that Hank would have spoken so openly if Dick had not reassured him of his position with the firm?

6. What do you think of Dick's solution to the problem?

7. Which technique did Dick employ in his performance evaluation of Hank?

Pete Tempelton had spent his first month as a sales trainee in the men's apparel department. His manager, John Hammersmith, was reviewing his performance during that period.

"Pete," John began, "you give the appearance of thoroughly enjoying what you are doing. My experience in retail selling has shown me that by watching the facial expression of the customer, you can usually determine the attitude of the salesman. A friendly face, coupled with a genuine smile by the salesman, almost always will have a similar impact upon the buyer. What do you enjoy most about this type of selling, Pete?"

"Well," Pete thoughtfully began, "it's the first opportunity in my life to provide a service I feel is important to someone else. When a customer asks my advice on matching a shirt with a tie, I know that it's important to him to be well dressed, and that his appearance will reflect upon him in a variety of public activities. It also gives me a good feeling to know that he has accepted me as an expert in my field and relies upon my judgment."

"Sounds like you have a good future with our firm, Pete," John replied. "Is there anything I might be able to do to help you?"

"Yes, there is, John. During this first month I've had a large number of customers who, when I approached them, indicated that they were just looking. Often they continued to browse the department as though intent upon making a purchase. I hesitated to follow them, for fear of antagonizing them. Yet, I can't help but wonder if I was passing by a sales opportunity."

John smiled knowingly, "That's one of the toughest retail sales obstacles to overcome. We know that the customer has a degree of interest, but how much is difficult to ascertain. I have found some success with this approach. Upon first seeing the customer, get some idea of what interests him. If he looks toward the shirts, that could be a clue. If he examines one, you can be reasonably sure that there is a degree of interest in shirts. As you approach the customer, casually place one of your newer styles before him and ask if he's tried, for example, this new winter color shade with his suits. If he is interested in shirts, he'll reply to your question in one of several ways: 'Yes, that does interest me, do you have a 15 neck?' or 'I like the style, but prefer it in brown tones,' or 'I had in mind something more conservative,' or 'No, thanks, I'm just killing time waiting for my wife.' In the first three situations you have sufficient customer commitment to continue the discussion. In the last situation you would be wasting your effort. Does that give you an idea of how to handle the situation?"

"You bet it does," replied Pete. "I'll be looking forward to using that approach tomorrow."

PROBLEMS

1. One of the principles of the attention step states that enthusiasm begets enthusiasm. Explain how John applied this principle as a retail sales manager.

2. Evaluate Pete's attitude toward retail selling. Will Pete develop into a professional salesman?

3. Is there a good working relationship between John and Pete?

4. Do you feel the idea of need fulfillment is important to the salesman *and* the customer? How does Pete express this relationship to himself?

5. How would you evaluate John's handling of the "just waiting" customer?

In November 1970 Bill Hayden, Mobil Oil Corporation's senior lubrication engineer for the Pacific Northwest, received an urgent memo from the New York office indicating that Mobil's industrial division had received word of a new steel rolling mill to be built in Palmer, Alaska. At his earliest opportunity Bill should travel to Alaska to determine lubrication requirements during construction, start-up, and operation. Bill promptly made a telephone call to Palmer and was soon speaking with the construction engineer, C. A. Morford. He indicated to Bill that the firm was planning initial construction as soon as the spring thaw permitted laying a foundation. Bill made an appointment for Wednesday of the following week to determine more specifically the requirements of Alaska Steel. The following Engineering Service Report[1] is the result of Bill Hayden's investigation of this potential customer's needs.

MOBIL ENGINEERING SERVICE REPORT
Issued by Commercial Sales Department, West Coast Division

Date   April, 1971

Alaska Steel Rolling Mills, Inc.
Palmer, Alaska

Attention: Mr. C. A. Morford

Gentlemen:

This report will describe the Engineering and Sales Services we propose to provide for your new steel mill in Palmer, Alaska.

As a matter of convenience, information is indexed in the following sections:

I. Mill Lubrication
   A. During Planning Stages
      1. Lowest number of correct lubricants
      2. Warranty protection through Mobil Equipment Builder services in United States and abroad
      3. Lubrication devicing

---

[1] Reprinted by permission of the Mobil Oil Corporation.

    B. During Construction and Start-up
       1. Cleaning and flushing instructions
       2. Installation of correct products
       3. Corrosion prevention where needed
    C. During Operation — the Mobil Industrial Program
 II. **Storage and Handling**
    A. Lubricants
    B. Paints
III. **Attachments**
    A. Typical reports for Mobil customers

Mobil has had many years experience in servicing the steel industry both in large primary plants, i.e., Kaiser Steel, Fontana, U.S. Steel, and in mills similar to your new mill, such as Etiwanda Steel, Etiwanda, California; N.W. Steel Rolling Mills, Seattle and Auburn.

We appreciate your interest in Mobil, and look forward to discussing this important program with you in detail.

                             Very truly yours,

                             W. A. Hayden
                             Senior Lubrication Engineer

                             W. K. Watson
                             Senior Marketing Representative

cc: Mr. Ken Hinchey
     Northern Supply

 I. **Mill Lubrication**
    A. *During Planning Stages*
       1. Mobil's qualified engineers will study blueprints and engineering documents to insure the use of correct lubricants and recommend lubrication control systems. Consolidation of types of lubricants will be a primary goal, consistent with engineering considerations under this phase of our service.

2. In the event that your mill may be equipped with some foreign equipment. Mobil has the largest engineering staff in the oil industry located throughout the world, whose primary function is working with equipment builders. Through this Equipment Builders Department, we have direct contact with the builders to assure you of warranty protection and the recommendation of the correct product for your machinery. We attach sample pages from domestic and foreign Equipment Builders books for your information.
3. Lubrication devicing. Recommendations will be made to install various types of application devices to more effectively lubricate your equipment and reduce oiler labor time. Many thousands of dollars can be saved if installation of this type of equipment is made during the construction phase.

B. *During Construction and Start-up*
Our goal is to help you achieve a smooth, trouble free start-up, and to insure maximum component life so far as it is affected by lubrication. To attain this goal, a qualified Mobil Engineer will be on hand to help you in several important areas:
1. Cleaning and flushing
Check preference of machine builder, then prepare written instructions for cleaning and flushing major systems. Supervise the cleaning procedure; make on-the-spot checks to determine degree of cleanliness. Advise disposition of used flushing oil.
2. Installation of correct products
Lubrication charts are prepared, specifying correct lubricants and service procedures. Where required, he affixes a recommendation tag on individual reservoirs. He is available for on-the-job training, insuring use of the correct lubricants and lubrication methods.
3. Corrosion prevention
We carry a full line of rust preventives. Where needed during storage, or between installation and start-up, correct products and methods will be recommended.

C. *During Operation — the Mobil Industrial Program*
The total economic purpose of the Mobil Industrial Program is directed to cost reductions. We are confident, and will show to you throughout this report, that with Mobil as your lubricant supplier you will be able to operate your facilities and produce your products at lowest unit cost.

The basis for the Mobil Industrial Program is the principle that a sound Preventive or Planned Maintenance system in any plant is the only desirable maintenance system. Numerous articles on the subject of PM have been written in every trade magazine, and they all point out the advantages and benefits to be derived from this system versus a breakdown maintenance program.

To put maintenance in the proper perspective and show how much it directly affects corporate profits, *Factory* magazine, a few years ago, ran an extensive industry survey in the United States and found that all industry spends each year on maintenance an amount equal to 66% of their net profit. Chances are this figure would not be out of line for your Company. With so much money at stake, it is imperative that the lubricant supplier offer not only proven premium quality products, but have a sound set of objectives and goals to assist in installing the never ending preventive maintenance program. Only in this manner can unit costs be decreased.

An effective lubrication program is truly the keystone of a good Preventive Maintenance system. Regular inspection of machines, continuing analysis of operating conditions, examination of all high cost areas, and other preventive maintenance measures are all keyed with the lubrication program.

With a sound goal oriented Preventive Maintenance Program, it is easily conceivable that, if maintenance costs were reduced only 5%, this would approach and possibly even surpass the total amount paid for all lubricants purchased.

The Mobil Industrial Program works into a complete PM program by producing benefits in one or more of the following areas:
1. *Reduced Unscheduled Downtime* — through elimination of equipment failure due to faulty lubrication and maintenance.
2. *Increased Production of Acceptable Products* — through improved machine performance and reduction of scrap caused by malfunction of inadequately lubricated equipment.
3. *Lower Maintenance Labor Costs* — by reduction in machine repair labor and through effective methods of lubrication scheduling, lubricant handling, and application.
4. *Fewer Machine Replacement Parts* — that have resulted because of execssive wear or failure due to faulty lubrication on maintenance practices.
5. *Reduced Lubricant Consumption* — by eliminating over-lubrication, minimizing, and extending lubricant life.
6. *Low Purchasing Cost* — through taking full advantage of quantity buying and recommendations based on the requirements of the equipment and operations performed.

7. *Assurance of Effective Maintenance Control* — by establishing supervisory and lubrication controls and by the training of plant personnel in efficient lubrication methods.

The way in which one or more of these seven benefits becomes a reality is by Mobil personnel continually analyzing over and over the following ten areas:

1. *Fewest Correct Lubricants* — A study of plant equipment and lubrication practices is made in which manufacturers' recommendations are balanced against over-all plant requirements and operating conditions. The objective is the use of the fewest number of correct lubricants consistent with sound lubrication and engineering practices.

2. *Lubrication Instructions* — Oilers must have complete, simple, well-organized instructions if efficient lubrication of equipment is to be accomplished. Mobil methods of charting, scheduling, and routing provide simple controls yet flexible enough to meet all plant needs. Scheduling with the use of data processing equipment will be discussed under the section "MI/DAC."

3. *Lubrication Organization* — Organization for lubrication is often such that no responsible person has complete authority. Supervision of oilers, inspectors, and repairmen is split among various departments. Good organization assures that all instructions and plans are carried out.

4. *Lubricating Devices* — When replacing less modern methods, automatic and semi-automatic lubricating devices can pay for themselves in a short time in labor and in the reduction of errors and waste. Mobil will advise of up-to-date ways to get more efficient application of lubricants.

5. *Storage and Handling* — Improved handling, storing, and dispensing of petroleum products reduces waste and confusion; minimizes fire and safety hazards; and reduces labor, storage, and warehousing costs. Mobil will recommend storage and handling procedures facilities to maximize savings in this area.

6. *Lubricant Life* — In hydraulic and circulating systems, special preventive maintenance measures should be taken. When proper inspection methods are set up to reveal contamination and to establish filtering and drain schedules, definite benefits result; fewer production shutdowns for oil changes, reduced labor costs, and extended oil life. We will analyze causes of leakage to save oil and secure long life of quality oils. Our Customer Service Laboratory will be used as necessary to determine oil condition in large systems.

7. *Oil Purification* — Purification of lubricating oils, either by filtering or centrifuging, is a practical means of extending the useful life of

oil in machine systems or in reclaiming used oil drained from machines. Mobil will investigate installation of proper filters in circulating systems to extend oil service life. Also, the use of reclaimed oil for less critical applications will be studied.

8. *Lubrication Controls* — Control of costs through lubrication records helps keep lubricant costs and lubrication application labor at a minimum. Such records initially provide a baseline to show where improvements are needed and, later, what results have been accomplished. Lubrication Controls, with the use of data processing equipment, will be discussed under the section "MI/DAC."

9. *Training of Plant Personnel* — Today management is more and more conscious of the need for proper training of personnel to carry out their duties. The training of oilers, maintenance men, and machine operators helps achieve greater effectiveness in lubrication, arouses interest in lubrication, and provides correct information. The use of Mobil clinic material is a vital tool in this training effort.

10. *Preventive Maintenance* — Mobil will work closely with plant personnel in continuing to up-grade the Preventive Maintenance Program by anticipating trouble spots, locating high cost areas needing correction, recommending inspection procedures, and providing a lubrication plan as a basis for a Preventive Maintenance Program.

As each of the ten points is analyzed by the Mobil Marketing Engineer, he will prepare an Engineering Service Report indicating the present conditions or baseline, the proposed conditions or goal, and the recommendation necessary to achieve the proposed results, and the cost reducing benefit that will result.

By following this format, we will be able to keep your management fully appraised at all times of the progress being made in reducing costs through the Mobil Industrial Program.

MI/DAC

In the plant location where the benefits and economics of employing high speed data processing equipment for maintenance procedures are present, Mobil pioneered a unique program called MI/DAC over eight years ago. To date, there are over 350 plants in the United States reducing maintenance costs with the aid of MI/DAC.

MI/DAC, meaning Management Information for Decision And Control, utilizes data processing equipment to give management meaningful, concise information on the location of high cost areas of maintenance.

MI/DAC is twofold in its capabilities. First, it is used to schedule all lubrication functions; other PM items can be added to the scheduling phase. Second, MI/DAC can be built into a full cost control system where all high cost areas can be identified. Once the high cost areas are identified, they can be analyzed, decisions made, and controls effected.

In order to install and insure the successful operation of this program, your Data Processing Systems personnel will be consulted regarding capability and adaptability to your machines, and their assistance will be required to fully implement the program.

Steps to Be Taken

1. *Complete Lubrication Study of all Equipment*
   This includes selection of the correct product, determination of application, method and interval, and optimum drain interval. (By Mobil)

2. *Design of Scheduled Maintenance Word Order Card*
   This form (ADP Card) will serve as a work order for all craft PM functions and may be designed to capture costs and other data. (By Mobil and Alaska Steel Rolling Mills)

3. *Determination of Type and Scope of Reports*
   As various departments will require different reports, a determination of the format and content will be necessary at this stage. These will define the nature of input data required. (By Alaska Steel Rolling Mills)

4. *Preparation of Initial Input Data*
   Based upon the requirements of the Scheduled Maintenance Work Order card (Step 2), Mobil will assist in the preparation of the input data for the master lubrication schedule. This basic format will be used by you to add other craft PM functions to the system. (By Mobil and Alaska Steel Rolling Mills)

5. *Preparation of Master Deck-lubrication Schedule*
   Your systems people will complete this phase.

6. *Implementation of MI/DAC Program*
   This will include introduction to personnel on the mechanics and operation of the program. (By Mobil and Alaska Steel Rolling Mills)

It is planned that a single form (see Step 2) will be designed to serve as *both* the Scheduled Maintenance Word Order and Unscheduled Maintenance Work Order. This one form will then provide input data for all maintenance costs (labor and materials).

Full assistance will be rendered by Mobil in the adoption of the MI/DAC Program, including de-bugging, report analysis, instructions, etc.

MOBIL ENGINEERING SERVICE

Mobil will assign two individuals to your plant. One is the Marketing Representative who will coordinate all Mobil activities, and the other is the Senior Lube Engineer. The engineer will be responsible for the installation of the Mobil Industrial Program. As the installation progresses, he will make regularly scheduled Planned Engineering Service calls on a periodic basis. During these PES calls, he will continually look for ways in which costs can be reduced. The guidelines for these investigations are listed under the Ten Phases shown in the section "Mobil Industrial Program."

The objectives for the Engineer to work on are in many cases worked out up to a year in advance. Close coordination with plant personnel helps assure that the objectives are of a significant nature. The Engineer is also available to assist in the implementation of many of the cost reducing ideas.

As problems are uncovered in the plant and necessitate rapid handling, both the Marketing Representative and/or the Engineer can be available for assistance. Habitual problem areas offer excellent subject sources for Mobil clinics.

CUSTOMER SERVICE LABORATORY

As part of our complete Engineering Service, the facilities of the Mobil Customer Service Laboratory are available to assist in analyzing oil samples to determine suitability for continued use. In addition, failed parts may be analyzed to determine the cause of failure to prevent further machine failures.

II. STORAGE AND HANDLING – LUBRICANTS AND PAINTS
A. *Lubricants*
We propose to ship products direct to you from our Consignee, Northern Supply Co., Anchorage, Alaska. We will insure adequate back-up stocks for your mill at all times.

B. *Paints*
In addition to a full line of lubricants, including fire resistant fluids, a subsidiary, Mobil Chemical Company, has a full line of paints and industrial coatings, which are available through Northern Supply Company.

PROBLEMS

1. After reading this report, list the functions Bill Hayden performs as a company representative.

2. Discuss three points which illustrate the depth of Hayden's efforts to provide consumer need satisfaction.

3. Do you feel that Hayden has the professional background to make the recommendations found in this report? Discuss your answer.

4. Give five important services provided by Mobil. Could these services become selling points?

5. Do the seven benefits offered through Mobil lubrication have merit to Alaska Steel Rolling Mills? Discuss.

6. In reading the section "Steps to Be Taken," what was your impression of Hayden's ability and professional background? Does he seem to know his product well and know how it relates to this firm?

7. Do you think that a sales representative of this background is of value to the Mobil Oil Corporation? Why?

Lee Marshall, advertising salesman for the feature department of *The Daily Globe,* is fighting homebound traffic while en route to the office.

"Four-fifteen," Lee mutters impatiently to himself. "I've got to get back to the office in order to call the out-of-town accounts before the ten-thirty deadline. Thus far this week, I've sold close to $3,500 in advertising for the fall hunting section. At five percent commission, that should give me a pretty fat bonus this month.[1] I know there's at least another $2,000 in the outlying area, particularly the farming communities, where most of the hunters will spend their time. I have a copy of last year's issue in my desk; all it will take is a phone call to each account. They should all buy again, certainly the motels and restaurants! If I can finish the calls by seven this evening, that will leave me three hours to get the copy ready for the copyroom."

Lee arrives at his office close to 4:45. After making a list of the rural accounts he wishes to call, he reaches for the phone, asking for a sequence operator. For the next five minutes he gives the operator fifteen telephone numbers in various towns. Almost immediately the telephone rings. Merle Masson, owner of the Lucky Friday motel/restaurant, is on the line.

"Hello, Merle, this is Lee Marshall, *Daily Globe.* Haven't had a chance to visit with you since that fishing trip last summer. We sure enjoyed the Lucky Friday food! We're putting our hunting edition 'to bed' around ten-thirty this evening, Merle, and I couldn't go home without giving you an opportunity to run your annual spot.

"What does it look like? Well, last year you used an excellent picture of the restaurant, and in the upper corner there's a colored map showing the proximity of your restaurant to the best deer hunting in the state. Did you fill up last year? How much was that worth to you? That much, huh? Well, I don't see why we couldn't run the same one again this year. I still have the plate on file, so there wouldn't be a charge for artwork. The cost? Same as last year, Merle, $250. Use the same ad, you say? Has your phone number changed? Thanks, Merle, have a good hunting season. I'll see you next year during trout season."

PROBLEMS

1. How would you evaluate Lee's telephone technique? Discuss.

2. Under these circumstances, would you work until 10:30 P.M. for the additional sales?

3. How did Lee utilize planning and realistic objectives to support his telephone technique?

---

[1] Lee receives a flat salary of $600 per month, plus 5 percent commission on all sales.

4. Why did he use a sequence operator?

5. Do you think Lee enjoys his work? Why?

Professor Ainsley was holding a discussion with a group from his sales class. Members of the class described sales organizations which they felt had achieved a high degree of success. After they all had an opportunity to give examples, the professor made the following comments.

"From what you have all said, it becomes apparent that the successful sales organizational structure is one which is capable of working with reality — there is nothing more real than determining the sales revenue earned for a specified period of time! Yet, in order to be a successful sales organization, one which attains positive results in a real, factual manner, there are certain organizational concepts which have an important bearing upon how well that sales organization deals with reality. I am here referring to the importance of developing clear objectives which reflect the customer needs the firm's products can fulfill; to the utilization of well-thought-out policies which give the necessary guidance to the organization in reaching these objectives; to a plan of action which utilizes *all* the resources of the organization to match the product benefits with the consumers' needs.

"I would like to present to you what I think is also a good example of a sales organization which utilized these three management constructs most effectively. The firm is Ford, the product the Pinto. As a background to this example you must understand the tremendous impact of the Volkswagen. It was about 20 years ago that the first Volkswagen appeared on the streets of New York City; that beetle turned out to be the nose of the camel! By the end of the decade, not only the camel but the whole caravan was within the tent, for by 1959 sales of imported cars in the United States stood at 621,000 units. Although the compacts helped recapture a portion of those sales, by 1969 the imports were taking 13 percent of all new-car sales. The Maverick, which was introduced by Ford in the mid-1960s, wasn't an import stopper, but it did perform its objective of constituting a holding action until the Pinto was ready to trot.

"The objective in developing and selling the Pinto was to match product characteristics with consumer characteristics, as follows:

Product characteristics:

Subcompact size

Subcompact weight

Low cost of ownership, in terms of:

Initial price

Fuel consumption

Reliability

Serviceability

Clear product superiority, in terms of:

Appearance

Comfort

Features

Ride and handling

Performance

Consumer characteristics:

Median age, thirty-three

Median income, $12,100

College education

"The policy which Ford employed to assure this was to develop a product which met the consumer's needs, at a price under $2,000. Using this as a guideline, Ford planned to sell the Pinto at a retail price of $1,919.

"There was a great deal of planning which went into effectively presenting the Pinto to the buyer. To illustrate the type of planning that went into this sales organization, let me tell you a little story. The little Pinto colt was a great help in registering the name of the new little car in the buyer's mind. Being at the right place to photograph a *real* pinto was quite a challenge, however. The problem was to find a newborn pinto and photograph him next to *Ford's* Pinto! In order to have the proper time, Ford staked out practically every pregnant pinto mare in the country. But the Creator didn't work to their schedule and specifications. The first born was solid black without a trace of the pinto patches. The photographers had to break camp quickly to get to the next location, where they found their subject. The little guy was only 3 or 4 hours old when they began photographing him. By the time the crew was finished, he was a real ham, more at home with the car than with his own mother!

"On the more serious side, Ford included its dealers in a really big way. Las Vegas was selected as the site to give over 10,000 dealers and staff the Pinto story. The first weekend the Pinto was on sale, 2,912 were delivered and another 12,023 were ordered; at the end of the first month Ford dealers had sold 18,797 and taken orders for 22,846. Pinto sales through the first 3 months climbed to 71,965 units, as compared to 59,415 for Maverick.

"Sales analysis indicated that the Pinto had taken giant strides in reaching Ford's objectives of stemming the erosion of the domestic manufacturer's market share by relating specific production characteristics to a well-defined customer group."

PROBLEMS

1. Define Ford's sales objectives in this case. Do they relate to specific customer's needs?

2. Does the case suggest that Ford was utilizing the potential strength of its sales organization? Give an example.

3. Did Ford, as Professor Ainsley suggests, deal with reality in relating objectives, policy, and planning to its sales organization?

4. Would you like to work for a sales organization such as Ford? Why?

Ten acres of choice land were made available to Properties Unlimited Land Development Corporation. It was an unusual offer, since the owner at that time had just been awarded the land as his share of an estate willed to him by his grandfather, Vincent E. Smothers. Smothers had been a pioneer to the area and in the 1890s had purchased a large section of choice view property overlooking the Puget Sound, near Seattle. The 10 wooded acres were entirely surrounded by homes worth from $45,000 to $60,000 in an exclusive residential area called Timberline.

Rockford Morgan, sales manager for Properties Unlimited, had a "gut feeling" that this land was a wise investment, but his selling experience in real estate also told him that when his firm planned to commit itself to an investment of $125,000 for the 10 acres, a more purposeful evaluation was essential.

To determine a market potential for 10 acres of prime view property (zoned residential and class AAA apartments, no more than three stories high) required an analysis, or "tearing apart," of the sales potential in terms of these three alternatives: (1) Sell the lots individually, allowing the buyer to build his own house. Lots would sell in 1/2-acre increments. Morgan felt there was a possibility that some might wish to buy as much as a 2-acre lot. (2) Build homes on the lots, selling completed units to the buyers. (3) Build apartment houses on the property, or a combination of homes and apartment houses.

In making a survey of the homes around this 10-acre area, Morgan found that these owners had purchased in that particular location in order to take advantage of the panoramic view of Puget Sound; because of their association with other members of the community, both on a group and individual basis; and because of the quality schools in the area and ease of shopping. This survey also indicated the characteristics of those presently residing in Timberline tabulated on page 298.

Based upon this information Morgan felt that the market for this property site fell into two selling segments: (1) The age group of thirty-five to forty-four, having on the average three children ranging from eleven to fifteen years of age. This sales potential comprises college graduates who are still reaching toward their earning potential but nevertheless have sufficient experience to warrant an above-average yearly income. (2) The age group of forty-five to fifty-one, having on the average two children living at home and one married. This group has reached its earning potential and has maximum job security. Morgan felt these two sales groups offered the best sales potential, for they were most likely to benefit from the needs which this property fulfilled for those residences in Timberline. Specifically, Morgan stated the primary needs that would be fulfilled as:

CHARACTERISTICS OF PRESENT RESIDENTS OF TIMBERLINE

Age	Percent of Residents	Number of Children	Percent of Residents	Age of Children	Percent of Residents
25–34	10	1	15	1–5	5
35–44	35	2	35	6–10	20
45–54	30	3	30	11–15	35
55–64	15	4	10	16–20	20
65–Over	10	5	5	21–25	15
		Over 5	5	26–Over	5

Work environment

85% of the husbands had a 4-year degree from a college or university, with a minimum of 5 years' experience in their chosen profession. 25% included professional men — doctors, dentists, lawyers, and educators. 85% of the sample were employed by firms which transferred frequently.

1. Outstanding view of Puget Sound and Olympic Mountains

2. Large lots making it possible to enjoy family life in privacy

3. Opportunity to find reference groups of similar values

To best satisfy the potential customers and make the highest profit for his firm, Morgan concluded that the best sales potential was found in selling the lots individually with the 1/2-acre lot selling for $10,000. The only expense incurred by Properties Unlimited would relate to developing improvements such as sewers, streets, and lighting. Morgan felt it best to allow the buyer an opportunity to build a home in harmony with his personal tastes, thereby giving the purchaser a high degree of individuality.

PROBLEMS

1. Do you agree with Morgan's evaluation of consumer needs in terms of his product? Discuss.

2. Did Morgan take into consideration the benefits (personal values) of potential buyers in reaching his decision?

3. Relate Maslow's hierarchy of needs as motivational factors affecting the purchase of property in this area.

4. List all the statistical characteristics Morgan used in this study.

5. Will the statistical information acquired from those presently living in Timberline be of value in selling the lots? How?

6. Give an evaluation of Morgan as a sales manager.

INDEX

Conviction step:
  analysis process, 61–64
  case study, 77–79
  principles of, 64–66
  techniques, 66–75

"Deaf duck," 97–98
Decision making:
  case study, 158–160
  I-M-P system, 157–160
  methods, 156
  systematic approach, 156–157
Del Monte Corporation, 211
Demonstration, 70–71
  participation in, 71–72
  verbal, 72
Descriptive language, 72
Desire step:
  analysis process, 84–86
  case study, 90
  principles of, 86–88
  techniques, 88–90
Dichter, Ernest A., 28
Distribution:
  by age, 228–229
  geographic, 230–232
Drucker, Peter, 221

Empathy, 122
Esteem needs, 32
Estimating, 207
Example, the, 66–67

Family:
  beginning, 242
  expanding, 242
  launching, 242–243
  middle-age, 243
  old-age, 243
Fears of buying, three, 124–131
Ford Motor Corporation, 228, 230
Frazier, Joe, 26
French, Wendell, 7

General Motors Corporation, 27
Goals:
  congruency of, 219
  importance of, 95

Handshake, proper technique, 41
Household characteristics, 242–243
Hyman, H. H., 130

Indecision, impact of, 158
Interest step:
  analysis process, 47–49
  arousing in customer, 48
  case studies, 53–56
  principles of, 49–50
  techniques, 50–51
International Business Machines, 17
Intrasubjective, 33
Introduction, methods of, 42

Knowledge:
  application, 33–36
  case study, 35–36
  definition, 33
Kornhouser, Arthur W., 27

Laws of behavior, 128–129
Leadership:
  case study, 163–165
  definition, 163
  sales meetings, 165
  styles of, 167–168
  training and development, 163–164
Leisure time, 235–238
Love needs, 32

McGee, John F., 145
McGregor, Douglas, 27
Maier, Norman R. F., 173
Maslow, Abraham H., 31
Maverick, 294
Mercedes-Benz, 259
Moore Business Forms, Inc., 223–226
Motives:
  application, 9–10
  case studies, 10, 36–37
  definition, 31

Name memory, 42
Need:
  awareness of, 13
  developing, 14